DEADLY THUNDER

Through the open hatch, Masters heard the deafening roar and crackle of gunfire. Dropping heavily to the ground, he turned to what he thought was the north and began a slow, staggering run. He had to make it back to his command post, not because he was afraid of being taken prisoner, but because his sense of duty demanded that he take control of the bitter struggle of his Knights against the Jaguars.

I'm never going to make it. Masters rebuked the thought the moment it sprang into his head. *I have to make it,* he told himself. *I have to.*

A dull throbbing rumble blanketed the battlefield, drowning out even the clamor of battle. Masters looked up, trying to locate the source of the prolonged thunder. A few hundred meters to the southeast hovered a huge, spherical shadow, lit from beneath by the blazing drive flares of its massive engines. Smaller jets of flame showed where dropping BattleMechs were descending onto the battlefield. Some were landing almost on top of the Jaguar positions.

The Com Guards had arrived. . . .

BATTLETECH®

Twilight of the Clans V

SWORD
AND FIRE

Thomas S. Gressman

A ROC BOOK

ROC
Published by the Penguin Group
Penguin Putnam Inc., 375 Hudson Street,
New York, New York 10014, U.S.A.
Penguin Books Ltd, 27 Wrights Lane,
London W8 5TZ, England
Penguin Books Australia Ltd, Ringwood,
Victoria, Australia
Penguin Books Canada Ltd, 10 Alcorn Avenue,
Toronto, Ontario, Canada M4V 3B2
Penguin Books (N.Z.) Ltd, 182–190 Wairau Road,
Auckland 10, New Zealand

Penguin Books Ltd, Registered Offices:
Harmondsworth, Middlesex, England

First published by Roc, an imprint of Dutton NAL,
a member of Penguin Putnam, Inc.

First Printing, August, 1998
10 9 8 7 6 5 4 3 2

Series Editor: Donna Ippolito
Cover art by Bruce Jensen
Mechanical Drawings: Duane Loose and the FASA art department

ROC REGISTERED TRADEMARK—MARCA REGISTRADA

In memory of Octa Bluetooth;
I'm sorry you won't get to read this one.
We're going to miss you, my friend.

Thanks again to Blaine Pardoe and Bill Keith for all their encouragement, and to Bryan Nystul, Mike Stackpole, and Donna Ippolito, who forced me to think about what I was doing and to be the best I could. The author would also like to thank all those other persons, too numerous to mention here, for their technical expertise. Thanks to Brenda for her patience.

And, as always, thanks to You, Lord. I know where my talents and opportunities really come from.

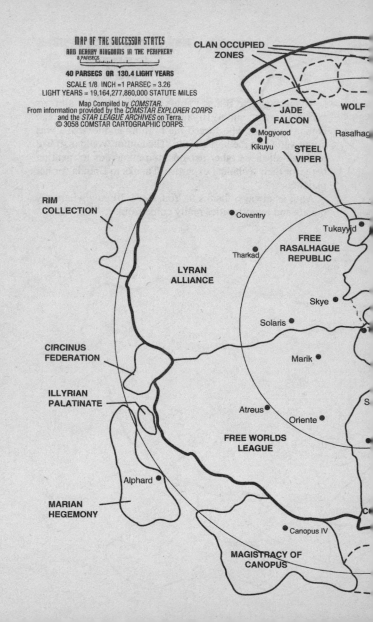

MAP OF THE SUCCESSOR STATES
AND NEARBY KINGDOMS IN THE PERIPHERY

8 PARSECS

40 PARSECS OR 130.4 LIGHT YEARS

SCALE 1/8 INCH =1 PARSEC = 3.26
LIGHT YEARS = 19,164,277,860,000 STATUTE MILES

Map Compiled by *COMSTAR*.
From information provided by the *COMSTAR EXPLORER CORPS*
and the *STAR LEAGUE ARCHIVES* on Terra.
© 3058 COMSTAR CARTOGRAPHIC CORPS.

CLAN OCCUPIED ZONES

JADE FALCON

WOLF

Mogyorod

Kikuyu

Rasalhag

STEEL VIPER

RIM COLLECTION

Coventry

Tukayyid

FREE RASALHAGUE REPUBLIC

Tharkad

LYRAN ALLIANCE

Skye

Solaris

CIRCINUS FEDERATION

Marik

ILLYRIAN PALATINATE

Atreus

Oriente

S

FREE WORLDS LEAGUE

Alphard

MARIAN HEGEMONY

Canopus IV

C

MAGISTRACY OF CANOPUS

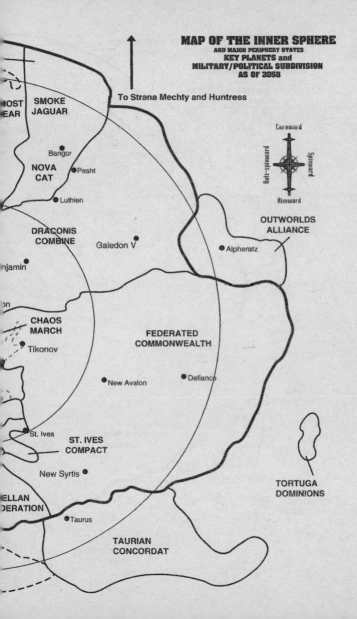

MAP OF THE INNER SPHERE
AND MAJOR PERIPHERY STATES
KEY PLANETS and
MILITARY/POLITICAL SUBDIVISION
AS OF 3058

To Strana Mechty and Huntress

Coreward

Anti-spinward — Spinward

Rimward

NOST EAR

SMOKE JAGUAR

Bangor

NOVA CAT

Pesht

Luthien

DRACONIS COMBINE

Galedon V

OUTWORLDS ALLIANCE

Alpheratz

njamin

on

CHAOS MARCH

Tikonov

FEDERATED COMMONWEALTH

New Avalon

Defiance

St. Ives

ST. IVES COMPACT

New Syrtis

TORTUGA DOMINIONS

ELLAN DERATION

Taurus

TAURIAN CONCORDAT

Prologue

The year is 3060.

When the leaders of the Inner Sphere gathered for the Whitting Conference in late 3058, they signed a charter to re-form the Star League so that under its aegis the Inner Sphere could carry the fight to the Clans and end their threat forever. The plan was to totally destroy a single Clan, and the Smoke Jaguars was the one chosen.

Armed with secret data provided by a Smoke Jaguar defector known only as Trent, the heads of the Great Houses planned a two-phase attack. The first, codenamed Operation Bulldog, and led by Prince Victor Davion, was aimed at driving the Smoke Jaguars from their Occupation Zone. The second prong of the operation was named Task Force Serpent. Commanded by Marshal Morgan Hasek-Davion, it was composed of forces drawn from the elite units of all the Successor States, bolstered by two crack mercenary units.

While Operation Bulldog diverted the Jaguars in the Inner Sphere, Task Force Serpent would make a long, round-about march through the Periphery and beyond, to strike at the Jaguar's heart, the planet Huntress. Thanks to the mysterious Trent, the Inner Sphere had at last learned the route to the Clan homeworlds, a path through the stars that the Clans had named the Exodus Road.

As Operation Bulldog drove the Smoke Jaguars from the Occupation Zone, Task Force Serpent continued its long trek through the depths of space. After nearly a year of travel and but a few jumps from their target, Morgan Hasek-Davion is found dead, the apparent victim of an assassination.

Now, his second in command, General Ariana Winston, commander of the elite Eridani Light Horse mercenary brigade, must step into his place. With dozens of starships and scores of Drop-Ships and nearly sixty thousand soldiers under her command, cut off from any help, she stands poised on the brink of launching the greatest military operation ever attempted by the Inner Sphere, with an assassin running loose in her fleet.

1

***Battle Cruiser SLS* Invisible Truth**
Task Force Serpent
Unnamed Star System, Deep Periphery
03 January 3060

"**C**'mon, Andrew," Ariana Winston said gently. "He's gone. There's nothing more we can do here."

Redburn turned to look at her. For a moment, anger flickered in the dead space behind his red-shot eyes. Then, he shook his head sadly. "Yeah, I guess you're right."

Winston laid a comforting hand on his shoulder, feeling the faint quivering of the muscle under his drab green jacket. She knew that it was neither fear nor fatigue causing the trembling, but the strain of holding back strong emotion. She was wrestling with the same feelings of shock and grief, but Andrew Redburn had been Morgan Hasek-Davion's closest friend. His sorrow had to be far greater than hers.

She had come to know Redburn well during the past year of training and travel, and it was no secret how much he loved Morgan. In some ways the two men had been closer than brothers. His grief was natural, but it would do him no good to remain in Morgan's flag suite even an instant longer.

Gently, she guided him toward the door to the outer office, and Redburn yielded to the pressure of her hand, though he moved with unsteady legs. At the door, Winston glanced back into the empty stateroom where, not twelve hours earlier, Marshal

Morgan Hasek-Davion, commander of Task Force Serpent, had been murdered. With a heavy sigh, she turned and followed Redburn out.

As they passed through Morgan's outer office, she let Redburn go on ahead as she paused to speak with Captain Roger Montjar, commander of the AFFC's elite commandos known as the Rabid Foxes. The closest thing the task force had to a chief investigative officer, Montjar had promised to conduct as thorough an investigation as possible. Orderlies had removed Morgan's body to the *Truth*'s sick bay only minutes earlier, and Montjar had gone straight to work searching the flag suite for clues. She and Redburn would only be in his way.

"Let me know the minute you find anything, Captain," Winston said in a voice husky with emotion, then she too went out into the corridor, where Redburn was waiting for her.

"Why don't you come into my office for a bit?" she said softly. "We can just sit a while. If you feel like talking, I'll listen. If not, that's okay too."

Redburn nodded silently, which Ariana took for a yes. She crossed the corridor and was just keying in the combination to the door of her office when Montjar poked his head out the door of the flag suite.

"General?" his voice sounded flat and unnatural in the starship's steel-walled corridor. "I've finished my preliminary examination of the Marshal's quarters. I'm heading back to the *Rostock* to analyze and evaluate the evidence. I'd like to request that the flag suite be sealed until I finish my investigation. I may have to go over it again, and I don't want anything disturbed in there."

"Very well, Captain," Winston said. "Anything else?"

"Yes, now that you mention it." Montjar came out into the corridor and set the heavy plastic case he'd been holding carefully on the deck. "Be careful who you talk to," he said, dropping his voice. "We don't know who killed Morgan, who ordered the hit, or why. Whoever it was went to an awful lot of trouble to make it look like a natural death, and we don't want to tip our hand."

"The command staff has been told," Winston said.

"Yes, ma'am. I'm not saying don't tell them. I'm saying it might be wiser to hold off a bit. They all know you ordered an autopsy. Let Doctor Donati finish the job, then tell them."

"Why?"

Montjar rubbed his chin thoughtfully. "If we tell everyone how the Marshal was murdered, whoever killed him may get the idea that we're on to him. If word gets out, well . . . who knows what might happen?"

"What do you mean?" Andrew Redburn had stepped in closer to catch everything Montjar was saying.

"He may just go to ground," Montjar said. "You know, dump any evidence he has, and then just sit tight. That sort of thing. Then again, he might consider us a threat to his continued existence, and take steps to relieve that threat. Do you want to spend the rest of this mission living with a couple of guards in your hip pocket, looking over your shoulder the whole time?"

"You're serious," Winston whispered, shocked.

"You bet I am." Montjar half-laughed. "That's not the worst of it. We're dealing with a heavy hitter here. If he thinks he's about to be caught, he may take drastic steps to prevent it."

"Such as?"

"Such as blowing up the ship. Ha! Don't look at me like that. I saw it happen once. Just after the Fourth War, a couple of Capellan Death Commandos tried to snatch an MI-7 section chief off Monhegan. Somehow, the whole thing got malfed up, and when the bad guys found out the Rabid Foxes had been called in, they grabbed a DropShip and demanded clearance to boost. When Port Control refused to clear them, the Capellans totally wasted the ship. Blew it up. Used forty, maybe fifty, kilos of pentaglycerine, and splattered the *Monarch* and a hundred and fifty passengers all over the tarmac. I'd rather not take the chance that we're dealing with that kind of fanatic. How about you?"

"All right, Captain, we'll play it your way," Winston said. "For now. But get back to me as soon as you've got something, all right?"

"Yes, ma'am." Montjar sketched a salute, retrieved his case, and disappeared around a bend in the passageway.

"General, I should be going, too." Redburn sighed, sorrow gouging deep furrows in his face. "My place right now is with the Uhlans. They're going to want answers, and I guess it's up to me to give them."

"Do what you have to do, Andrew." Winston put her hand on

his shoulder again. "Don't worry. We're going to bag this bastard. And when we do, you'll be the first to know."

Redburn nodded his thanks for her attempt at sympathy. Then, pulling himself erect, he straightened his uniform jacket and strode off down the corridor.

"Blast." Winston breathed the word like a curse. "I hope I didn't just lie to him."

With a shake of her head, she turned and entered her office. Crossing the steel deck, she considered the events of the past twenty-four hours and what they meant to Serpent and its mission. The fleet was only a few jumps from launching one of the most important operations in the history of the Inner Sphere—the invasion of Huntress, homeworld of Clan Smoke Jaguar.

Then, on the figurative eve of the attack, the task force commander, a well respected and well loved man, was murdered in his bed. As Morgan's second-in-command, the responsibility of leading the task force had fallen squarely on her shoulders.

Her office was small and sparsely appointed. A gray-painted steel desk cluttered with hard-copy reports, datachips, and manuals was bolted to the deck near the office's far wall. Two filing cabinets and a couple of plain chairs completed the furnishings. Only a framed photograph and a few other personal effects distinguished this office from a dozen others aboard the *Invisible Truth*.

Winston made straight for her desk, and collapsed into the thinly padded chair. For several moments, she sat staring wearily at the wall. She hadn't known Morgan Hasek-Davion nearly as long as Redburn had. Still, she had an eerie feeling, almost as though she could feel him standing behind her, just out of her peripheral vision. Twice, she caught herself turning around, hoping to see Morgan, his green eyes gazing levelly at her. Of course, the feeling was ridiculous. Morgan was dead, and she didn't believe in ghosts.

Winston leaned back in her chair. The thought that she was now in command of the task force kept rolling through her mind. A soldier all her life, she'd planned plenty of large operations before, but there was something different about this one. In almost every previous mission, she'd been in command of her own troops, the famed Eridani Light Horse mercenaries. Now, she was commanding House troops drawn together from across the Inner

Sphere. For all her adherence to the traditions of the Star League, she was a mercenary, and as such lacked Morgan's political stature. Would she be able to hold the various pieces of the task force together? Was the mission itself in danger?

Stretching, she reached across the desk, taking the silver-framed holopic in her hands. The image was of a much younger Ariana Winston, mugging for the camera with an older man wearing the moon-and-star crest of the 21st Striker Regiment. Despite the fact that his skin was somewhat lighter than the dark brown of her own, the family resemblance was unmistakable. Sadly, she gazed into her father's eyes, as though she could find an answer in their image. There was no answer now, anymore than there had been solace or explanations when he himself had died.

With a weary sigh, Winston leaned across the desk and tapped a code into her desktop intercom.

"Yes, General?"

"Patch me through to the *Gettysburg,* please."

After a slight delay, the Officer of the Deck aboard the Light Horse's command JumpShip answered the hail.

"Mr. Koll, please have my aide pack my gear for transfer to the *Invisible Truth.*" Winston was not all that eager to move over here, but the *Cameron* Class battle cruiser was the flagship of Task Force Serpent and her place as commander was aboard.

Without waiting for a reply, she severed the connection and leaned wearily against the back of her chair. The circumstances surrounding Morgan's death nagged at her. Who would want to kill him? Granted, Morgan Hasek-Davion was the cousin of the Archon Prince of the Federated Commonwealth. But Prince Victor Davion had two brothers, not to mention two sisters, one of whom seemed to have disowned him. Though Morgan had a distant claim to the throne, there was no real chance that he would ever have ascended to it.

Maybe that, in itself, was a motive for political murder. Morgan's father, Duke Michael Hasek-Davion, had been a pretender to the throne, back when the Davion realm still consisted only of the Federated Suns. Much to his father's dismay, Morgan had never wavered in his allegiance to Hanse Davion, or later, to his son Victor. Morgan had even dropped the Davion name from his children's official records. Could it be that some follower of

Duke Michael's was still bitter over what might be interpreted as Morgan's betrayal of his family? Bitter enough to arrange his assassination?

What about the Clans? There were reports that they had finally created their own intelligence arm, naming it "The Watch." Was it possible that the Clans had slipped an agent into the task force with orders to eliminate its leaders? The prospect seemed so unlikely that Winston discarded the thought almost instantly. Such a thing would mean that the Clans had discovered the existence and purpose of Task Force Serpent even before the force had gathered on Defiance. If that were true, why wait so long to strike? Why use an assassin at all? Why not simply mass a war fleet and intercept the task force as soon as it crossed the truce line? Besides, assassination didn't seem to fit in with their strict code of honor.

Winston levered herself out of the chair, carefully replacing the holopic of her father as she did so. She crossed the room to the bulkhead-mounted coffee maker and poured herself a cup of the bitter, soy-based substitute, which was all that was left to drink because they'd been gone so long. As the hot liquid warmed her from the inside, she resumed her contemplation of the mystery before her.

Could the murder have been a personal matter? Who hated Morgan enough to wish him dead? Whoever it was, it had to be somebody inside the task force with access to the Marshal's quarters.

For several minutes, Winston sat staring blankly at the pile of papers on her desk, sipping absently from the cup, considering all the implications of Morgan's death. She realized that she would soon have to make a formal statement to the other commanders, telling them that Morgan had been murdered.

No, let it wait until we have proof more concrete than Andrew's suspicions, or at least until we have a probable cause.

Three hours later, Ariana Winston had her probable cause.

The caustic buzz of the intercom grated on her nerves like a file. Slapping the annoying black box, she snapped an acknowledgement.

Captain Joel Donati, the *Truth*'s chief medical officer, responded. The intercom speaker gave his voice an odd, tinny quality.

"General, I've just completed my preliminary examination. I'm still waiting for some test results, but I think I've got a probable cause of death. It looks like—"

"Hold it, Doctor," Winston said. "I don't want this going out over an unsecured line. Report to my office. We'll discuss it here."

A few minutes later, a sharp rap sounded at her door. As it slid open, Dr. Donati strode into the room and went directly to take one of the chairs facing Winston's desk without bothering to wait for an invitation.

Winston didn't care. She was as eager to hear what he had to say as he was to tell her. She leaned forward with her elbows on the desk. "I'm all ears, Dr. Donati. You said you had a preliminary cause of death?"

"Yes, sir, uh, ma'am. Preliminary toxicology reports indicate that Marshal Morgan Hasek-Davion died of a lethal dose of a variform tetraodontoxin."

"Say that in English," Winston said.

"That *is* in English," Donati returned. "Tetraodontoxin is a naturally occurring nerve agent found in the internal organs of certain types of fish. On Terra, and among certain worlds of the Draconis Combine, it's called 'fugu.' A few thousand people die every year from eating improperly prepared pufferfish, because of the toxin in it."

"So you're telling me it was something he ate?"

"No, ma'am. It was probably something he drank." Donati smiled thinly. "Remember, I said it was a variform. The chemical composition of the toxin I found in the Marshal's blood was somewhat different from that of 'ordinary' fugu. Near as I can tell, the poison was derived from Breegan's toadfish, a species found on only three worlds: Yorii, Rigil Kentarus, and Altair. This toxin is about five times more powerful than that occurring in fugu, and acts faster."

"How much faster?" Winston asked, feeling an odd fascination. Like most professional soldiers, she knew nothing about poisons. She considered them to be a coward's weapon.

"Well, fugu acts in about ten minutes. Symptoms begin with numbness around the mouth and lips, and mood elevation. As the toxin sets in, you get difficulty in speaking, general paralysis, and death. The whole process takes between fifteen minutes and a couple hours.

"But this stuff? Onset is about ten seconds, with death in a minute or so."

"So he probably didn't know he was poisoned," Winston said.

"Not likely. Especially if, as General Redburn suggests, the killer put the poison in his scotch. The burn of the alcohol would cover up the numbness."

Winston nodded as she considered the doctor's report.

"Is it possible the poisoning was accidental?"

"Not a chance," Donati said. "Breegan's toadfish is inedible. The presence of its toxin automatically makes it murder."

2

Battle Cruiser SLS **Invisible Truth**
Task Force Serpent Flagship
Unnamed Star System, Deep Periphery
03 January 3060

Ariana Winston gave Donati the benefit of a level stare for a few moments before she turned away to call the bridge.

"Communications officer," she commanded. Then, as the man came on the line, she continued. "Establish a secure lasercom line to the *Rostock*. I want to speak with Captain Montjar."

It took several minutes to establish the linkup Winston had requested. Using a relatively low-power laser as the signal carrier, the officers could speak to one another with relative assurance that no one could eavesdrop on their conversation.

"Montjar," the commando leader answered at last.

"Captain, have you got anything for me yet?" Winston demanded.

"I was just about to call you, General. We were able to lift a few fingerprints off the whiskey bottle and the transfer system. They belonged to Morgan Hasek-Davion and his cabin steward. No big surprise there. What is surprising is what we found in the tubes of the transfer system."

"What transfer system?" Winston asked.

"You know, the pressurized gizmo that sucks the whiskey out of a bottle and into a squeeze bulb."

"Oh, yes. I was thinking about something else. Now, I remember," she said, rubbing her forehead. "What did you find? Tetra-odontoxin?" She stumbled slightly over the unfamiliar word.

"Yeah, that's right. How did . . ." Montjar paused briefly. Then he guessed. "Donati found it in the Marshal's blood."

"Uh-huh," Winston said. "Anything else?"

"Not yet. We're still running some tests. I'll let you know as soon as I've got something concrete. In the meantime, may I suggest that you have a little talk with the Marshal's cabin steward?"

Then there was silence on the line for a moment. Montjar seemed to be hesitating over what he would say next.

"General, I'd also suggest that you call Major Ryan and get him and his DEST people to help with the investigation. They get the same kind of investigative training as Fox Teams, but a lot more of it. As an arm of the Draconis Combine's Internal Security Force, they're sometimes called on to augment the regular investigative branches."

"Captain," Winston said flatly. "Need I remind you that the Draconis Elite Strike Teams are not above suspicion in this matter?"

"Excuse me, ma'am, but I'd say they are." Montjar's voice carried the proper note of respect due a commanding officer, carefully mixed with a mild lecturing tone. "The DEST teams were a sort of gift from Theodore Kurita, partly to Morgan and partly to Prince Victor. I hardly think the Coordinator of the Draconis Combine would personally hand-pick a team of special forces troopers, assign them to this task force, and then order them to murder the task force commander. That would be like robbing a bank and using your own car for the getaway."

Winston briefly weighed Montjar's arguments. She hadn't really considered the Combine special forces troops as serious suspects in Morgan's murder, though she knew that others might disagree. Everything Montjar said was true. It wasn't likely that Theodore Kurita would assign troops with assassination orders to Morgan and the task force. The assistance of the DEST teams would double the investigation's manpower, and there was no denying their competence.

"All right, Captain, you'll get your Dracs." Winston severed the connection without waiting for a reply. For a moment, she pondered how much information she should release and to whom. The command staff had a right to know what was going on. She had also been informed that rumors concerning Morgan's death were already making the rounds of the fleet. The scuttlebutt apparently ran the gamut from a simple heart attack to a crime of passion to an act of mutiny on her part to gain command of the task force.

Winston snorted bitterly at that tale. Anyone who had commanded a body of troops larger than a squad knew the profound headaches associated with leadership. And those were magnified, in geometric progression, the higher up the ladder you went. A commander was responsible not only for himself, but for his troops. He had to look out for their safety in battle, their conduct during down-time, their equipment, provisions, and health, both physical and mental. A good officer had to have the qualities of a leader, father-figure, teacher, counselor, and disciplinarian. The real balancing act came in knowing which of these roles to play at what time.

"No, let them wait," Winston said aloud, but to herself. "I don't want to malf up the investigation because I opened my mouth at the wrong time."

"Beg pardon, General?"

Jerking erect with a start, she half-reached for the laser pistol nestled in a nyleath shoulder holster under her drab green uniform jacket.

On the other side of her desk, Dr. Donati wore an expression of surprise mixed with fear.

"I'm sorry, Doctor," Winston said. "I forgot you were here. You kind of startled me." She felt the blood burning in her cheeks. "I was just thinking out loud that I should let the other commanders wait until you and Montjar finish your investigation, then I'll give them the particulars about Morgan's death."

"All of them, ma'am? What about General Redburn?"

"Oh, you're right. He deserves an explanation, and so does Commodore Beresick."

Turning again to the intercom, Winston rang through to Alain Beresick's ready room. After speaking briefly with him, she placed a similar call to Andrew Redburn's quarters aboard the *Truth*. Moments later, both officers were seated in the uncomfortable, steel-framed chairs facing her desk. Donati stood, leaning against the bulkhead.

"Gentlemen, I don't quite know how to phrase this, so I'll

come right out and say it. I hope you'll excuse me if this seems a bit rough, but . . . all indications suggest that Morgan's death was deliberate."

"Dammit, I knew it," Beresick spat, almost before Winston had finished speaking. "When Morgan died so suddenly, I half-expected it was murder. In fact, I've already had to quash half a dozen rumors to that effect." Beresick was a Com Guard naval officer now holding the Star League rank of Commodore. He was also the *Invisible Truth*'s captain and commander of the task force's naval assets.

"General," Redburn interrupted stiffly, fury and renewed sorrow warring in his eyes. "How did Morgan die?"

"Autopsy results and testing on the transfer system taken from his nightstand revealed traces of a rare and extremely powerful neurotoxin. The poison is derived from an inedible breed of fish found only on a few worlds—Altair, Rigil Kentarus, and Yorii. Doctor Donati assures me that there is no chance the Marshal ingested this substance by accident."

"Katherine!" Redburn hissed.

"What?"

"Katherine Steiner. She hates Morgan because he was so close to Victor. She'd do anything she could to hurt her brother. You said yourself that the poison came from Yorii or Rigil K. Those are Alliance worlds."

"True enough," Winston said. "But Altair is under Combine control, and Yorii is occupied by Combine 'peacekeepers.' The culprits could just as easily be part of Major Ryan's DEST team. Or, given the proximity of those three planets to the Capellan Confederation, the assassin might have come aboard with Kingston's Legionnaires.

"When you get right down to it, Andrew, nobody—*nobody*—is above suspicion, not even me, especially given the arguments I've had with Morgan over the past few months."

"If I may, General?" Beresick interjected. "The rarity, and therefore, the cost of this poison rules out a crime of passion. So, unless you've been plotting to kill Morgan ever since this operation began, I think we can scratch your name off the list of suspects."

"I don't think we should rule anyone out, not completely," Winston answered. "None of us here is an experienced investigator. The closest thing we've got is Captain Montjar and his team.

They, at least, have the basic training necessary to conduct the investigation."

"The DEST teams receive similar training," Beresick put in.

"That's right, Commodore, they do. Captain Montjar recommended that I ask the DEST boys to help out. Though I'm still not certain whether to scratch them off the list of potential suspects."

"I think we can," Beresick said. "I'd say the killer has to be part of the *Truth*'s crew, at least as a cover. No one else could move around freely and not be noticed."

"That's pretty much the conclusion I came to myself." Winston rubbed her eyes, more in frustration than fatigue. "I was planning to ask Ryan to help out anyway. Let's leave the investigation to the professionals. That's their job. Right now, our job is rumor control.

"I want you to go back to your commands and inform them that Morgan's death is still under investigation. I'll pass along the same information to the other unit commanders.

"And, gentlemen? Let's try to keep a lid on the rumor factory. We're all a little on edge, and things are only going to get worse the closer we get to the Clan homeworlds. We don't want to be fighting among ourselves only a few jumps from our target. Got it? All right, dismissed."

As the door closed behind the withdrawing officers and Donati, Winston lowered her face into her hands. For a long while, she remained that way, feeling a mixture of shock, grief, and exhaustion. Then, collecting herself, she flipped on the intercom, asking the bridge communications officer for a line to the *Haruna*, the Combine WarShip transporting the DEST teams.

Andrew Redburn didn't go straight to the shuttle that would take him to the *Ericsson*, the Kathil Uhlans' *Invader* Class Jump-Ship. Instead, he made his way down to the *Invisible Truth*'s number two cargo deck. As a battle cruiser, the vast WarShip was designed to fight other combat vessels rather than haul Drop-Ships, but she also boasted two "docking collars," the massive locking rings capable of clamping down onto the outer hull of a DropShip and securing it to the WarShip's hull. DropShips and other small craft were the only way of traveling from deep space to a planet's surface. No JumpShip ever built was capable of landing, or grounding, as warriors tended to call it. At the same time, no DropShip was capable of making star-spanning leaps through the netherworld of hyperspace. It was an imperfect system, but then it was an imperfect universe.

Mated to the *Truth*'s forward docking collar was the *Honor*, a *Union* Class DropShip belonging to the ComStar contingent. The Com Guards had a tradition of giving their DropShips a diminutive form of the name of their parent vessel. The ships assigned to the *Invisible Truth* followed this tradition: they were called *Honor* and *Integrity*.

As Redburn reached the forward cargo bay, a pair of Com Guard marines, dressed in heavy ballistic plate combat armor, snapped onto guard. As soon as the men realized that the newcomer was General Andrew Redburn, and not an aggressor, their postures changed from readiness to rigid attention. Redburn returned their formal salutes and passed through the cargo bay into one of the small secondary access tunnels flanking the main accessway. These tunnels were essentially long airlocks connecting the *Truth* to her DropShips. The secondary accessways were intended for the passage of personnel and small items of cargo. Larger payloads were moved between the vessels through the main tunnel. At the other end of the accessway, which led into the *Honor*'s engineering deck, a single Com Guard crewman met him.

"Good afternoon, General. Can I help you?"

"No, Private. Thank you, I'm all right," Redburn heard himself say. His tone was as hollow and lifeless as an empty shell casing. He saw a look of concern cross the young soldier's face. The youth had apparently picked up the note of anguish and loss in Redburn's voice. The expression of worry was a natural human reaction.

Redburn forced a smile, which he realized probably looked like a death rictus, given his mental state. "I just wanted to take a look at Morgan's 'Mech, that's all."

"Yessir." The crewman seemed unconvinced about the condition of Redburn's sanity. "I think it's in Bay Four, upper deck. I can check for you."

"No, son. Don't bother. I'll find it."

Giving the crewman what he was sure was another death-like grin, Redburn stepped aboard the *Honor*'s starboard elevator and punched the button for the upper 'Mech bay. As the doors closed, he caught a glimpse of the crewman looking concerned and leaning against a control console.

He's probably about to call for a straight jacket, Redburn thought ruefully.

When the lift doors opened again, he was met by a sight that never failed to awe him. Bathed in the harsh glow of the work lamps illuminating the bay, eight huge BattleMechs stood as though at attention.

Massive combat machines, mostly bipedal and humanoid in form, BattleMechs mounted as much armor and firepower as a battalion of conventional tanks. 'Mechs had ruled the battlefield for centuries, ever since the first successful combat test more than six hundred years before. The armies of the Inner Sphere had believed that their ten-meter-tall war machines were the pinnacle of military technology. Then came the Clans and they learned they were wrong.

When the Clans first swept in across the Periphery in 3050, they brought with them a level of technology that the Inner Sphere had believed lost. The invaders had apparently spent their self-imposed exile improving their military technology. Clan 'Mechs, called OmniMechs by their owners, were faster and better-armored than their Inner Sphere counterparts. Designed around modular weapons systems, they could be fitted out with a mix of lasers, PPCs, missile launchers, and quick-firing autocannons to meet the specifics of a particular mission. Like those of the Successor States, Clan 'Mechs were usually bipedal, and weighed from twenty to one hundred tons.

Redburn walked past the Com Guard technicians where were tinkering with the innards of a tall, gaunt-looking *Black Knight*. The heavy 'Mech's design was an old one, stretching back to the time of the Star League. Weighing seventy-five tons, the *Knight* mounted a PPC, backed up by a six-pack of lasers. Like good race car mechanics, who were never satisfied with the machines under their care, the techs had pulled a number of access panels from the *Knight*'s armored surface and were going over its systems, trying to coax just one more gram's worth of performance out of the war machine.

All by itself, in a transport cubicle that seemed too small to contain its 100-ton bulk, stood Morgan's *Daishi*. The Japanese word, meaning "Great Death," had supposedly been given to that particular 'Mech type by a member of the yakuza, the criminal underground operating in the largely Japanese Draconis Combine. Though it was later learned that Clan designers had christened the design *Dire Wolf*, the name *Daishi* stuck. It became the standard reporting name all across the Inner Sphere. Whatever you called it, the machine was one of the largest and most powerful Clan OmniMechs. This one had been captured during the Clan invasion. Morgan, through long, hard practice, had learned to pilot the enemy-built 'Mech as well as he could any Inner Sphere design.

Redburn pulled himself up a narrow steel ladder, which was part of the cubicle's service gantry, and swung himself into the black and gold *Daishi*'s cockpit. Powered down as it was, the machine seemed no more dangerous than a ground car or a private aircraft. Carefully, he ran his hands over the controls, touching each in sequence, as though he were going to bring the 'Mech to life.

Power plant to preheat.

Gyro to active.

Sensors and targeting systems to standby.

Escape system armed.

Redburn had watched Morgan go through the start-up procedure so many times that he could almost see his friend doing it. There was so much of Morgan still in the *Daishi*'s cockpit. An open pack of mints rested on the narrow lip surrounding the front viewscreen. The advanced neurohelmet tucked into a cubbyhole behind the command couch lacked the unit crests and bellicose nicknames and slogans that most helmets sported. Instead, it bore the simple inscription "Morgan."

Something glittered faintly in the shadows next to the 'Mech's primary weapon control panel. Redburn reached out and picked up a gold locket. It looked, to his untrained eye, to be made of real gold. The soft luster and exquisite craftsmanship told him that it was probably a family heirloom.

Touching the tiny catch, he opened the locket. Inside were a pair of old-fashioned photographs. On the left was an image of Kym Sorensen Hasek-Davion, Morgan's wife. Her blonde hair was shot with silver, and there were a few lines on her face, but she was still as beautiful as the day Morgan had wed her. The second picture wrenched Andrew's heart. It was the image of a handsome young man holding a boy of about five years on his knee. Redburn recognized them as easily as he did Kym. They were George Hasek and George Junior, Morgan's son and grandson.

It was not often these days that a soldier ever actually had to face the human cost of warfare. Even looking at a battlefield after a bitter and bloody fight, all Redburn saw were the burned-out wrecks of BattleMechs. The dead were viewed as objects to be disposed of and the wounded as assets to be repaired. As cold and cruel as that sounded, he knew that such detachment was necessary, especially in a commander. Otherwise, a soldier would lose his will to fight. Andrew Redburn had never thought he would lose that detachment. There, in that cold cockpit alternately lit garishly by the flare of welding torches and then plunged into an oppressive semi-gloom, he felt the first creeping edges of an emotion that he had never experienced before.

Grief.

When Hanse Davion had passed away, there was a sense of national loss and mourning. When his own father died of pancreatic cancer, it was a mercy. When Ariana Winston informed the command staff of Morgan's death, shock had insulated Redburn from the initial pain. But now, seeing the wife and family Morgan had left behind, the full impact of his friend's death came crashing down on him. Hurriedly, he locked the *Daishi*'s cockpit hatch from the inside. Then he let his head drop helplessly against the control panel. Great, wracking sobs shook him.

How long he sat there, mourning his dearest friend, Andrew Redburn couldn't say. When at last he undogged the hatch, the 'Mech bay was quiet. The technical crew had gone. The overwhelming grief that had consumed him had also passed. In its place was weariness, and an emptiness that might never again be filled. There was something else, a coldness, a bitterness in the core of his soul, which he had never known before. It was some moments before he could put a name to the feeling. It was a hunger for revenge.

Redburn grasped the swing bar above the hatch with tear-stained hands, preparing to leave the cockpit, then stopped. Quickly, he turned in the narrow confines of the cockpit and snatched the locket.

"Goodbye, Morgan," he said aloud. "I'm going to get that son of a bitch. And when I do, I'm going to break his neck with my own hands."

Lifting the gold case with its tiny images, he stared into the faces of the family left behind. "And don't worry about Kym or the kids. As long as I'm alive, I'll look after them."

Then Andrew Redburn snapped the locket shut and pulled himself out from the cockpit.

3

Battle Cruiser SLS Invisible Truth
Task Force Serpent
Unnamed Star System, Deep Periphery
10 January 3060

Ariana Winston looked across her office at the glowing numbers on the wall-mounted clock. Oh-five-forty-three, a quarter to six in the morning. It felt as though she hadn't gotten to sleep at all. She had been staying aboard the *Invisible Truth* rather than shuttling back and forth between the task force flagship and the Eridani Light Horse command ship ever since Morgan's body had been found. The nights she had spent in her office. The grief and deep sense of loss she felt over Morgan's death weighed heavily upon her, but, as the second-in-command—*no,* she amended, *as the task force's new commander*—she couldn't give in to her emotions.

It had been much the same when her father died. Colonel Charles K. Winston, former commander of the 21st Striker Regiment, had been one of the best-loved warriors the mercenary outfit had ever seen. Physically, he was almost a negative image of his daughter. Where she was tall, dark-skinned, and well built, with the muscles of a decathelete, he had been short, light-complexioned, and possessed of a runner's build. Ariana believed, however, that she had inherited the Colonel's thunderous voice and innate ability to inspire troops, as well as his warrior's skill and deep love for the Light Horse. Her closeness with him had sometimes caused tension between Ariana and her only sister, Gloria, who exhibited no interest in becoming a warrior, developing instead a passion for history.

At times, Ariana still felt the emptiness at her side, where her father had so often stood. Now, that hollow, echoing space was enlarged, magnified by the loss of a man who, in a few short months, she had come to count as a friend. Pushing aside the feeling, Winston closed her eyes again, trying to will herself back to sleep, but sleep, like a disobedient pet, refused to come.

"Dammit!" She jerked apart the sleep harness' fastenings. Free of the restraining nylon web, she roughly wadded the blanket into a ball and shoved it into the tiny locker beneath her bunk. "Lights!"

The *Invisible Truth*'s central computer responded to her barked command in less than a second. Voice-recognition software brought the flush-mounted overhead illumination strips to life, and the room was flooded with eye-straining light.

A second *sotto-voce* curse sounded in the quiet office as Winston screwed her eyes shut against the glare.

No sense in lying here not sleeping, she thought, as she rummaged in an upright locker for a fresh uniform. *I might as well get up and try to get some work done.*

But concentration proved to be just as elusive as sleep. Half an hour's worth of desultory pecking at the keys of her computer console yielded little more than three deleted documents and a mounting feeling of blind anger. Unfortunately for Ariana, there was no outlet for channeling her emotions. There wasn't even a real object for her anger. She was angry at Morgan for dying and for leaving her in charge. She was angry at the assassin, who had taken the life of a great commander and a good and decent man. She was angry at herself for the feelings of frustration and loss she couldn't seem to control. She was even angry at her father who, like Morgan, had died, leaving her behind.

"*Faaugh,*" she growled, slapping the computer's power stud without going through the normal shut-down procedure. Snatching up a green nylon duffel bag and her uniform jacket, she stormed out of the office, heading for the *Truth*'s central elevator bank.

The *Invisible Truth,* like all starships, was laid out around the central shaft of the Kearny-Fuchida jump drive. The K-F drive was the heart of the system scientists had developed for traveling instantly between the stars nearly a thousand years before. Massive energies generated by the drive literally tore a hole in the fabric of space, through which the starship was hurled. It was possible to travel thirty light years in a single jump, with the ships departing and arriving at carefully plotted zenith or nadir "jump points" above or below a system's sun.

There were two drawbacks to the system, however; the incredible amounts of energy needed to power a K-F drive could not be created quickly. Giant solar energy collectors, called jump sails, were required to gather solar radiation, which was then shunted into massive storage coils, from whence the energy could be tapped to power the drive. The problem was that it took a number of days to build up a sufficient charge. A JumpShip's own fusion plant could be used to power the drives, but it took just as long to build up a charge as it would using a sail. "Hot-loading," as it was sometimes called, *was* possible, but was not recommended. Quick-charging the drive could be done in as little as sixteen hours. The problem was that, for every hour shaved off the normal recharging time, the risk of charge loss, or even the destruction of the delicate K-F core, increased dramatically.

The second drawback to interstellar operations lay in the sheer size of the vessels themselves. With the smallest JumpShip measuring nearly three hundred meters in length and massing some ninety thousand tons, it was virtually impossible for a JumpShip to land on a planet's surface. Most lacked any kind of maneuvering drive more powerful than attitude-control thrusters. To deal with the problem of interplanetary and intrasystem travel, a second type of vessel, the DropShip, was developed. These spacecraft, some massing up to fifty thousand tons, were employed to ferry troops, vehicles, and cargo from the JumpShip to a planet's surface.

Until recently, JumpShips used by the Inner Sphere had been unarmed transports; most still were. With the coming of the Clans, a new breed of starship was developed. Bigger, with thicker, armored skins and potent weapons, WarShips used the same Kearny-Fuchida system, but had the added feature of powerful maneuvering drives. Most of the Inner Sphere's WarShips had recently been built from scratch, some using new designs, others constructed from plans dating back to the Star League. A few, the *Invisible Truth* included, had been hidden away by

ComStar in the asteroid belts of uninhabited systems. They were brought out when the Clans threatened to overrun the Inner Sphere.

Because of their construction, JumpShips and WarShips were both laid out around the K-F drive core. Most systems, the ship's elevators included, which had to service all areas of a vessel, were usually laid out alongside the core.

When the lift car arrived, Winston stepped aboard, sliding through as soon as the doors began to open. Without looking, she stabbed the touchpad next to the door, selected Deck Seven, then leaned heavily against the elevator car's side.

The trip took only a few seconds. When the doors hissed open again, she had regained some of her accustomed calm. Moving quickly along the deserted corridor, she soon found herself facing a steel door that bore a small red sign reading, "Grav Deck 1. Exercise Caution Upon Entry."

In response to her touch on the lockpad, the door slid aside. With practiced ease, Winston slipped through the opening, executing an odd forward somersault. Suddenly, the magnetic boots she wore to counteract the lack of gravity aboard a JumpShip in space had become a hindrance.

The *Invisible Truth*'s two grav decks were the only places aboard the massive starship where one could be free of the effects of weightlessness. In most parts of the ship, the *Truth*'s decks were laid out across the vessel's hull, with "up" and "forward" being the same direction. Grav decks—large, doughnut-like sections set on ring mounts encircling the vessel's hull—were rotated at a speed sufficient to produce what was called "rotational gravity," which was, in reality, centrifugal force. In these areas, the deck was actually the inner face of the ship's outer hull, and "up" was toward the vessel's central core. This artificial gravity was approximately one G force, mimicking an environment that would be comfortable to most humans.

Winston clambered down the short ladder just below the hatch and hopped lightly to the deck beneath. Swiftly, she unfastened the magnetic boots, an action that gave her a strange feeling of lightness. Stuffing the boots into her duffel, she made her way barefoot along the corridor toward a door labeled "Women's Locker Room." The deck shifted almost imperceptibly under her feet as she walked, reminding her that the corridor also doubled as a jogging track for off-duty crewmen. She had other things in mind.

Like the elevator and the jogging track, the locker room was uninhabited. Winston was glad to have the place to herself. At 0650, most of the *Truth*'s crew and passengers were standing watch, preparing for the day's duties, or asleep. Selecting a locker at random, she tossed her boots into it. Swiftly, she stripped off her uniform, exchanging the khaki tunic and pants for dark green sweats with a faded Eridani Light Horse crest silk-screened onto the front of the hooded shirt. A pair of battered sneakers completed the outfit.

Moving quietly through a connecting door, Winston entered one of the *Truth*'s small, but well-equipped, gymnasiums. At the far end hung a heavy canvas bag, suspended by a chain, from the exercise room's overhead. A meter and a half in height and half a meter across, the bag showed signs of heavy use. A thick rubber mat covered the floor beneath the bag. Stepping up to the bag, Winston pulled a pair of worn leather gloves out of her sweat-shirt's kangaroo pocket and pulled them over her hands. The gloves had a layer of padding over the knuckles.

Winston took up a front stance, her left foot a bit in front of her right, her shoulders relaxed, torso erect. Exhaling through her mouth, she brought her hands up into a guard position, leading slightly with her left. Then, as though responding to a signal that only she could hear, she lashed out with her right fist. The impact produced a flat slapping sound. The bag swayed slightly. A second punch followed the first; a third; then, a short hooking kick, as she dropped back half a step to give her strike space to develop.

More blows rained on the bag. Her breath came in short bursts. Sweat beaded on her forehead, threatening to run into her eyes. A contemptuous toss of her head shook it away. Her face, which had begun the exercise calm and impassive, twisted into an angry mask of exertion.

After a short time, Winston halted her assault on the bag as suddenly as she had begun. She wiped her face with the hem of her sweatshirt, thankful that she had the gym to herself.

The workout had helped. She still felt a little lost, but the over-whelming sense of despair that had kept her from sleep was gone. She checked the shockproof watch on her wrist. Twenty minutes after seven. There wouldn't be any point in returning to her cabin now. By the time she showered and dressed, it would be just about the time she usually got up. With a short laugh and a shrug, she headed for the locker room. The physical exertion of the workout had helped her put the situation in perspective.

Thirty minutes later, Ariana Winston strode through a set of pneumatically operated doors onto the *Invisible Truth*'s bridge. As a *Cameron* Class battle cruiser, the *Truth* was the last of her kind in the Inner Sphere. Nearly eight hundred forty meters long, excluding her jump sail, and massing over eight hundred-fifty thousand tons, she was the largest vessel in the task force fleet. Her hide was thickly layered with armor and bristling with weapons, and the two thick, reinforced docking collars along her spine were currently occupied by a pair of spheroid *Union* Class DropShips.

Winston had seen the mighty starship often enough from the outside, through the bridge viewscreen of the shuttle that carried her back and forth between the *Gettysburg* and the *Invisible Truth*. The ship's size and appearance reinforced the impression that she was a powerful combat vessel, though her bulk gave no hint of her speed and maneuverability. Such an impressive fighting ship should have an equally impressive captain, Ariana thought. Going by appearances, the commander of the *Truth* didn't fit the picture.

She had first met Alain Beresick on Defiance, the Federated Commonwealth planet where the various units of Task Force Serpent had rendezvoused for staging and training before jumping off on this mission. Back then, the man had failed to impress her. Beresick was below average height, with thinning, dull brown hair that fell lankly across a high, domed forehead. He reminded her of a low-level tax examiner rather than the commander of a WarShip.

Though she had not been aboard the *Invisible Truth* when the Task Force had unexpectedly run into a small flotilla of starships belonging to Clan Ghost Bear a few short weeks ago, Winston had learned how very wrong she'd been about Beresick's ability to lead a battle fleet. In its first engagement with the Clan enemy, the task force had handed the Ghost Bears a stunning defeat. They had even managed to capture one enemy warship, a *Whirlwind* Class destroyer named *Fire Fang*, relatively intact, losing only a few vessels.

"Commander on deck," a petty officer shouted.

"As you were," Winston said, following the age-old tradition. The idea was to forestall any crewman who might be coming to attention, although, from long experience, she knew that no attempt at a salute would be made by the bridge personnel. Still, it was a tradition that stretched all the way back to the sail- and steam-powered blue-water navies of Terra's distant past, and the Eridani Light Horse revered tradition. If any of the bridge crew were aware of her presence, they hid it well.

"Morning, General. Sleep well?" The dark smudges under Beresick's unremarkable brown eyes showed that he had not.

"Morning, Commodore," Winston answered. "No, I didn't sleep well, and neither did you, it would appear."

"Hmm," Beresick said noncommittally.

"Ah, God, I hate what I've got to do now," Winston said reluctantly. Then, taking a deep breath, she said, "Open a channel to all task force ships."

"Channel open," a technician responded.

First giving herself a moment to collect her thoughts, she then signaled and began to speak.

"Attention, all commands. This is General Winston. By now, you have all heard that Marshal Morgan Hasek-Davion is dead. The cause of his death is under investigation." She paused, cleared her throat and continued. "In accordance with mission orders, as of now, oh-eight hundred hours, ten January, thirty sixty, I am assuming command of Task Force Serpent. All ship captains and unit commanders will so note in their ship's or mission logs.

"Memorial services for Marshal Hasek-Davion will be held in a day or so, here aboard the *Invisible Truth*. Following that service, I will want to meet with the command staff to resume operational planning.

"That is all."

Her quick nod toward the communications console signaled the tech to close the channel.

She turned to Beresick and said, "Commodore? I'd like you to accompany me to the Marshal's quarters. It's time we opened his safe."

Beresick nodded unenthusiastically. "Mister Lake, you have the conn," he said.

"Aye, sir. Third Officer has the conn."

Beresick turned back to Winston with a rueful expression. "Let's get this over with," he muttered.

Moments later, Winston and Beresick stood in the corridor facing the locked door to Morgan's stateroom. The brief elevator ride had been marked by uneasy silence.

"You know," Winston said, "I'm really not too eager to do this. It seems like I'm jumping right into his seat, before the body is even cold, as the saying goes. Do you think I should wait until after the memorial service?"

"I don't want to do this any more than you do, General," Beresick said, shaking his head. "But, we can't leave this task force without a leader, and you're the one who was appointed second in command. You've got to step up and take control."

"Yeah," Winston dragged out the word. Her reluctance was not an attempt to shirk her responsibility. She was just loathe to take the place of a man whom she had come to know and admire as a comrade and a fellow soldier. Taking control meant, to her mind, that she was shutting the door on Morgan Hasek-Davion. To Ariana Winston—the woman, not the mercenary general—it seemed that the moment she opened the stateroom door, she would be forever consigning Morgan to the cold pages of history.

She didn't feel ready to do that just yet. Still, Beresick was right. They were less than two hundred light years from their objective, the Smoke Jaguar homeworld of Huntress. No one could falter now, much less her. This mission was the most important any of the thousands of men and women of Task Force Serpent had ever undertaken. The fate of the Inner Sphere could be riding on whether they succeeded or failed. Now that they were but a few short weeks away from arriving at the world toward which they'd been traveling for almost a year, it was time for her to boldly accept the responsibility for which Morgan himself had selected her.

Shaking her head, Winston tapped a four-digit code into the cryptolock mounted in the wall next to the door. The electronic keypad clicked three times and let out a pleasant low-pitched tone. The red indicator turned green as the door hissed open.

The office was not quite as they had left it. Morgan's data unit had been removed by the Fox teams, who were evaluating its contents, searching for some clue to the identity and motive of the assassin. Many of the non-classified hardcopy files had been likewise removed. Morgan's cabin steward, an old-time ComStar ship's crewman, had straightened up the clutter. The coffee-maker had been cleaned and a new pot installed. When Morgan's steward had found him dead, there'd been a thick sludge of boiled-down coffee in the glass urn. It was easier to replace the pot rather than try to clean the gunk out of the old one. Winston could still smell the odor of burnt coffee, faint as it was.

Putting the smell out of her mind, she slipped warily behind Morgan's desk and opened a panel set into the front of the side-board. Built into the credenza upon which the coffee maker rested was a heavy, reinforced steel safe. During their search for clues in Morgan's suite, the Rabid Fox investigators, and, later the DEST teams, had confirmed that the killer, whoever he might have been, had not attempted to open the safe.

"Do you know the combination?" Beresick asked.

Winston nodded. "Morgan insisted that I learn it." Her voice was toneless and flat. "Just in case, he said. I guess this is the case."

The safe was constructed of the same material as a Battle-Mech's armor, although not as thick. It was fitted with an old-fashioned, dial-type combination lock. Winston had thought the large chromed knob, with its tiny black-enameled numbers, quaint. Morgan had explained to her that, with the proliferation of electronic locks keyed either to a magnetic strip or a series of numbers punched into a keypad, few people with nefarious purposes in mind would be able to open the archaic lock.

The lock clicked faintly as she manipulated the dial through the series of left and right turns until she had completed the sequence.

No wonder they quit using this kind of lock. It takes forever to enter the access code.

A final turn of the knob and a twist of the L-shaped handle resulted in the muted thud of the safe's bolts retracting from the steel frame. It took a certain amount of strength just to swing the door open. It probably weighed twenty kilos, she thought.

Inside the strongbox was a stack of chip- and hardcopy files. Winston knew that these contained the task force's operational orders and strength reports, as well as in-depth profiles of each unit commander assigned to the task force. As she pulled the records from the safe, she resisted the urge to pull her file and read what the Federated Commonwealth's Department of Military Intelligence and ROM, ComStar's spy wing, had written about her. Instead, she reached for a small plastic case with a hand-lettered label reading "To Ariana Winston." For a few seconds, she examined the case, peering closely at the three-centimeter-square black plastic chip within. Aside from the tag on the chip case, there were no other markings. Winston slipped the case into her right breast pocket, intending to read it later.

For a few moments she leafed through the hardcopy file tagged "Operational Orders," mechanically scanning the pages of mission orders, strategic doctrines, and tactical outlines. Looking up, she saw Beresick watching her closely.

"I don't know if I can pull this off," she said in a small voice.

"Nonsense," Beresick said matter-of-factly. "You've been a soldier all your life, and you've planned major campaigns before, including the Light Horse's part in the Coventry operation."

"Yeah, and look at how *that* turned out. The Seventy-first Regiment got so mauled by the Jade Falcons that we almost disbanded it."

"General . . ." Beresick smiled gently. "Ariana, you'll do fine. Morgan wouldn't have made you his second-in-command unless he thought you were up to the job. You're just feeling a little overwhelmed by his death. We all are.

"You'll do just fine," he repeated, getting to his feet. "You're going to want some time alone to read that chip." Winston hadn't realized that Beresick had been able to read the crabbed handwriting on the case. "I'll leave you to it."

Without another word, he turned and left the room.

Winston busied herself with a closer read-through of the task force's general orders, trying to delay the moment when she would have to read the chip. Finally deciding to get it over with, she pulled the case from her pocket and fed it into the data unit built into the desk.

The screen blinked once, then settled into an image of the late Marshal Morgan Hasek-Davion. From the off-gray wall behind him, Winston could tell that he had recorded the message while sitting in the chair she now occupied. Her skin crawled a bit at the thought.

"Hello, Ariana." Morgan gave in to a burst of embarrassed laughter. "This is really strange. I don't quite know what to say. 'If you're watching this, then I must be dead' seems so trite, but it's got to be true.

"I know you're probably upset right now, not to mention confused, apprehensive, and more than a little scared. That's all right. No matter how many times I went into a fight, either alone or leading an army, I was always scared: scared that I'd malf up, scared that I'd get my people killed, scared that I'd fail my Prince. Most good commanders feel that way. It's the ones who aren't afraid that you have to worry about.

"Anyway, it's your task force now."

For the next several minutes, Morgan's image ran down all the details that Winston would need to know as task force commander: timetables, troop movements, intelligence summaries, and so on. He ended by reminding her that there were chip and hard copies of those materials in the safe.

"Now comes the really strange part," Morgan's image said. "If my body can be recovered, I'd like to have it shipped back home, to New Syrtis, for burial. I left some instructions in the safe regarding a memorial service. I don't want anything too grand, just a simple soldier's goodbye."

The image stopped just long enough to make her wonder if the recording had run out, then it continued.

"General Winston, if you're not alone, please stop this recording immediately. What follows is for your ears only." Morgan paused as though he was waiting for her to clear the room.

"Listen very carefully to what I am about to say. Just before I left New Syrtis for Defiance, I received a personal, confidential message from Theodore Kurita. He told me that, with Victor's approval, and, in addition to the Draconis Elite Strike Teams, he was sending me a special gift as task force commander.

"That gift was a team of four nekekami agents."

Winston slapped the data unit's Pause button and stared openmouthed at the frozen image. Wanting to be certain that she'd heard correctly, she rewound and replayed the last few seconds of the recording. There was no doubt about it. Morgan had actually said that four nekekami agents had been assigned to Task Force Serpent.

She knew that the nekekami were the inheritors of the techniques and traditions of the ninja of feudal Japan. The word, loosely translated, meant "spirit cat." Winston was also familiar with the legends surrounding them. It was said that they were unkillable, the apprentices of Death himself. Stories said that they could walk through walls, make themselves invisible at will, and kill with a glance. They were paid agents, trained from childhood to be spies, saboteurs, and assassins. Her flesh crawled at the thought of having hired killers under her command. True, she was a mercenary soldier, but she was bound by a rigid code of honor. She felt that people like the nekekami would have no code to restrain them.

"According to Theodore," Morgan continued, "the nekekami will be completely loyal to the task force, and may be used in any way the commander sees fit.

"I originally had them slated to hunt down and assassinate whatever high-ranking Jaguar officers might be on Huntress at the time of the invasion. Trent gave us enough intelligence on these officers for the nekekami to carry out the assassinations. Unfortunately, that information will be two years old by the time you arrive, and may be useless.

"Theodore sent along a list of code words and a sort of send-only 'pager' unit. It was the only way I would be able to communicate with the nekekami. I've never met with them face to face. I'm going to recite those code words for you. Memorize them. *Do not* write them down, *ever*. They may not make such sense to anyone other than the nekekami, but there's no sense in taking any chances."

For several minutes, Morgan repeated the words and short phrases, along with what the ciphers would mean to the spirit cats. After each, he paused, giving her time to fix it all in her memory. When he had gone over the list several times, he resumed his narrative.

"Of course, you're going to have to keep all of this to yourself. Especially don't let Paul Masters or Sharon Bryan find out. They'd both be yelling their heads off so loud that you could hear it all the way back to Terra."

Again, he paused. Winston could see Morgan fighting to maintain control of his emotions. Until that moment, she had not considered how difficult it must have been for him to record a message that would only be seen after his death.

"Ariana, I have complete confidence in you," he continued, after mastering himself. "Otherwise, I wouldn't have asked to have you appointed as my second-in-command. You're a good soldier and a good officer. It's hard to find someone who's both these days. Hang on to that thought, and you'll pull this off."

Another pause.

"Say goodbye to Andrew for me. Tell him there was never a man who was a truer friend and that it was an honor, as well as my great pleasure, to call him one." Again, Morgan's voice threatened to break. "And Ariana? Assuming that you survive the mission, will you please call on my wife and family when you get back to the Inner Sphere? There's a package in my desk. I'd appreciate it if you would give it to Kym, personally. Tell her I love her, and I'll be waiting for her."

Mercifully, the recording ran out. With tears in her eyes, Ariana Winston shut the reader down.

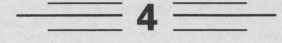

4

Battle Cruiser SLS Invisible Truth
Task Force Serpent
Unnamed Star System, Deep Periphery
11 January 3060

I hate this. The thought flashed through Ariana Winston's mind so rapidly, and with such vehemence, that she glanced quickly at the faces of those around her, fearing she might have spoken aloud. None of the people gathered in the large rec room of the *Invisible Truth*'s number one grav deck seemed to have heard. Winston reached up and tugged at the high collar of her drab green dress jacket. The movement was not as surreptitious as she had hoped. Edwin Amis, one of the Eridani Light Horse's regimental commanders, seemed to have caught the movement out the corner of his eye. He half-turned his head and gave her a thin smile accompanied by a tiny nod. The gesture seemed to say, "I agree with you, General. I'd rather be anyplace else."

The rec room, though large, was full, but not crowded. Present were the commanders of all the combat units that made up Task Force Serpent. Andrew Redburn, his face drawn, stood next to Major Michael Ryan of the Draconis Elite Strike Teams. Redburn's green dress uniform, with its golden sunburst covering the left half of his breast, contrasted strangely with Ryan's orange-piped white dress tunic.

It struck Winston as odd that ComStar, whose leaders had seemed so concerned that the mission be seen as representing the

Inner Sphere as a whole—in fact, as the renewed Star League—had issued the men and women of Task Force Serpent combat fatigues, but had failed to provide "Class-A" uniforms. The result was a hodgepodge of color and style, which—once she thought about it—was more fitting to the purpose for which they'd gathered than having everyone in identical uniforms.

Marshal Sharon Bryan, her light blue jacket immaculate, represented the Eleventh Guards of the Lyran Alliance. Colonel Samuel Kingston, whose green-gray outfit declared his allegiance to the Capellan Confederation, stood next to Colonel William MacLeod of the Northwind Highlanders. The Highlander uniform was similar in many ways to the drab green worn by the Eridani Light Horse—hardly surprising, given that both units had close ties to the Star League. The Highlanders managed to relieve the muted appearance of their dress greens by adding a kilt in one of the many colorful plaids associated with their Scottish ancestry.

Alain Beresick and Colonel Regis Grandi, both Com Guard members, were dressed alike in the gold-edged blue adopted by their order. Perhaps the most formal-looking of all was Överste Carl Sleipness of the Free Rasalhague Republic. His dress uniform, with its starched white shirt and high-collared black cloak, seemed to belong to the nineteenth rather than the thirty-first century. There was an elegance to the costume that spoke of a simpler time. Colonel Paul Masters was resplendent in the gold-trimmed white uniform of the Knights of the Inner Sphere.

As Winston glanced around the room, an older man, dressed in the black and gold uniform of the Kathil Uhlans, stepped to the front of the room, where the *Truth*'s crew had set up a podium. The assembled men and women quickly found their seats.

"Friends," he began. "We have gathered here today to honor the life and memory of a great man, Morgan Hasek-Davion." For the next few minutes, Father Jonas Pavlik delivered a beautifully crafted eulogy, praising Morgan for the soldier, leader, husband, and father he had been. He told of Morgan's many achievements in both war and peace and of his unwavering devotion to the Davions as well as to the Federated Commonwealth over which they ruled. Winston was moved by the chaplain's words, even more so because his speech wasn't just the empty tribute so often heard following the death of a great man like Morgan. Father Pavlik had known and loved the man he was now laying to rest.

When Pavlik stepped away from the podium to resume his seat, Andrew Redburn took his place. He coughed nervously and fumbled with the pages he had taken from his dress jacket. Then, after another cough, he began.

"I probably knew Morgan better than anyone in this room, maybe even better than his wife, Kym. Many of you already know the facts of his long and distinguished military service. The important events of his career as the soldier, the general, the public figure. At first, all I knew about him was that he was Michael Hasek-Davion's son and Prince Hanse Davion's nephew. But, over time, I learned so much more. What can you say about a man like Morgan that doesn't sound trite? Not much, because he *was* the man that preachers always talk about at funerals.

"Morgan Hasek-Davion was, first and foremost, a man totally devoted to his family. I know that sounds strange when you consider the amount of time he spent *away* from his family. He told me once that spending that much time apart from Kym and George was not time lost, but time sacrificed. He said that by giving his time and talent, his sweat and blood to the Federated Suns, and later the Federated Commonwealth, he was securing his family's future. This security wasn't financial. He came from one of the richest families in the Inner Sphere. He didn't have to rely on the relative pittance he earned as a soldier. No, the security he fought for was far more precious, and far less tangible, than money. Morgan fought, and bled, and died for a future secure from the threat of tyranny and oppression.

"I know in my heart that Morgan is sitting somewhere in Heaven, probably under one of those trees the Bible says line the streets of gold, looking back at us. I can almost see his careworn face, his green eyes, that crooked smile. I can almost hear him say, 'Stick to it. Run the race. Fight the good fight. It's all worth it. If even one person lives free for one hour, it's all worth it.'

"For myself, I lost my best friend, a man whom I'd come to love even more than I realized.

"Goodbye, Morgan, I . . ."

Unable to continue, Andrew Redburn shook his head and stepped away from the podium. Winston moved to his side in a single, long-legged stride. Taking him by the arm, she guided him gently to his seat.

"It's okay, Andrew," she murmured, speaking so quietly that only he could hear. "We all understand. We've all been there."

"I'm all right." His voice was a strained whisper, but strength began to creep back into his tone. "I'll be all right."

Winston gave him a brief, encouraging smile and a nod. Then she took her place at the podium.

"We all know that Morgan was a soldier, but who ultimately reaps the benefit of a soldier's life? It is those he leaves behind: his family, his friends, his countrymen. Even those who hate him for the uniform he wears, and for the weapons he carries, and for the blood he spills, have a share in the prize he wins. All partake, in equal measure, of the freedom and peace that only a soldier can provide.

"Now, I don't have the gift for crafting beautiful words that Father Pavlik has, nor do I claim the long-time friendship of Andrew Redburn. What I do have is a sense of history. Morgan Hasek-Davion was one of those souls who left a lasting impression on everything he touched. You may not see it right away, but it *is* there. He was the last of his kind, and the world is much the poorer for his passing. We will never see his like again."

As she found her seat, Captain D.C. Stockdale, the Light Horse's chaplain, stepped forward. He and Father Pavlik had agreed to share the memorial duties. Opening a small, cloth-covered book, Captain Stockdale read aloud the words of the Commitment, which were unchanged after more than three thousand years.

"I know that my redeemer liveth, and that he shall stand in the latter day upon the Earth. Lord, we commit to your keeping the soul of Morgan Hasek-Davion, in the sure and certain hope that one day, the grave will give up its dead. Ashes to ashes, and dust to dust. The Lord giveth, and He taketh away. Blessed be the Name of the Lord."

As Stockdale stepped back from the podium, Ariana Winston snapped out a call to attention. Almost as one, the assembled warriors shot to their feet. The sound of their heels coming together was like a single pistol shot in the crowded rec room.

From the back of the room, a high, thin, wailing sound was heard. Winston, from her vantage point, could see a young man dressed in the uniform of the Northwind Highlanders, with green and red plaid warpipes pressed under his left elbow, and tears streaming down his clear, young face. The tune he played almost escaped her for a moment. Then she remembered it from childhood, *Almighty Father, Strong to Save*. She hadn't heard it in years, though it had been one of her father's favorite hymns.

As the skirling sound of the pipes faded away, she saw another young man, this one clad in the black and gold of the Kathil Uhlans, step forward. In his hand was a silver-plated bugle. He snapped the mouthpiece to his lips. Each warrior in the room brought his or her right hand up in a last salute to a fallen comrade as the haunting notes of the old, old bugle call *Last Post* sounded across the crowd.

When the last notes died away, Winston barked out "Two," and the saluting hands were lowered.

"Dis . . ." The papery whisper caught in Winston's throat. She coughed once, and tried again. "Dismissed."

For a moment, no one moved, as though each felt that, by dispersing, they would be guilty of forgetting Morgan. Then, in ones and twos, they began to drift out of the room.

Winston went back to her chair and sat down next to Andrew Redburn.

"He's gone, Ariana."

"Ria," she said, wanting to comfort Redburn, but feeling in need of some comfort herself. "I know he's gone, Andrew. And I know it hurts. Do you want to be alone so you can say goodbye to him? Or do you want me to stay?"

Before Redburn could answer, the intercom crackled to life.

"Bridge to General Winston."

Ariana cursed the bridge officer for his poor timing, lousy judgment, and lack of compassion. Briefly, she considered not answering the page. Then she realized that the *Truth*'s third officer, who had the watch, would not interrupt the memorial unless he had a *very* good reason.

Patting Redburn on the shoulder, she said, "I'll be right back."

"Bridge, Winston." She allowed a note of irritation to creep into her voice as she keyed the intercom unit. "What is it?"

"General, maybe you'd better come up to the bridge," the Officer of the Deck answered. "Communications is picking up a weird signal."

"Can you patch it through here?"

"Yes, ma'am."

Almost immediately, a ghostly voice hissed from the intercom. There was something uncomfortably familiar about it, as though Winston had heard the speaker somewhere before.

"To all citizens of the Inner Sphere do I, Aleksandr Kerensky, send greetings."

Aleksandr Keresnky! The revelation set the flesh over her spine to crawling. That was where she had heard the voice before—in the dozens of holotapes she and everyone else in the galaxy had seen of that famous general's speeches, lectures, and personal appearances, all recorded long before the collapse of the Star League had prompted him to take his armada beyond the farthest known reaches of space.

Kerensky's disembodied, gravelly voice continued.

"Know that I have taken the remnant of the Star League Defense Force which has remained true to its purpose beyond the boundaries of the Inner Sphere, beyond the Periphery. I have done this, neither out of disappointment with those whom we leave behind, nor out of spite or disdain, as some will say. No, we have left the Inner Sphere because we love it too much to see it destroyed. In the wake of the Usurper's coup, and the long, bitter fighting that came with it, I fear that my forces would do incalculable, possibly irreparable, harm to our society. We are sworn to ward the Star League and its subjects, not destroy it.

"Thus, we have left the only homes we have ever known to place the destructive capability of this armada beyond the reach of those who would use it, not for defense, but for conquest. Perhaps, with the might of our 'Mechs and ships out of their reach, the leaders who now grapple with one another will relinquish their dreams of subjugating their neighbors and learn to live in peace with them.

"Perhaps, one day, should mankind step back from the brink of the abyss, we, or our children, or our children's children will return, to once more serve and protect and guide the Star League in mankind's quest for the stars.

"Fare well."

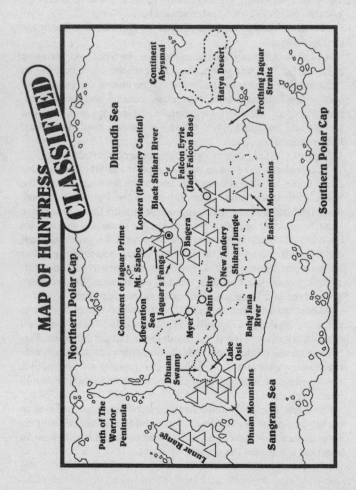

5

Battle Cruiser SLS **Invisible Truth**
Task Force Serpent
Unnamed Star System, Deep Periphery
15 January 3060

News of the unearthly message intercepted by the task force quickly made the rounds of the fleet. All of Serpent's ships picked it up and recorded it. Several of those recordings had been copied, and the copies made their way into the hands of individual soldiers, some of whom had plans to exploit what was coming to be known as the "Voice of Kerensky" for their own enrichment. Thankfully, each of the unit commanders was eager to deal with profiteers.

For Ariana Winston, however, the Voice prompted entirely different questions.

"So what are you telling me, Commodore?" she asked Alain Beresick, seated at the desk in the center of the *Invisible Truth*'s ready room. Like most large WarShips, the *Truth* boasted a relatively spacious combination cabin, office, and lounge adjacent to the main bridge. Called the Captain's ready room, it was the sole province of the ship's commanding officer. Though Beresick had offered it to both Morgan and Winston, each had declined, for the same reasons. Morgan, and later Winston, as task force commander, had chosen to occupy the *Truth*'s flag suite, one deck below. The ready room was traditionally for the ship captain's use, and neither had wanted to deny Beresick that privilege.

"What I'm telling you, General, is that I'm not sure," Beresick shot back in exasperation. "I'm not a commtech, I'm a ship's captain. I don't think I could give you more than a thumbnail sketch of how half the systems on this bridge work, let alone the whole ship. Beyond that, I simply couldn't tell you how hyperspace communications work, as opposed to rational space communications.

"I do know that there's some connection between HPG communications and Kearny-Fuchida jump drives, but that's about it. I can surmise that the same technology that opens a 'gate' in the fabric of the universe for a JumpShip to move through is used by a hyperpulse generator to send interstellar messages.

"Once a ship is back in rational space, it has to rely on the same technology they were using back in the twentieth century to send their little bug-ships to Luna and back. I'd have to guess that R-space communications are the same way. We use an HPG to send messages between systems, but we're stuck with radio, laser, and microwave communicators when we're in-system.

"Part of the problem with HPG messages is their limited range. Sure the signal is transmitted almost instantly, but it *does* have a range limit, about fifty light years. So, without a series of HPG-equipped relay ships, Kerensky's message would never have reached the Inner Sphere.

"But I think there was probably another reason he chose to send his 'maybe I'll come home someday' message via an ordinary communicator, in this case a broad-band microwave transmitter. If he did establish that chain of relay stations, his message would have arrived in the Inner Sphere shortly after he left. The Successor States were still at war with each other, and the storm of barbarism he sought to escape was still raging. If he'd sent the message then, what effect would it have had? We can't know for certain, but I'd have to say not much. Some of the warring states might have tried to capitalize on the message, tweaking it here and there for their benefit. Somebody might have tried to launch an expedition to find the armada, to try to convince them to come back or throw in with one faction or another. Most likely the message would have been ignored or maybe denounced as a fake.

"Now, by using normal microwave communications, he could send his message out at sub-light speed, with the reasonable assurance that in time, a *long* time, the signal would reach the Inner Sphere. I'm just speculating here, you understand. I think he hoped that by the time his message reached the Inner Sphere, the wars would have sputtered to a halt, the destruction would have ended, and mankind would have come to realize how wrong they were in ripping the Star League apart.

"Do you realize that if Morgan hadn't been killed, we'd have jumped out of this system long before 'the Voice' ever got here, and it's going to take a long time for that signal to reach the nearest human outpost. It was blind luck that we were around to hear it."

"Yeah, 'luck.' "

Winston's answer revealed a level of dispirited weariness that surprised Beresick.

"General, is something wrong?"

"No, Alain, not really. It's just that the past few days are starting to catch up with me. And now this." She tapped the hardcopy printout of the "Voice." "Intercepting the 'Voice' right after Morgan's memorial kind of gave me the creeps. I mean, the similarities are a little too close for comfort. Both Morgan and Kerensky led an armada off into the 'deep dark' in hopes of preserving what was left of the Inner Sphere. And here we are following in Kerensky's figurative footsteps, and what do we hear? The voice of a long-dead General, at about the time we're saying goodbye to our own recently dead general."

Winston shivered. "It just gave me the creeps."

She shuddered again, this time with the decisive shake of one throwing off an uncomfortable garment.

"How soon do we jump?"

The sudden change in Winston's demeanor seemed to take Beresick by surprise.

"As soon as you give the word, General. The engines are all charged up, and we're ready at any time."

Winston inhaled deeply, then blew the air out again in a long breath.

"All right, let's go," she said. "The sooner we're away from this system, the better I'm going to like it."

In many ways, the *Invisible Truth*'s bridge was identical to the control deck of every other starship Ariana Winston had ever seen. The main difference was its size. Where the average transport-type JumpShip, like the Eridani Light Horse's own

Monolith Class *Gettysburg,* had a bridge supporting only a few control stations, the *Truth* boasted over a dozen. The center of her spacious control deck was dominated by a high-resolution holotank. Smaller vessels seldom had the space to install such a device. The three-dimensional laser-generated image of the task force, its ships hanging motionless in space above the system's KII sun, was easily six meters across.

Surrounding the tank's raised platform were a series of smaller flat-screen and three-dimensional monitors displaying everything from the current tactical situation to the status of the jump sail. A second battery of instrument panels ran around the outside of the bridge deck. These were occupied by still more ComStar techs going about their routine tasks. The most alert of the bridge personnel were those peering closely at the various "waterfall" displays linked to the ship's sensors. Given their current position so far from the Inner Sphere, early detection of an incoming starship could spell the difference between life and death for the men and women of Task Force Serpent.

"Commander on deck. Captain on deck."

Winston had long since grown accustomed to the age-old shout raised by the petty officer stationed next to the bridge door. But, up until a few days ago, that honor had been Morgan's, not hers.

Beresick seemed not to have noticed the salute. Instead, he went straight to work.

"I have the conn," he barked.

"Captain has the conn," replied the *Truth*'s second officer.

"Report all contacts."

"Sir, my only contacts are those of the task force." The officer in charge of the sensor technicians didn't look up from his master panel as he gave his report.

At Beresick's command, another bridge tech opened a communications channel.

"All commands, this is Spanner. Recall Combat Air Patrol and prepare for jump. Report when ready."

Slowly, the ships comprising Task Force Serpent checked in with the flagship. The first was the *Haruna,* a *Kyushu* Class frigate built in secret under the Draconis Combine's Phoenix Program. That WarShip, along with the elite troopers of the DEST teams, were the Combine's only contribution to the task force.

The majority of that state's military strength had been dedicated to Operation Bulldog, the Inner Sphere phase of the operation.

Winston found a place where she could observe the goings-on without being in the way. Though she had witnessed the task force's preparations for jump many times before, from both the *Truth* and the *Gettysburg,* the organized chaos of the operation never failed to amuse and astound her. Amuse, because, for all the drama of the moment portrayed in countless holovids, the entertainment industry never seemed to get it right. Nowhere were the steely-eyed men and women sitting tensely at their consoles. No frenetic cries rang across the bridge, reporting as various systems came on-line.

A casual observer would find the scene anti-climactic, after a steady diet of techno-thrillers. Calm, self-possessed professionals relayed their reports to and through the appropriate officers. They spoke quietly into head-set microphones.

What astounded Winston about the jump preparations was the fact that Commodore Beresick and his officers were able to make sense of the dozens of brief reports forwarded to their stations not only from those men and women around them, but from every other ship in the fleet. Her astonishment turned to disbelief when she noticed that Beresick seldom consulted the repeater displays set in his command console. He seemed to be keeping track of the many, sometimes conflicting, reports in his head.

When the last vessel had checked in, Beresick turned to face Winston. "All stations report manned and ready, sir."

"Good." Winston took no offense at the male honorific. She knew that tradition reaching back to the blue-water navies of Terra dictated that all officers aboard a combat vessel be referred to as "Mister" or "Sir," regardless of their gender. "Let's get away from here."

"Aye, sir." Beresick bobbed his head in acknowledgment. Then, turning to face his console, he began rapping out the orders that would eventually send the 850,000-ton starship hurtling across thirty light years through a tear in the fabric of space.

"To all commands, initiate jump procedures. Mr. Hivlan, lock course into the navputer. Mr. Ng, engage the K-F drive."

"Course plotted and laid in."

"K-F drives charged and on-line, sir."

"Sound the horn."

In response to Beresick's order, a raucous klaxon honked three times.

In the miniature world of the holotank, a scarlet flare of light bloomed and vanished in less than a second, leaving flash-bulb afterimages swimming before Winston's eyes. More crimson flashes dotted the projection as the WarShip's powerful computers translated the electromagnetic and tachyon flares of all the departing JumpShips of Serpent into a visible-light display.

"Sir, we are ready to jump."

Winston nodded sharply. "Jump."

"Aye, sir. Jump," Beresick repeated. Gesturing to the chief engineering officer, he snapped, "Mr. Ng, activate field initiator. Jump."

"Initiator active, sir." The officer's fingers danced across the control panel. "Jump in five . . . four . . . three . . . two . . . one . . . Jump!"

Ng's final exclamation slurred, as though played through a recorder that had suddenly run out of power. The field initiator, a massive system of electronics and quantum mechanics buried deep within the *Truth*'s hull, drew power from the ship's engines, and, focusing it through the Kearny-Fuchida drive, translated it into an expanding field of energy that soon enveloped the ship. In a burst of electromagnetic and tachyon radiation, the gate snapped closed, and the WarShip materialized at the nadir jump point of its destination system, nearly thirty light years away.

Winston's senses cleared quickly, throwing off the disorientation that often accompanied being hurled across the void between stars. The holotank was still flickering, with bright red flashes proclaiming the arrival of the rest of the task force.

Winston knew that Task Force Serpent fielded fifty-five thousand men and women, over a thousand 'Mechs, aerospace fighters, and armored vehicles, scores of DropShips, and dozens of starships. They came from thousands of worlds across five greater and two lesser states. Four regiments worth of troops, her own Eridani Light Horse and the Northwind Highlanders, were mercenaries, but they were mercenaries with ancient ties, often including personal ancestries, back to the Star League. Then there were the Com Guards, the warrior arm of ComStar. Each unit comprising the task force had its own traditions, doctrines, and agendas. Some, the DEST teams, for example, had different languages and cultural backgrounds. These were all problems that had to be overcome.

Some of these difficulties had been ironed out somewhat before the task force left the training base on Defiance. Further refinements in troop integration had been accomplished as Serpent made its slow, steady "flank march" through untracked space.

Winston didn't often think about the terrible void through which the task force had come. She understood the necessity of moving so far around the Clan-held occupation zones. The reason was the same for any strategic flanking maneuver: to move as many troops as far behind the enemy's front lines as possible, with the least risk of detection by the enemy. What had given her moments of anxiety was the realization that, if anything major went wrong along the way, such as a jump drive failure, the task force would have to abandon the crippled vessel.

What unnerved her the most was the possibility that the Clans might discover Serpent before it reached its objective. They had dodged that particular bullet once already. The task force had jumped into a Deep Periphery system, where a flotilla of Clan Ghost Bear starships was recharging its jump engines. A short naval battle had ensued, the first in two hundred years of Inner Sphere history.

Serpent had been lucky that day. In a battle that a rather unimaginative Com Guard officer had dubbed "Trafalgar" after a blue-water battle between sail-powered warships of Terra's ancient past, the task force had defeated the more experienced, but numerically inferior, Clan force. The battle had resulted in the loss of one assault-type DropShip and a handful of aerospace fighters. One of the task force's WarShips, the *Starlight,* an *Essex* Class destroyer, had taken heavy, but repairable damage. The Ghost Bears fared less well. Two WarShips and one JumpShip had either been destroyed or badly damaged. One Clan destroyer, a *Whirlwind,* along with a handful of fighters and DropShips, had been captured and repaired by the task force, upping their WarShip complement to eight.

The victory at Trafalgar had left the task force with an unforeseen problem, however. The Ghost Bears had been transporting civilians to that Clan's occupation zone in the Inner Sphere. From what the few captured Clan officers were able to tell their captors, the plan was a semi-secret move by Khan Bjorn Jorgensson to transfer large portions of his Clan to worlds of the Inner Sphere. The result was that there were over a thousand noncombatants aboard the Clan ships. The Inner Sphere force was not prepared to handle such a large number of prisoners, so far from their own destination. The only option available was to maroon the Clan captives on a habitable planet, and send for them once the operation was completed. The solution was not perfect, but it was more acceptable than simply executing hundreds of helpless civilians and those warriors who refused to take a bond-oath to "Clan Serpent."

That had happened once already, when the task force encountered a ragtag band of Periphery pirates. The leaders were tried for crimes against humanity and executed. Winston understood the need for justice, and, for the most part, had agreed with the sentence. The pirates were criminals. They had murdered, raped, robbed, and enslaved helpless people. The punishment fitted their crimes. What bothered her was the fact that the pirates had been prisoners of war. The task force was a military expedition, not a law-enforcement operation. The prisoners should have been turned over to "the proper authorities" for their trial. She knew that the only real course of action open to the task force was the trial, execution of the ring-leaders, and the abandonment of the pirates spared from death. The forced dichotomy of her deeply held personal convictions and the need for military expediency still bothered her. She wondered what other challenges to her convictions she would face now that she was in charge.

"General, all commands report in-system. The BARCAP has been deployed, and we are beginning recharge operations."

Winston jumped. "Very well, Commodore." She felt a little foolish, as though she had been caught daydreaming. "Do we have a survey report on this system?"

Beresick tapped keys on his command console.

"Yes, we do. Explorer Corps mission five-five-six-oh-one survey of this system reports three planets, none inhabited, none capable of sustaining Terra-type life. Are you thinking of a naval fire-support test?"

"Uh-huh. Any of those rocks down there look like a suitable testing ground?"

"Hold on a second." Beresick scanned the data before him. "Yeah, number two. It's far enough away from the central star that a spotter crew could survive. Of course, they'll have to wear environment suits, but that shouldn't be too much of a problem. How soon do you want to start?"

Winston looked at her watch. "Let's make it two hours. I'd like to give everybody a chance to settle in after the jump. Let anyone with TDS get their legs back. Yeah, two hours ought to be soon enough."

"Mmm . . ." was the Commodore's reply.

TDS, or Transit Disorientation Syndrome, was simply a fifty C-bill medical term for jump sickness. Most doctors believed that the malady was a psychosomatic reaction to the sudden and unnatural shock of being hurled across thirty light years of space in less than a heartbeat. Many people felt only a moment's disorientation or a sinking feeling in the pit of their stomachs. Some people had a more severe reaction. Otherwise healthy men and women became dizzy or nauseous after a jump. An unfortunate few were subject to severe reactions. Painful abdominal cramps, blinding headaches, and stabbing arthritis-like pains in the joints could incapacitate a TDS victim for as long as thirty minutes after a hyperspace jump. Medication could control, or at least lessen, the effect. A synthetic meclizine analog was the drug of choice. Unfortunately, the cure was in some ways as bad as the disease. Meclizine caused drowsiness. Most warriors suffered the effects of jump sickness rather than having their fighting ability impaired.

Winston knew that only about two percent of the task force suffered from the severe effects of TDS. She also knew that number included Sandra Barclay, her junior colonel, commander of the 71st Light Horse Regiment.

"Let me know when you're ready to start the test," Winston said, heading for the bridge door. "I'll be in Morgan's . . . ah, my office."

Not two, but sixty hours later, a bleeping intercom dragged Ariana Winston's attention away from the mound of paperwork that had accumulated on her desk over the past few days. It amazed her that Morgan had ever gotten anything accomplished, given the number of reports that had to be reviewed by the task force commander. There was an old saying that an army traveled not on its stomach, but its paperwork, and she was finding that to be true.

"General Winston, we're about ready to start the fire-support test," Beresick said.

"Okay, Commodore, I'm on my way." Winston replied, happy to have a legitimate reason for putting off the reports. As she made the short trip to the bridge, she reviewed the plans for the test firing in her mind.

The command staff had decided to assign the job to the destroyer *Starlight*. Her skipper was a fairly experienced officer, and had been going over the fire procedures developed from the data taken from the Clan WarShips captured at Trafalgar. Lacking a docking collar—the heavy ring of machinery, interlocks, and seals that held a DropShip to the JumpShip—the *Starlight* was forced to rely on small craft for ferrying men and material from ship to surface. In this case, the men, a fire-direction team drawn from the 2nd Com Guards, and the materiel, a Swift Wind scout car belonging to that combat battalion, were crammed aboard a K-1 type drop shuttle.

Under real combat conditions, the fire-control party would be grounded aboard a larger, better-armored DropShip, but for the purposes of the test, the two-hundred ton shuttle was sufficient.

Moving under a normal one G's worth of acceleration, it took the *Starlight* about sixty hours to make the trip from the system's zenith jump point to a geosynchronous orbit above the target planet. The unusually short trip was accounted for by the fact that the destroyer was only traveling as far as the second planet in the system. Had the system's only planet that *might* have supported life been the destination, the trip would have taken twice as long.

When the bridge doors hissed open, Winston saw that Commodore Beresick had been joined by Colonel Regis Grandi, commander of the 2nd Com Guards. He was carefully reviewing the fire procedures for the naval officer.

"As soon as they get the Swift Wind unpacked and an uplink established, the fire-direction team will pick out a target, probably a hill or a large rock outcropping. We're going to try to call in fire two ways; first, the old-fashioned way, by calling coordinates in to the ship's Fire Direction Center. Assuming the *Starlight* manages to hit the mark in no more than four rounds—and I have no real hope of that—the spotters will switch targets and try again, using the designator and uplink mounted in the Swift Wind."

"How soon will they be in position?" Winston asked, moving to the holotank, which was set to display a graphic representation of the test-fire area.

" 'Bout ten minutes," Grandi replied. "They've got to get the scout car emplaced and the antenna aligned. After that, it's just a matter of pointing at the target and saying make that disappear."

"What's the lag time on your graphic?" Winston knew enough about surface-to-space operations to realize that what she was seeing was not real-time imagery.

"Given that we're using a direct two-way communications link, and considering the distance, not too long. Fifteen minutes, give or take," Beresick answered. "Now that's from the *Starlight* to the *Truth*. The *Starlight* is in-system and we're still sitting at the jump point. Ship-to-surface will be so close to instantaneous as won't matter."

Winston was vaguely disturbed by the detached interest in the proceedings. If the test was successful, the task force would have another weapon in their arsenal against the Jaguars. If the exercise failed, they would be forced to fight a more conventional campaign. She wasn't sure which outcome she hoped for. If the task force had the option of orbital fire-support at their disposal, an otherwise losing battle might be turned into a victory. On the other hand, she, like most military leaders, had seen the vids smuggled out of Turtle Bay.

In March of 3050, the Smoke Jaguars had assaulted Turtle Bay, a backwater world in the Draconis Combine's Pesht Military District. During the fighting, the Jaguars unknowingly captured Prince Hohiro Kurita, heir apparent of the Draconis Combine. Members of the local yakuza took it upon themselves to rescue the Prince and his companions. Furious at what they considered an affront to their honor, the Jaguars withdrew their troops from Edo, then moved the *Saber Cat*, an *Essex* Class destroyer into geosynchronous orbit above the planetary capital, and leveled the city with a naval artillery barrage. It was an act of unparalleled barbarism. Tens, if not hundreds of thousands, died as a result of the bombardment. Disease and starvation followed. To this day, the exact death toll was still uncertain.

Though Winston knew that the task force was planning to

employ naval gunfire against specific targets, and only as a last resort, she couldn't shake the images of burned-out buildings and sick, starving civilians from her memory.

"General?" Beresick's concerned tone jolted Winston out of her reverie.

"Oh, pardon me, Commodore, you were saying?" she said, trying to bring her mind back to the task at hand.

"I was saying that the spotting crew is on-line. They've got an uplink with the *Starlight*. They're ready to proceed."

"Okay, let's do it."

Several million kilometers away, a Com Guard lieutenant, who was still getting used to his new rank, selected a small rocky hill about three kilometers away from his fire-direction team's position. A pair of binoculars fitted with a laser range-finder and a basic magnetic compass provided him with the data he needed.

"Range: three-zero-five-three meters. Azimuth: two-six-seven."

A corporal seated in the back of the six-wheeled scout car repeated the figures as he entered them into his communications gear. Lacking a sophisticated global positioning system, the fire-direction team had to rely on the ancient method of range and compass bearing for calling in support fire.

"*Starlight* reports coordinates received, ready to fire," the noncom reported a moment later.

"Fire."

High above the scout car's position, the destroyer *Starlight* unleashed a single blast from her starboard naval laser.

On the planet's surface, an eye-searing flash obliterated a patch of rocky soil almost one hundred meters away from the target hill's summit.

"Splash," the lieutenant called, indicating that the shot had landed where he could see it. "Correction. Up thirty, left twenty-five, and fire again."

Again, a brilliant flare erupted on the hill, this time only a few meters from the target.

"I'd call that on-target, wouldn't you, Corporal?"

"Yes, sir."

"Okay." Satisfaction was evident in the lieutenant's voice. "Switching targets. Let's try it again using the microwave designator."

Not long after the first laser shot impacted the test range, the fire-direction team secured their equipment and boosted for the *Starlight*. Aboard the *Invisible Truth*, the command staff reviewed the test's results.

"First of all," Commodore Beresick read from his noteputer-displayed report, "Lieutenant Bales, the man in charge of the fire-direction team, reports he had difficulty in establishing an uplink with the *Starlight*. The problem was a misaligned uplink antenna. Although the team located and solved the problem quickly, the glitch took almost ten minutes to correct."

"That's not good," Ariana Winston interjected.

"No, General, it's not," Beresick agreed. "In combat, especially if things are desperate enough to call for naval fire support, ten minutes is a long time.

"However, once the problem was corrected, the team reports that they were able to designate and correct naval support fire quickly and easily. The team shifted targets rapidly, calling for different types of fire, different barrage patterns, and so on. In each case, the fire-direction officer was able to talk the naval gunners onto the target in three rounds or less."

"Mm-hum." Winston peered closely at her hard-copy of the direction team's report. "What does your spotter think? Could a fire-direction team call in accurate orbital support fire during a high-stress situation?"

"He thinks so," Beresick said guardedly. "He thinks that anyone familiar enough with normal fire-direction procedures could call in support fire. The main difference is where the shots are coming from. Granted, there is a much smaller margin of error, given the relative power of the weapons we're dealing with here. Lieutenant Bales thinks, and I concur, that an inexperienced spotter would have real trouble coordinating fire accurately."

"Commodore, I see that you tested naval lasers, PPCs, and autocannons," Major Marcus Poling, CO of the 2nd St Ives Lancers, chimed in. "What about your big missile launchers, like the white sharks? Couldn't they be fired against ground targets?"

"Sure. But why would you want to?" Beresick asked. "Capital missiles like the white shark are far more accurate than other ballistic weapons, but the problem is that they're in kind of short supply. We fired a dozen or so back at Trafalgar, and we've got to figure that there will be at least a few WarShips guarding the

Huntress system. Do we engage the Jag WarShips all out, or do we hold back some of our missiles for bombardment?

"Even if we had missiles to spare, they aren't suited to planetary bombardment. Their warheads are designed to penetrate heavy naval armor plating before they detonate. You'd get some blast effect, but not a lot of shrapnel."

Beresick paused, and, rubbing his chin, called up a map of Huntress on the conference room's holotable.

"I guess you might want to fire missiles at a really big, nasty bunker or major installation, say . . . like Mount Szabo." The mountain reported to house the Huntress system's command and control headquarters glowed red on the holographic map. "Anything less, and you're swatting mosquitoes with a sledgehammer."

At the same time, another meeting, far less formal, and comprised of ordinary space-hands was taking place. In the age of sail of Terra's blue-water navies, the gathering might have been called a "fo'c'sle council." The fact that the *Invisible Truth* had no forecastle, and that, even if she did, her crew would still be housed in dormitory-like quarters instead of a common berthing space didn't matter. Like those "crewmen-only" conferences of old, the subject of the rather heated discussion was the shortcomings of the ship's officers.

"I don't really care what 'Old Berry' says," said jump drive astech Lucas Penrose, who was lying on his bunk and lifted his head a bit as he spoke. "There's something more going on here than they're telling us."

Penrose's roommate, an ordnanceman rejoicing in the unlikely name of John Smith, bristled slightly at the Commodore's lower-deck nickname. His devotion to the *Truth*'s commander didn't prevent him from agreeing with Penrose.

"That's what I was trying to tell you, Luke. Anytime the brass start passing around 'official statements,' you can bet your last C-bill that the truth is something other than 'official.' "

"So what are you saying? That Beresick lied to us?"

"No, nothing like that." Smith leaned closer to Penrose. "You know, they might be keeping something back for security reasons."

"What security reasons?" Another man, this one wearing the khaki and gray uniform of a DropShip crewman, interjected. "As far as we know, the Marshal had a heart attack. Even if he didn't, who are we going to tell all the way out here?"

"Phil, I think that's just what Smitty is saying. Isn't it, Smitty?" Penrose heaved himself into a sitting position, facing the other men. "He was just wondering if they'd say anything different if there were anything different to say."

"Something like that," Smith concurred.

"Something like what?"

"Well, for instance . . ." Penrose hesitated, looked around, then asked, "What if the Marshal didn't die of natural causes? Right, Smitty?"

"Uh-huh." Smith picked up his roommate's theme. "I mean, what if someone had a grudge against the Marshal and did him in? They wouldn't tell us about that, would they?"

"Not on your life they wouldn't," Penrose said emphatically.

"Oh, come on!" Phil said, exasperated. "Who would want to kill Morgan?"

"Who would want to kill Morgan?" Smith said. "Let's start with Sun-Tzu. The Kathil Uhlans made his granddad look kinda sick during the Fourth War, didn't they? The Marshal was the Uhlans' commander, wasn't he? For all we know, Sun-Tzu's just as cracked as the rest of his family. Is it that far-fetched that he'd take a crack at the Marshal, just out of spite? Or how about Teddy Kurita? Huh? Or even Katrina Steiner? It's no secret that neither of them ever really liked the Marshal. If they had him killed, it'd weaken the Federated Commonwealth, and Prince Victor."

"Smitty, you're starting to sound a little paranoid."

"No, I'm not, Phil. Just think about it for a minute, will you? What if I'm right? What if there's some 'unknown power' at work here? How safe is this task force? How safe are we? I mean, if they could have the Marshal assassinated all the way out here, what's to say they won't sell us out to the Clans?"

Before Smitty could continue, Lucas Penrose levered himself off his bunk.

"Well, fellas, as interesting as all this is, I'm on duty in twenty minutes, and I want to get a shower first."

As Penrose closed the cabin door behind him, he heard Smitty offering, as proof of his conspiracy theory, the fact that the Draconis Elite Strike teams had "wormed their way onto the investigation team."

"I mean that's the perfect cover-up, isn't it? You kill the Marshal, and then conduct the investigation into the murder. By the time you're done, there either isn't enough evidence, or they've pinned it on some poor guy who never had anything to do with it."

Only a few hours after Penrose had closed the stateroom door, most of the *Invisible Truth*'s enlisted crewmen had heard Ordnanceman Smith's conspiracy theory. The ship-board rumor mill was in full operation.

6

Battle Cruiser SLS Invisible Truth
Task Force Serpent
Unnamed Star System, Deep Space
19 January 3060

The investigation into Morgan Hasek-Davion's death had grown to a size and scope where it threatened to take on a life of its own. Captain Montjar, the officer originally assigned to look into the assassination, had first requested the help of the Draconis Elite Strike Teams, and then stepped aside in favor of the more experienced DEST commander, Major Michael Ryan. Secretly, Ariana Winston approved of the change. Being a mercenary, she had none of the usual baggage that went along with being a member of one of the House units of the Successor States. While she respected Captain Montjar, and considered him a competent officer, Winston actually liked Ryan.

She wasn't quite sure why, though. She usually found Combine officers rather stiff, and overly formal, a product of their somewhat monolithic culture. Ryan, however, was different. While in public, he adhered rigidly to the code of conduct set down in the Draconis Combine's Pillar of Teak, one of the five disciplines that figuratively supported the Draconis Combine. Privately, in some of his few relaxed moments, Ryan was a real person in the body of a trained, cold-eyed killer.

It had surprised Winston to learn that he enjoyed music and could even play the *shakuhachi*, the traditional Japanese bamboo flute. Ryan respectfully reminded his commanding General that the code of bushido required all warriors to learn at least some of the fine arts as well as the arts of war.

Perhaps it was this pleasant, wholly human trait that made Winston accept Montjar's recommendation that Ryan be placed in charge of the investigation. The fact that the ship's gossips held that Ryan and his men were up to their necks in a far-reaching assassination plot did not shake her faith in the rightness of the decision. In fact, Ariana Winston had done everything she could to quash the rampant and somewhat outrageous stories coming out of the *Truth*'s rumor-mill.

Like most soldiers, she had developed an ear ever alert for the slightest bit of information that might come along. As a commander, she came to loathe the unsubstantiated reports that tended to make the rounds of any military unit. The paradox failed to amuse her when she'd been a lieutenant commanding her first lance of BattleMechs. Now as the leader of what amounted to a reinforced division, in task force, she absolutely hated the wild, potentially dangerous, speculations and flawed conclusions that were making the rounds of the units comprising Task Force Serpent. That intense disgust had even begun to color her normally even temper.

Thus, as she sat uncomfortably behind what had been Morgan's desk, listening to Major Ryan and Commodore Beresick interviewing Morgan's cabin steward for perhaps the fifth time, her mood was blacker than anyone outside the Eridani Light Horse had ever seen it. Andrew Redburn sat in an armchair in the far corner of the room. He seemed to be exhausted. Winston had suggested that he get some sleep, leaving the interrogation to the command staff. Redburn would have none of it. Instead he perched zombie-like on the edge of the nyleath-upholstered chair.

"You're sure about the Marshal's habit of taking a drink before he turned in?" Ryan had taken a seat in front of the former Com Guard crewman. Winston recognized the positioning for what it was. Ryan's knees nearly touched the steward's. By invading the young man's "personal space," the commando leader put the steward on the defensive. There was an implied menace in Ryan's closeness. The steward's face revealed that he understood the threat, at least subconsciously. "You're sure he never missed a night."

"I told you he didn't *always* have a nightcap." The steward was defiant in his words, if not his attitude. "Sometimes he was just so tired that he went straight to bed. Sometimes he'd barely remember to fasten his restraining straps. I was always afraid that he'd turn over in his sleep, float off the bunk, and crash into something."

The steward's fears were not unfounded. Many people experiencing space travel for the first time forgot to tie themselves into their beds at night. Lacking any significant type of artificial gravity, starships had to rely on such measures. Those not properly restrained often tossed themselves across the room where they either got hurt, damaged the furnishings, or both. Winston knew that the steward was more concerned for the former than the latter of these potentials.

"So ka?" Ryan's tone suggested disbelief. The Japanese phrase added to the implied threat by reminding the steward exactly who and what Ryan was. "But what about the bottle, why can't we find it?"

"How should I know?" the steward growled in sudden irritation. "The last time I saw that bottle was when I put it back into the sideboard. The Marshal was forever leaving it out."

"And when was this?" Ryan interrupted.

The steward glanced at his commander before answering. Alain Beresick returned the steward's gaze impassively. Only a slight tightening around his eyes betrayed his sympathy for his young crewman.

"Just the day before." The man's tone left no doubt that "the day before" meant the morning before the murder. "I clearly remember putting it back into the nightstand. I had to do that a lot. The Marshal had a habit of leaving it out, sometimes not even in a rack. I was worried about the bottle drifting free and smashing against something. He'd even leave that pressurized transfer system or the squeeze bulb he drank from lying around. I was forever after him about cluttering up his cabin. It's funny, as neat as he was about the office, he never could seem to keep his stateroom in order."

"There was a full, unopened bottle of whiskey in the Marshal's nightstand. You said it was there the day before when you put the open one away, *neh?*" Ryan's voice was sharp, and his eyes never left the steward's even as he tapped entries into his noteputer. "What happened to the open bottle?"

"I don't know."

"And you can't tell us how the poison got into the transfer system, or what happened to the squeeze bulb?"

A spasm of righteous anger twisted the steward's face.

"I don't know!" he shouted. Moderating his angry tone, he turned in his seat to appeal directly to his commander. "Honest, Precentor, I didn't do it. I don't know what happened to the bottle or who killed the Marshal."

Beresick showed no reaction, other than a millimetric nod, which the steward obviously missed.

Looking at Winston, the hurt and fury still evident in his voice, the steward amplified and expanded his plea. "General, you believe me, don't you?"

Speaking for the first time since the interview began, Winston got to her feet, crossed the room and laid a hand on the young man's shoulder.

"It's not a matter of what *I believe,* son. It's a matter of what we can *prove.* Right now, all we can prove is that Morgan is dead. He was poisoned, and the poison was in his whiskey. We're trying to find out who put it there."

The steward sagged under her hand.

"I don't know what else to tell you." Then his drooping head snapped erect, a sudden fire blazing in his eyes.

"I don't even know why you're asking *me.* You ought to be asking *him.*" The steward's finger pointed straight between Ryan's eyes as though he wished it were a gun. "He's a *Drac.* He was probably in on it."

Winston's own temper nearly snapped.

"That is enough, mister," she hissed between clenched teeth. "Frankly, I'm surprised at you. Your record says you've been in the service for nearly ten years. You should know better. You shouldn't be getting 'rumoritis.'

"If nothing else, remember that Mister Ryan is a ranking Major in the new Star League Defense Force, and as such deserves your respect, not some baseless accusation. What about me? Are you going to accuse me next?"

"No, sir . . . er . . . ma'am," the crewman stammered. "You're right of course. I'm sorry, Major."

"Shigata ga nai." Winston, ever alert, caught the trace of a smile on Ryan's lips as he answered the steward in formal Japanese, and with a slight bow. Telling the man that what he had said mattered for nothing, the formal way of saying "that's all right," excused him for his poor manners. At the same time, Ryan's unaccustomed use of the Japanese formality was a not-so-subtle dig at the steward's suspicions.

"Er . . . um . . . *arigato.*" The steward fumbled over the proper, formal reply. The stricken look in his eyes told Winston that he also got the gibe.

"Is there anything else you'd like to tell us?" Beresick asked.

"Yes, sir." The steward was obviously relieved at having someone other than Ryan ask a question. "On . . . that night, I went to the Marshal's cabin, just after he turned in. I let myself in. The office was pretty neat, like I said, that's how he always kept it. I knocked, kinda quiet, on his stateroom door, but he didn't answer. I figured he'd already gone to sleep. Maybe if I'd been there a few minutes sooner . . ."

The steward's voice caught in his throat.

"That's all right, steward. That wasn't your fault," Winston said, not knowing what else to say. "You're dismissed."

"I've got to apologize for his attitude," Beresick said as the door closed behind the retreating steward.

Ryan began to say something, apparently intending to deflect the apology.

"No, Major," Winston cut him off. "There was no cause for such an outburst. He's an experienced man, and he ought to have known better." Ryan and his team had worked hard to build up a degree of trust between themselves and the rest of the task force. The steward's frustrated outburst was shaped by a long history of hatred, prejudice, and open warfare between the Draconis Combine and the Federated Commonwealth. It was hard to eliminate old hatreds in just a few months.

Winston had seen in Ryan's eyes that the man's comments had stung him, but there wasn't much they could do about it now except try to counter such displays of blind hatred any time they reared their ugly heads.

"Anyway," she said, turning the conversation back onto less painful ground. "Have you got anything new to tell us?"

"Hai," Ryan answered, obviously glad of the change of theme.

"I asked the ship's computer to run a records check on who opened the Marshal's door lock, and when. One of those times cannot be accounted for. It occurred when the Marshal was in a staff meeting and the steward was off duty. I already checked, and we've got about a dozen people who saw him. In fact, a few thought I was suspicious of them and referred me to the steward for an alibi. I was beginning to think we were looking in the wrong place with him.

"Then, I checked out the lock itself. Those prints that Montjar and his men lifted off the cryptolock were all pretty good. We've got a whole lot of smudges, and plenty of partials, but we also have two beautiful sets of intact prints." Ryan stopped giving Winston the benefit of a soft, sly grin.

"Whose prints were they, Major?"

"The prints belonged to Marshal Hasek-Davion and his cabin steward. We couldn't bring up anything else. The prints were just too smudgy."

"Like someone had wiped the pad after he was done?" Beresick asked.

"Possibly," Ryan said. "The smudges are more a factor of the way people tend to punch buttons. They just kind of peck at them, with their fingertips. That makes a kind of smear rather than a good, clear print."

"So the steward was in on it?" Redburn's voice was dull and lifeless as he spoke for the first time.

"No, sir," Ryan answered. "At least I don't believe so."

"So what *do* you believe, Major?" Winston asked.

"When we couldn't lift any prints off the cryptolock's keypad, I had a sudden impulse to unscrew the lock's faceplate and take a look at its inner workings. When we looked at the wiring, there were tiny, but discernible creases in the insulation of the leads running from the keypad to the lock mechanism. That kind of crease is caused by powerful, saw-tooth, spring-loaded alligator clips, the kind used on most electronic lock-breakers.

"I checked the maintenance logs, and found out that there had never been any work either ordered or done on the Marshal's door locks. Therefore I can only surmise that the assassin, probably disguised as a maintenance crewman, unscrewed the lock faceplate, hooked up an electronic lock-breaker, and ran a random series of numbers through the system until the door opened."

"How long would that take?" Winston sat forward, leaning her elbows on the edge of her desk. A gentle tug across her lap reminded her that, with the ship in freefall, even so simple a gesture as leaning forward in the chair might have sent her spinning off uncontrollably, were it not for the wide restraining belt holding her to her seat.

"How long?" Ryan repeated. "It would depend."

"On . . ."

"On many things. I'm assuming that this lock is the same as the rest used on the ship. It uses a five-digit code, right? Well, using a five-digit code gives you a hundred thousand possible combinations. There's a type of lock-breaker that runs a random series of numbers through the system, hoping to hit on the right one."

"You know, Major, we've all seen the vids."

Ryan either didn't hear, or ignored Beresick's acid comment. In either case, he continued his homily on electronic lock-picking.

"Now, most cryptolocks have a delay time built into them, which gives the system time to reset itself after a bad combination. Let's call it a two-second delay. That means to run all one hundred thousand possible codes would take two hundred thousand seconds, or about fifty-six hours. The problem is that most cryptolocks only give you two or three tries before they shut themselves down and set off some kind of internal alarm. We all know there were no alarms of any kind the night the Marshal was killed."

Winston was incredulous. "So what are you telling us? Either our boy used a lock-breaker and failed, or he got the combination right on his first three tries, out of a possible hundred thousand combinations?"

"No, General. What I'm saying is that the assassin wasn't using a 'standard' sort of lock-breaker. There is a somewhat more sophisticated model available to . . ." Ryan paused as though he was embarrassed by what he was about to admit. ". . . some of the better known security agencies. Instead of relying on the brute-force method, these advanced breakers sort of con the code out of the system. They work slower, but actually take less time because they aren't trying every possible number."

"What do you mean, Major, they con the system?"

"Well, General, instead of running a series of complete five-digit code strings, they run five series of numbers, one for each code digit. When they hit the right number for that slot, they stop that string. Eventually you have the right code, and you only have to input one number."

"How big are these lock-breakers?" Beresick was obviously impressed even with Ryan's somewhat sketchy knowledge of the sophisticated code-breaking system.

"About fourteen centimeters, by eight, by two. A little smaller than the average pocket computer."

"I take it that these devices are rare?"

"They are. So far as I know, there are only a handful of them in existence among the Combine's Internal Security Force and House Davion's Ministry of Intelligence, Information, and Operations. The DEST teams just got them before we shipped out for Defiance. The ISF people are holding on to them very tightly. I gather the Fox teams have one or two of their own, but that ought to be all. Like I said, they're brand new, lifted from captured Clan tech, pulled straight out of the NAIS memory core.

"Now, the 'simpler' version is available on the black market. I guess there could be a hundred of those things floating around the task force. The basic electronic lock-breaker is about the size of a pack of cigarettes. If someone on this ship has one, it could be hidden practically anywhere."

Winston nodded slowly to cover what she considered to be an appalling lack of knowledge about the shadier side of modern warfare. Like many MechWarriors, she believed herself to be above the "dirty" business of espionage, sabotage, and assassination, which was so often assigned to people like Michael Ryan. When suddenly and brutally confronted with the last of that unholy trio, she found herself with no solid point of reference.

"So is it possible that someone on this ship, aside from you and Montjar, might have one of these newer lock-breakers?" Beresick asked.

"Possible, yes. Probable? No." Ryan shook his head. "Like I said, they're pretty much limited to the intelligence community. You might, just *might* if you were *very* lucky, get one on the black market, but you'd expect to pay fifty to sixty thousand C-bills for it. Even then there would be no guarantee it would work."

"Hmm," Winston grunted. For some time she leaned on her elbows, not speaking. Then, her mind made up, she turned to Alain Beresick.

"Commodore, I think we have to accept Major Ryan's estimation that the assassin is aboard this ship. I don't know how he got here, but there's no way anyone on one of the other ships could be assured of getting a clear opportunity to make their move."

"What are you suggesting, General?" Beresick's tone indicated that he already knew the answer, and merely wanted Winston to say the words.

"I'm suggesting that we make a concerted effort to find our only two positive links between the assassin and the murder—the poison and the lock-breaker.

"Now it's possible that the assassin may have used up his whole stock of fugu in one shot, but I doubt it. He'd have to be prepared to strike again if necessary. Or, having completed his mission, he may have just dumped the stuff into the waste disposal system. But, he'd never have gotten rid of the lock-breaker. That's an awfully pricey piece of equipment to throw away." Taking a breath, she fixed Beresick with a level gaze.

"I'm going to have to ask you to allow a stem-to-stern search of the *Invisible Truth,* including her crew's and officer's quarters."

"Uh-uh! No way in hell!" Beresick fairly shouted. "No way I'm going to allow *anyone* to conduct a search of my crew's quarters. Blake's blood, General, do you have any idea what that would do to morale? You start rooting through what few personal possessions my men were allowed to bring aboard, especially without telling them what you're looking for—and I don't see how you *can* tell them—and you're going to have some *very* angry spacers on your hands. If I gave that kind of permission, that'd be like saying we couldn't trust my crew. You try that on any other ship, by that I mean one that isn't ComStar, and you'd probably end up facing a mutiny."

"Commodore, one of your crew *might* be the assassin." Winston's gentle reminder stopped Beresick short. "We'll be searching every part of this ship. Not just the crew's quarters, but the marine barracks, passenger compartments, cargo bays, everywhere. We'll even be searching *my* quarters. In fact, we'll *start* with my quarters."

Beresick stared at her for a moment, then visibly relented.

"You're right, General." His tone was formal, and somewhat stiff. "You can conduct your search, but if, and only if, either I or my executive officer can accompany the search teams, and if they start in 'officer's country.' "

"Major Ryan?" Winston looked across at him.

"Fine with me, General." Ryan bowed his assent. "When can we start?"

"I'd say after change of watch would probably be best," Beresick said. "That way, you'd have six full hours to search without being interrupted."

"Dosihimasu," Ryan agreed. "That will give me time to get my team aboard the *Truth* and brief them on their task."

Ryan sketched a salute in Winston's direction and headed off to call in his search teams. Beresick left right on his heels. Only Andrew Redburn remained behind.

"General Winston," he began as soon as the door closed behind the withdrawing officers. "Are you sure it's a good idea to allow the DEST teams to conduct the investigation? Wouldn't it be better if it were kept 'in house'?"

"What do you mean, Andrew?"

"Well, let's suppose, just suppose, that Morgan *was* assassinated on Theodore Kurita's orders. If Ryan, or one of his men was responsible, we'll never know it. They'll be investigating the crime they committed."

"I'm surprised to hear you say that." Winston's dark face mirrored her words. "You sound just like the scandal vids after Melissa's murder, claiming that Prince Victor, or Morgan Kell, or even Jaime Wolfe had something to do with it."

Winston smiled gently to rob her words of any offense.

"I know you're upset, we all are, but you most of all. You've just lost your best friend, and if anyone has a right not to be thinking clearly, it's you.

"But, I just can't believe that Ryan and his men were responsible. Not only were they hand-picked by the Coordinator for this mission, but the Draconis Combine stands to lose more than any one else if this mission fails. Remember, the Jags seized a fair portion of the Combine, and the Inner Sphere part of this operation is aimed at kicking them out of Combine turf."

"I know all that, General." Redburn's voice was flat and dead. "But remember, just before we left, Victor was nearly killed by hard-core Dracs who still have this pathological hatred of the Davions."

Winston shook her head slowly. "I'm sorry, Andrew, but that's just too neat, too pat. Until the investigation turns up something to the contrary, I'm going to have to go with my gut, and my gut tells me that Ryan and his men had nothing to do with Morgan's death."

"Well, General, I hope you're right," Redburn said quietly as he turned and left Winston's office.

Watching the door close behind him, Winston's mind began to turn toward the shadowy figures described in Morgan's personal message. She began to wonder if perhaps those hand-picked nekekami agents might not be wearing two faces.

=== 7 ===

Battle Cruiser SLS Invisible Truth
Task Force Serpent
Deep Space, 180 Light Years from Huntress
22 January 3060

The *Invisible Truth* massed some 859,000 metric tons, had an overall length of 839 meters, and a beam of 139. With twenty-nine decks, and a crew of nearly three hundred, not counting her passengers, as the crew referred to the ground forces assigned to her, she was by far the largest WarShip in the task force.

Major Ryan's search teams took the better part of three days to go through the battle cruiser's berthing spaces, barracks, and cargo holds. As Alain Beresick had predicted, many members of his crew, not to mention the Com Guard MechWarriors and infantrymen housed in the vessel's two barracks decks, protested, some most stridently, the very idea of having their personal effects searched. The offense was made all the more grievous by the fact that the searchers were outsiders. Beresick's presence salved the wounded feelings to some extent, but the entire episode left the *Truth*'s crew with a rather bad attitude toward "the brass."

Led by Ryan's executive officer, and accompanied by Commodore Beresick, the team poked into every locker, rucksack, seabag, and packing crate they could lay their hands on. The commandos ruthlessly searched every berthing space, barracks, galley, recreation room, and cargo hold on the ship. They even opened every cockpit, ammunition magazine, and access panel of every BattleMech, tank, and aerospace fighter in the WarShip's transport bays. All to no avail.

When the search of the *Invisible Truth* herself turned up no sign of either the lock-breaker or the poison, the teams turned their attention to the DropShips mated to the battle cruiser's docking collars, and began the entire process all over again.

With each personal locker opened, every 'Mech cockpit invaded, the mood of mistrust and violation grew among the former ComStar personnel. Only Beresick's assurances that the search was being conducted for a very good reason, and his personal guarantee that the invasion of privacy would never be repeated salved the feelings of the increasingly resentful men and women.

Beresick himself grew short-tempered and irritable. On a number of occasions, he snarled first at his crew for resisting the search, then at the commandos for invading the privacy of men and women who were supposedly innocent until proven guilty. He hated the police-state tactic of a mass search, but he knew that the inspection might well be the only way of turning up any clues in the case of Morgan's assassination. More and more, he found himself praying for a quick end to the entire unpleasant business.

During the first few hours of the search, Ariana Winston had accompanied the search teams. She was impressed with their speed and efficiency. She had expected the searchers to simply open drawers and cabinets, dumping their contents onto the floor in their eagerness to find the lock-breaker, and thus Morgan's assassin. The exact opposite was true. Lockers and desks were examined with utmost care, leaving no item unexamined, but Major Ryan's troopers were calm and polite, treating the crewmen's meager personal possessions as respectfully as they would their own.

By the end of the second watch, she'd seen enough. Leaving the search operation to the DEST troopers, and explanations to Beresick, Winston retired to her office.

Three days later Ryan reported that his search was complete. Winston told him to come to her office following evening mess to report his findings. Not wanting the DEST officer to be seen loitering around the corridor outside her quarters, she asked that dinner be served in her cabin. It wasn't often that Ariana Winston took advantage of the privileges of her rank. Like many field commanders, she preferred to eat with her officers, taking a personal interest in their lives away from the world of battlefields and strategy sessions.

As the door hissed shut on its pneumatically operated runners behind the mess steward who had come to clear away the dishes, her desktop intercom gave out a muted bleep. Tapping the Answer key, she was confronted by the *Truth*'s Chief Quartermaster informing her that her personal effects had been transferred from the *Gettysburg* and were being held in the battle cruiser's number five cargo hold.

"We're jes waitin' fer yer okay 'fore we move yer gear inta th' Flag Suite." The man's gravelly voice was tinged with uncertainty. He, like most of the noncommissioned officers and enlisted personnel she had encountered since assuming command of the task force, seemed uncertain as how to proceed with their new leader.

"Well, Chief, if it's all right with you, I'd rather leave my gear in storage for a while, just until we finish up the official inquiry into the Marshal's death."

The Chief, a husky man with thinning gray hair and bright blue eyes, regarded her skeptically. He clearly suspected that something other than a routine "official inquiry" was being conducted, but he was too much of a professional spacer to say so.

" 'S awright with me, Gen'ral. You jes lemme know when ya want yer gear, and I'll get somebody move it."

As she was shutting down the intercom, her office door annunciator emitted a bell-like tone.

"Enter," she barked to the person awaiting her permission to do just that.

As it turned out, it was two persons, Major Michael Ryan and a rather disgusted-looking Alain Beresick.

"Beg to report, General," Beresick said with stiff formality. "The task force has completed recharging and is making preparations to jump. We will be ready to jump within the hour."

"Thank you, Commodore. Do so when ready. We can't delay the mission any further," Winston said. Beresick was obviously trying to cover his still festering irritation by conveying the rather mundane report of the fleet's readiness to jump. "What did your search turn up?"

"Well, General, you'll be happy to know that Ryan's boys have completed their sweep. We went through this ship from forepeak to sail-locker." Beresick passed Winston a datachip as he spoke. Despite the lightness of his words, there was an unmistakable tone of "I-told-you-so" and "we didn't find a thing" in his voice.

"Well, Commodore, that isn't, strictly speaking, true." Winston chuckled as she looked over the data contained on the chip.

"Have it your way, General," Beresick snapped. The angry retort was out of character. Having escorted most of the search teams himself, he was tired and clearly in no mood for humor, especially humor at his expense. "We turned up thirty-seven bottles of liquor, an even dozen contraband porno simchips, and three decks of marked cards. What we didn't find were any signs of poison or the lock-breaker.

"We spent three days pushing my crew and passengers almost to the point of mutiny, and for what? Nothing. We didn't find the lock-breaker, and I don't think we're going to. The assassin either spaced it or hid it so well that Ryan's people couldn't find it. We're working a dead end here."

Winston nodded thoughtfully.

"I think you're right, Commodore." Then she turned to Ryan. "Major, I have no doubt that your team did the best they could, but I just don't think we're going to find that 'breaker.'"

"*Hai*, General," Ryan said with a rueful shake of his head. "If my men couldn't find it in three days, it isn't going to be found. The assassin has covered his tracks admirably."

"So we're right back where we started."

"Not quite, General." Beresick passed a second datachip across Winston's desk. "While you had me out getting my crew primed for mutiny, my executive officer had a bit of a brainstorm. For some reason he ran a computer check on the *Truth*'s crew. We have pretty extensive computer-based files on all of our people. Now bear in mind that we've got nearly three hundred crewmen aboard this ship, so he had to use some pretty specific search parameters. One of those parameters was to check for any criminal or civil troubles dating back to the time *before* they joined ComStar. The computer red-flagged five files. Not because the individuals had been arrested or sued or anything like that before they joined the Order. No, they were flagged because they *didn't exist* before they joined the Order."

"What?"

"That's right, General." Beresick moved beside Winston's chair, then reached in front of her and scrolled the computer report down until the files he'd mentioned were displayed on the screen before her. "Those five persons have no records at all prior to their being initiated into ComStar."

"Cleary, Davis, Penrose, Ota, and Yee." Winston read the highlighted names in a tone that suggested she was talking to herself. "Know anything about any of them?"

"Not really," Beresick answered. "According to those records, they all transferred in to the Com Guards' naval branch shortly after Tukayyid. Cleary and Ota are both ABs. That's Able Bodies, just general shipboard hands. They're the people who do things like handle cargo, transfer stuff from storage to wherever it's needed, work damage control and general maintenance, that sort of thing. Davis is an armorer's mate, assigned to the *Banbridge*'s fighter lance. Penrose is an assistant jump-drive technician. Yee was an AB, but he was assigned to sick bay as an orderly when he was transferred aboard. I think we can rule him out, though."

"Why is that?" Ryan craned his neck to look at the computer screen from his side of the desk.

"Because he was one of the guys detailed to carry Morgan's body down to sick bay," Winston answered, sudden realization painting her features.

"That's right, how did you . . ."

"I bumped into the stretcher party as I was leaving the Marshal's quarters. I remember one of them was called Yee. I remember at the time thinking he looked awfully familiar. I wish I could recall where I've seen him before."

"I can't really say where you might have seen any of them before, except maybe Davis and Penrose. They're the only ones originally assigned to the *Truth*. The others were transferred aboard from the *Banbridge* during the personnel shuffle after Trafalgar."

"All three from the same ship?"

"Yeah, them and half a dozen others. We needed to make up our battle losses, so we sort of lifted crewmen from every ComStar ship in the fleet." Beresick rubbed his chin thoughtfully. "Still, I have to admit, it is a little suspicious, having five blanks assigned to the same two ships."

"May I look at those files, Commodore?" Ryan held out his

hand as though he had not the slightest thought that the naval officer might refuse.

Beresick hesitated at first, a result of ComStar's long history of treating any information in a proprietary fashion, then dropped the chip into Ryan's palm. Without asking Winston's leave, Ryan slipped the device into her data reader. He spent several minutes reviewing the information contained in the files before speaking again.

"Well, I think we should talk to all five of our, what did you call them, blanks? Just to be on the safe side. Though they were all aboard when Morgan was killed, I think we can probably rule out Ota, Cleary, and Yee. Since they weren't originally part of the *Truth*'s crew, there's no way they could count on being able to make the hit. We should still question them. I just don't think any of them had anything to do with the murder."

"So who do we start with?" Winston asked.

"Let's start with our two prime suspects." Ryan tapped the screen. "Davis and Penrose."

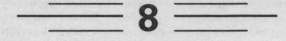

8

Battle Cruiser SLS **Invisible Truth**
Task Force Serpent
Deep Space, 150 Light Years from Huntress
23 January 3060

"**I**'m sorry, Commodore, I can't account for my whereabouts during the time of Marshal Hasek-Davion's assassination." The woman identified by the ComStar records as Julia Davis locked her brown, almond-shaped eyes onto Beresick's own. She had been specially trained to resist interrogation, even physical or chemical torture. Compared with those methods of extracting information, Commodore Beresick's mild questioning couldn't even be classed as an interview. "Doesn't that tell you something? Wouldn't you think anyone smart enough to assassinate the Marshal would be smart enough to engineer some kind of alibi?"

"Perhaps," Beresick agreed. "But perhaps someone smart enough to assassinate the Marshal would be smart enough to make just that assumption and leave herself without an alibi. We could dance around for quite some time, playing 'I-know-that-you-know-that-I-know,' but we're not going to. You're sure that no one can vouch for your whereabouts during the time in question?"

Davis shook here head. "I'm sorry."

"So am I, Adept Davis."

"Private Davis." The second man in the room spoke for the first time. "Do you have any idea why no record of your existence before your joining ComStar can be found?"

"Excuse me?" The young woman suppressed a thrill of anxiety. Davis, of course was not her real name, but that of a fictional Com Guard armorer's mate, the role created for her by her masters, and approved of by the unseen power who had hired them. As a *kunoichi*, a female nekekami, Rumiko Fox had been required to commit every detail of Adept Julia Davis' career to memory. She could converse quite freely about her involvement with the Order's military branch, even going so far as to complain bitterly that her unit had gone uncommitted during the battle of Tukayyid. Her cover had seemed to be as nearly perfect as any she had ever seen. Now, this dark-haired man wearing the stylized dragon's eye badge of House Kurita's dreaded Draconis Elite Strike Teams was telling her of a horrible gap in the background created for her.

"There is no record for you prior to the date you signed on with ComStar," Major Ryan repeated. "Why is that?"

"I don't know." Fox/Davis shrugged. Despite the posture, carefully sculpted of equal parts innocence and anxiety, her mind was racing, desperately trying to keep ahead of events. "Maybe they were lost when the Word of Blake seized Terra."

"That's awfully convenient, don't you think?" Ryan plainly didn't believe her excuse.

"Records *do* get lost, Major." The *kunoichi*'s voice held just the right mixture of frustration and anger. "They get lost all the time."

"Uh-huh."

"Major, I'm telling you the truth. If you don't believe me, I'll take a polygraph, voice-stress analysis, anything you like." Fox allowed a note of indignation to creep into her voice.

For several long minutes, Ryan locked a dark, level stare on Fox's eyes, as though he were trying to pry some deep dark secret out of the sealed vault of her mind. For a time she returned the gaze, then her eyelids fluttered and she turned away.

"General, you believe me, don't you?" The appeal carried an unspoken plea woman-to-woman.

"I'm sorry, Private. It's not a question of what I believe. It's a question of what can be proven." Winston sighed heavily, shrugging her shoulders. "All right, Davis, you can go, for now. Regretfully, I'm going to have to place you under house arrest until this matter is resolved." Winston glanced at her noteputer, which

Fox assumed displayed Julia Davis' personnel file. "Until this investigation is concluded, you are relieved of your duties. You will be restricted to your quarters. You will be permitted to go to the galley for your meals and to the rec room during your assigned periods. In short, Private, you may move freely around your quarters, but you may not leave Deck Fifteen. Understood?"

"Yes, General." Her tone was one of injured innocence mixed with equal parts fear and depression. Looking up, she gave Winston a tired smile. "I know you're doing what you think is best."

"That's right," Winston said. "Dismissed, Private. "She motioned for the DEST commando standing guard at the conference room door to escort Julia Davis back to her quarters.

As the door hissed shut behind the departing prisoner and guard, Winston looked pointedly at Ryan, who sat tapping industriously at his noteputer. When the commando officer failed to answer her wordless question, she spoke sharply.

"Well, Major?"

"Well, what?" Ryan answered distractedly, his attention still fixed on the data device before him. Winston looked in exasperation at the conference room wall. It had been Ryan's idea to conduct the "interviews," as he called them, in the large, relatively comfortable meeting room on the *Truth*'s number one grav deck rather than in her office. He claimed that the juxtaposition of a formal questioning taking place in an informal setting would help unbalance the subjects and put them off their guard.

"What does your fancy little toy there tell you about our Miss Davis?"

"Humph." There was a note of weary surprise in Ryan's grunt. "I have no idea."

"What do you mean, you have no idea?" Beresick moved to look over Ryan's shoulder at the confusing series of jagged lines and squiggles adorning the noteputer's screen. "I thought you said that thing could tell us if she was lying."

"What I said, Commodore, was that it might give us an indication if she wasn't telling us the whole truth." Ryan pushed his chair back, turning it to one side so he could face Beresick. "There is no such thing as a lie detector, at least not one that can ferret out every little half-truth and exaggeration.

"Voice-stress analysis picks up tiny, almost imperceptible

changes, micro-quavers and such, in a subject's voice, and compares them to a base line. That's why we always ask the subject questions to which we know the answers before we start the real test, to establish the base-line. Well, Private Davis, or whatever her real name is, couldn't even establish a base line. Her readings were jumping all over the place.

"Look here," he said, tapping the screen with his forefinger. "This is where you asked her for her name and service history. See how it's registering there? If we had a normal baseline to compare that to, I'd have to say the lady was lying."

"Now, here," Ryan keyed in a command, prompting the note-puter to display a separate set of squiggly lines. "This is where you asked her if she knew anything about the Marshal's death. She said no, and the lines remained pretty flat, indicating that she was telling the truth."

"So what are you saying?" Winston asked, following Ryan's explanation with great interest. "She killed Morgan, or she's lying about being part of ComStar?"

"Both. Neither. I don't know. At least not with any degree of certainty." Ryan shrugged. "If you ordered me to pin it down, I'd have to say she probably didn't have anything to do with the murder, but she's into some kind of really shady deal."

"Could she be ROM?" Winston wrinkled her brow in speculation. "Maybe Word of Blake ROM?"

"Could be." Ryan lifted his shoulders again at the suggestion that Julia Davis might be a member of the secret police branch of either the ComStar Order or Word of Blake faction. "I just don't get that feeling, though. *Neh,* there's something else at work here. Whatever it is, General, I think we're digging in the wrong place. For right now, I'd say keep an eye on her. Even if she didn't have anything to do with the Marshal's assassination, she's still up to something."

Winston nodded her agreement. All throughout the interview, a nameless anxiety had been nagging at her mind. If, as Ryan feared, the woman they knew as Julia Davis had been lying to them, what was she trying to hide? Why was there no record of her existence prior to her joining ComStar, and why hadn't she told the truth about that service? Was Davis even a member of the Order? As Winston contemplated these riddles, her mind was drawn back to the elusive memory of Chang Yee. As far as she knew, the first time she'd ever laid eyes on the man, now serving as an orderly, was in the corridor outside Morgan's stateroom, yet he had seemed so familiar to her. Then to find out that Yee, like Davis, had no pre-ComStar records made the feeling of *déjà vu* all the more disturbing. A shiver ran along Winston's spine.

"General? You still with us?"

"I'm sorry, Commodore. Someone just walked over my grave." Winston smiled, giving the superstitious explanation for the sudden twitch. "What were you saying?"

"I asked if you were ready to talk to Adept Penrose."

"Yes, I suppose we'd better."

Leaning across her desk, Winston passed an order to the Com Guard marines, asking that they fetch Private/Adept Lucas Penrose from his quarters. After receiving acknowledgment from the corporal of the guard, Winston sat back in her chair.

"You know, I just don't like this whole set up," she said, switching her gaze between Beresick and Ryan. "Regardless of the assassination, we've got at least five people on board who are mysteries in and of themselves. Who are they, and how did they get themselves assigned to this task force?"

Several decks below, a pair of Com Guard marines dressed in drab-green fatigues stepped into the quarters shared by the man called Lucas Penrose and three other crewmen. Penrose had been temporarily excused from his duties as an assistant jump-drive tech so that he might make himself available to the investigation team. At the command barked out by the corporal in charge of the detail, he got slowly to his feet, every detail of the motion bespeaking apprehension and not a little fear. He hadn't been told the purpose of the inquest, but he had guessed the reason accurately. The task force commanders were looking into Morgan Hasek-Davion's untimely demise. The presence of the marine guards told Penrose that not only did the officers consider the death suspicious, but believed he had something to do with it.

As he approached the door, the marines stepped cautiously back, allowing him to precede them along the short corridor leading to the centrally located elevators. Passing the men, he gave them a brief, uneasy glance. Neither marine was wearing body armor, yet they were concerned enough for their own safety to unfasten the flap covering their heavy auto-pistols.

It took several seconds for the lift to appear, during which Penrose tried to engage the marines in conversation. Each attempt was curtly rebuffed. Less than a minute after the elevator car arrived on Deck Thirteen, the trio stepped out into the access area leading into grav deck one. The elevator door closed behind them. One guard dropped into the grav deck corridor, leaving his partner to cover Penrose. Their "prisoner" went next and was followed by the second marine.

Suddenly, Penrose's knees started to buckle. The marine guards escorting him reached out to steady the apparently frightened man.

A ripping crack split the air. The marine gripping Penrose's right arm gasped and pitched onto his face. Before his companion could react, the once timid-seeming Penrose drove his left elbow hard into the marine's solar plexus. With an explosive cough, the guard doubled over, gasping for breath. Penrose continued to pivot on the ball of his left foot, allowing the force of the blow to carry him through a quarter-turn.

The guard scrabbling for his holstered weapon looked up just in time to see the over-and-under muzzle of a black gyrojet holdout pistol line up with his forehead. The second tearing report and brief gout of flame barely registered in his mind before the miniature rocket tore into his brain.

"What the hell was that?"

"Gunshots!" Ryan's shout was born more of long years of intensive training than as an answer to Winston's startled question. Sweeping his ever-present sidearm from its holster, he bolted through the door, closely followed by Alain Beresick.

Winston punched the intercom's emergency key.

"Bridge! General Winston. We have shots fired in the corridor, Deck Four." Knowing that the Officer of the Deck standing watch on the *Invisible Truth*'s bridge had received the urgent message, she didn't wait for a reply. Instead she drew her own weapon and darted through the still open door.

In the corridor, Winston saw Ryan and Beresick kneeling over a pair of blood-splattered forms lying on the deck halfway between the lifts and her office. The olive-drab jackets worn by both corpses revealed them to be ship's marines. There was the stink of burnt propellant in the air.

"What happened here?" Winston demanded.

Ryan reached into his jacket and extracted a pen, which he carefully inserted into the muzzle of a small black handgun.

"Hold-out pistol." He lifted the weapon for her to examine. "Gyrojet. Both barrels fired. See? Both the loading indicators read empty. Blasted things are small enough to hide just about anywhere. My guess is he pulled it from a concealed pocket, shot one guard at point-blank range. It would have taken the other guard a few seconds to react, and that was more than enough time. These men got careless, and he killed them. Looks like he grabbed both their guns too. I guess he *really* didn't want to talk to us."

Winston looked at the bodies, noticing for the first time that their holsters were open and empty.

"Where is he now?"

"I don't know." Ryan put the weapon back where he found it. "He's . . ."

A sudden fusillade of shots interrupted him before he could finish his sentence. His muttered curse broke off in a grunt of pain, punctuated by the thud of a heavy pistol bullet slamming into his torso.

Turning in the direction of the gunshots, Beresick snatched up Ryan's weapon and returned fire. Winston pivoted too, just in time to see Penrose's blond head disappear behind the door of a nearby recreation room.

"Hold your fire, blast it," Winston snapped, slapping Beresick's weapon aside. "I'd like to try to take him alive."

Cautiously, so as not to expose themselves to any further shots Penrose might care to loose in their direction, the officers slipped back into Winston's office, dragging the semi-conscious Ryan with them. From there they could keep an eye on the killer's hiding place, while using the WarShip's steel bulkheads as protection. Twice, large-caliber slugs whined off the bulkhead, leaving thick gray smears in their wake. It was unclear if the gunman was actually trying to kill them or merely keep them pinned down until some unknown accomplice arrived.

"It doesn't matter," Winston snarled in answer to Beresick's question. "So long as we stay behind this wall, he can't hit us. And, if we're pinned down, so is he. The marines will be here soon enough."

As though her saying it made it so, at that exact moment, the elevator doors whooshed open, emitting a squad of Com Guard marines, clad in camouflaged flak suits and carrying Rorynex submachine guns. Right behind them were a bevy of white-coated medical corpsmen.

"Commodore, General, are you all right?" The sergeant commanding the marines was almost painfully young.

"We're fine, Sergeant." Winston gestured to the groggy Michael Ryan lying on the deck. "Major Ryan needs a medic. He took a pistol bullet in the chest."

Gesturing to a corpsman, the sergeant knelt over Ryan, gently probing the hole in the commando's fatigue jacket. In a moment, he removed his remarkably unbloodied fingers, and with them a small, twisted piece of copper.

"Bullet jacket," he said in reply to the officers' questioning looks. "His body armor stopped the slug. He's gonna be pretty sore in the morning, and have a nasty bruise, maybe a couple broken ribs, but he'll survive."

As the corpsman arrived, shooing both the officers and sergeant away, the rest of the squad took up positions from which they could cover Penrose's hiding place.

"How do you want to handle this, General?" the sergeant asked.

After glancing at Beresick, Winston replied, "I'd like to take him alive. We need to know who's behind him. Let's try to not tear up the ship too badly."

Before the marine could begin issuing orders to his men, a sharp, commanding voice rang out from the opposite end of the corridor.

"Listen! You out there in the corridor! I want to talk to Winston. I know she's still out there. I want to see her. Now!"

The marine sergeant shook his head, silently advising Winston to refuse the gunman's demands.

"Tell him to forget it," Beresick whispered. "If you go out there, he'll kill you too."

"No stalling!" Penrose shouted. "I know you're out there, General. You may not care about your own life, but if you care about what happens to this ship, you'd better answer me."

"What do you mean, 'what happens to this ship'?" Winston

felt as though an icy, skeletal hand had just dragged its bony fingers along her spine.

"Ah. See there? I knew you'd talk to me. That's what I always liked about you, General. You always had time for the little people." Penrose laughed, a short, bitter, ugly sound. "If you want to keep having time for the little people, you'd better show yourself. The bomb I planted in the *Truth*'s number three magazine isn't all that big, but it doesn't have to be. One little twitch, and *bang*, we're all singing with the angels."

Winston shot a questioning look at Beresick.

"Cannon shells," he nodded. "If he's telling the truth, if there's a bomb in that magazine, and if he has some sort of remote detonator, all he'd have to do is push a button, or worst yet, release a deadman switch, and those shells would go up in a sympathetic detonation. The explosion might set off the rest of the magazines in a chain reaction, ignite the fuel cells, damage the drives. I'd rather not risk it."

"C'mon, General, time's-a-wasting!" Penrose yelled.

"I don't see we have much choice."

"We have a choice, General," Beresick countered. "We isolate and depressurize that room. It'll be kind of messy to clean up, but if we draw off the atmosphere rapidly enough, he won't have enough time to press any detonator buttons."

"Commodore, I'd like to take him alive, if possible. Remember?"

"And sir," the Com Guard marine sergeant added his support to Winston's argument. "What if he rigged the explosives up to a deadman switch? You go depressurizing that cabin, eventually he's gonna release the switch."

"You want to take that chance, Alain?" Winston asked, peering closely at Beresick. Seeing the reluctant agreement in his eyes, she said, "Good. Neither do I."

Letting her laser pistol fall to the deck, Winston stepped out into the corridor. Watching her over the sights of a stolen autopistol, from a partly open rec room door, was the handsome blue-eyed face of the man called Lucas Penrose. His right hand was out of sight, behind the door frame, but his left gripped the weapon with the easy confidence of an expert marksman. At a range of less than ten meters, it wouldn't take great marksmanship to put a slug straight through her forehead, so Winston moved slowly, keeping her hands in plain view the whole time.

"That's very good, General, just keep coming, right into the room." Penrose's voice, for all the polite phrasing, was dripping with sarcasm.

Winston heard Beresick softly urging her not to go, but she had no choice. If she refused, the best she could hope for was a pistol ball between the eyes. The worst consequence of defiance was almost too horrible to think about, an explosion in the ammunition locker, the fuel cells detonated, and over three hundred people dead, all because she refused to walk through a door. Waving Beresick to silence, she quietly complied with Penrose's orders.

It took a few moments for her eyes to adjust to the darkened room. Penrose had smashed the room's overhead lighting panels, leaving the room in a murky, shadowed twilight. At first the reason for the vandalism wasn't clear, then it came to her. It was harder to see into a darkened room than a lighted one, especially if you were standing in a well-lighted corridor. Like most of the systems aboard the *Invisible Truth*, the lights could be controlled by the ship's central computer, making it possible for the marines to switch on the office lights remotely. Destroying the overhead fluorescent panels ensured that Penrose's stronghold would remain in the dark.

As her pupils dilated, she was able to pick out, or at least guess at, some of the details of the room, and of the armed man before her. He was of average height, blond, blue-eyed, and relatively good-looking in a nondescript sort of way. His Com Guard uniform bore a heavy spatter of blood on the right sleeve, and there was a large rip in the breast where the guard, in his death agonies, had clutched at the tunic. Penrose held one big Federated Industries automatic pistol in an unwavering left hand. A second, identical weapon was thrust through the front of his belt, its grip turned toward the left. The killer's right hand was out of sight, held behind his back.

"What do you want, Penrose, or whatever your name is?"

"Oh, Penrose will do for now, General. Unless you'd rather call me Lucas?" The man's voice was pleasant, almost melodious, with a trace of an accent Winston couldn't place. "What I want is simple. I want you to detach a JumpShip to transport me back to the Inner Sphere. Once I'm away from the fleet, the task force will be free to continue its fool's mission. Of course, I can't risk some overzealous spacer getting delusions of being a hero and trying to, what is the phrase, take me down before I get where I'm going. So, I'll have to ask for the pleasure of *your* company for the trip."

"Is that all?" Winston said acidly.

"Well, there *is* one more thing. I'd like you to delete any records you may have of your suspicions concerning my involvement in the demise of Morgan Hasek-Davion."

Winston's eyes slowly adjusted to the dimness of the office, allowing her to pick out more details of the room and of the man standing before her.

"It *was* you, wasn't it?"

"You can't expect me to come right out and confess, can you?" Penrose laughed in amusement. "My dear Ariana, do you mind if I call you that? After all we *are* going to be spending a long time together. Whether I had anything to do with the Marshal's death or not isn't the question. The question is, are *you* going to be responsible for the deaths of the *Truth*'s passengers and crew, not to mention the destruction of the ship itself, or are you going to cooperate with me?"

Silently, Winston stared at Penrose, taking in every feature of his face and clothing. In every way, the man was as unremarkable as a holovid news anchor. Aside from the blood stains and tear, his gray and khaki Star League-style uniform was as ordinary as it could be.

A faint gleam on the wall behind Penrose caught her attention. Shifting her gaze, Winston realized that it was the light spilling weakly from the corridor, reflecting off the glass covering a framed laser-print of a *McKenna* Class battleship, dramatically highlighted against an eclipsed star. She had seen many such pictures adorning the living spaces aboard the ship. Still, it wasn't the heroically rendered spacescape that held her attention, but the reflected image of Lucas Penrose. The right hand, which he held so coyly behind his back, suggesting that it gripped the remote detonator that would blow the *Invisible Truth* out of existence, was empty. The man was bluffing.

For a fraction of a second, Winston felt the hot impulse to leap at him, to beat him into oblivion with her bare hands. But her rational, analytical mind kicked in. The distance between the smugly grinning assassin and Winston was more than three meters, and he would squeeze the trigger of that evil-looking pistol before she covered half that distance.

Keep talking, she told herself. *Get him to lower his guard.*

"All right, Penrose. Let's suppose I go along with this lunatic plan of yours. Once we get back, how long do you suppose it'll take the combined intelligence services of all five Successor States to track you down?" As she spoke, Winston made a show of pacing around to office. Purposely, she angled her track to inch her way ever closer to him with each step. "After all, you murdered Prince Victor's cousin, kidnapped a high-ranking military officer, stole a bloody *starship* for pity's sake, and jeopardized the most important offensive of all time. You think you can just walk away, do you?"

"Are you so sure that it'll be all five?" Penrose seemed to be enjoying himself. "How do you know I wasn't acting *for* one of the Great Houses? And, as for killing Victor's cousin—Victor killed his own mother, didn't he?"

"You know that's never been proven." Winston stopped pacing to fix the gunman with a black glare. "They never did catch the assassin. For all I know *you* might have been the one who planted the bomb."

"Me?" Penrose seemed genuinely surprised by Winston's accusation. His voice took on the injured, indignant tone of a master craftsman accused of shoddy work. "Bombs are crude, noisy affairs. They lack subtlety and imagination. Anyone can plant a bomb." He broke off suddenly, his face settling back into the unreadable mask it had been when Winston first entered the darkened office.

"This has all been very pleasant, Ariana, but I'm afraid it must come to an end, for now. We can discuss this at length during our trip back. But at the moment I must insist that you make arrangements for . . . Ow!"

Winston's pacing had brought her within a long arm's reach of Penrose. A short step forward and to her right took her out of his immediate line of fire. With her left hand, she chopped at his left wrist. There was a sharp, metallic clatter as the weapon flew from his suddenly weakened grip and skidded across a formica-topped table. Seizing the advantage, Winston lashed out with the fingertips of her right hand, flicking her nails across his eyes.

Penrose yelled again, as much in surprise as in pain from the unsportsmanlike, but decidedly effective poke at his eyes. Flailing blindly, he caught Winston by the open collar of her battle jacket. His target located, he drove a bony fist into her torso. His stinging eyes and Winston's twisting counter redirected his blow away from her solar plexus, but the powerful reverse punch landing on her short ribs was enough to drive the breath from her lungs in an explosive gasp.

The grappling pair tumbled to the deck. Winston sought to drive her knees into the assassin's groin, while he belabored her head and shoulders with his fists. A cupped hand slashed across her right ear, sending a dagger of pain deep into her skull. Her grip weakened, allowing the struggling man to fling her off. He managed to clamber to one knee before she spun to face him. Gathering herself, Winston sprang like a powerful, black-skinned cat. Penrose caught her diving body, rolling across the deck with her locked tightly in his arms.

She could smell the sweat of anger, exertion, and fear on the man, hear the breath rasping in his throat. The combatants smashed into the partly open rec room door, spilling out into the corridor beyond. Dimly, Winston heard Beresick yelling at the marines to hold their fire until they had a clear shot.

A short, back-fisted blow caught her in the face. She felt a tooth shatter. The coppery taste of blood filled her mouth. Grabbing the front of Penrose's tunic in both hands, Winston yanked him toward her and down, at the same time driving her head up and forward. The top of her skull smashed into his nose and jaw. Penrose staggered back, giving Winston enough room to lash out with her right foot.

The kick was well aimed. Had it connected as she planned, Penrose would have been left gasping for breath, writhing on the deck with the pain of broken ribs. But fatigue and pain slowed the attack. Rather than avoiding, or deflecting the kick, Penrose grabbed her ankle, pulling her off balance, and hurling her to the deck.

Spitting an obscenity between his smashed, bloody lips, the assassin yanked out the second gun, which had miraculously not fallen from his belt during the struggle.

So this is how I'm going to die, Winston thought as the black muzzle swung into line with her right eye.

Instead of a sharp explosive bark, she heard a high, thin hiss, followed by a meaty *thock*. Penrose stiffened, the weapon falling from his suddenly nerveless grip. Reacting on pure instinct, Winston snatched up the pistol, pointed it at the center of his body, and fired.

A single scarlet rose bloomed in the middle of his abdomen. With an odd, gurgling sound, he collapsed across her legs, his dead weight pinning her to the deck. With a strength born of anger and revulsion, she heaved the corpse off her body. As the lifeless form came to rest, Winston saw a small four-pointed star seemingly made of blackened steel jutting out of the dead man's back between his shoulders. The three exposed points had an oily glisten about them.

The corridor exploded into a chaotic whirlpool of noise and activity. The marines leapt forward, rolling the assassin's already stiffening corpse onto its face. Dragging Penrose's forearms together, they tightened a pair of thick nylon restraints around his wrists. The heavy plastic cuffs had no lock, but closed with a strong, ratchet-like fastener; they'd have to be cut off later. Their prisoner secured, one marine stepped back, his weapon covering the prostrate man, while his partner ran his hands along Penrose's arms and legs searching for any weapons he may have concealed about his person.

Doctor Donati, who had arrived while Winston was sequestered in the office with Lucas Penrose, rushed to examine her injuries, gently pressing her back down to the deck. A quick but thorough evaluation revealed only minor injuries.

"I still want to take you down to sick bay, so we can give you a good going over. You took a couple of pretty nasty hits."

"I'm all right," Winston protested, slapping away the medic's offer of support as she climbed stiffly to her feet. Upon gaining the upright position, she swayed unsteadily, the color draining from her face. "Then again . . ."

Gravity took over, and Winston once again found herself sitting on the deck, having made the trip through no conscious effort of her own.

"That's it. You're going to sick bay." Donati's tone of voice indicated that he would brook no further argument with his pronouncement.

Before Winston could protest again, he'd waved to a pair of corpsmen. Gently, aware that they were handling not only the task force commander. but an injured woman as well, the corpsmen carefully lifted Winston into a wire basket-type stretcher.

"Beresick."

"Yes, General." Beresick leaned over the stretcher. "I'm here."

"I know you're here, dammit. I'm beat up, not dying." Winston's growl expressed her feelings at being outranked, and properly so, by the doctor. "Who threw the shuriken?"

"What shuriken?"

"The one sticking out of his back. What are you, blind?" Winston's voice trailed off as a corpsman rolled Penrose's body toward her. The blackened metal star was gone.

9

Battle Cruiser SLS Invisible Truth
Task Force Serpent
Deep Space, 150 Light Years from Huntress
23 January 3060

It was several hours before Ariana Winston got to see Doctor Donati himself. The *Invisible Truth*'s chief medical officer had assigned one of his subordinates to tend to her relatively minor injuries while he saw to the wounded Major Ryan. The pharmacist's mate was gentle and skillful enough, though he talked incessantly throughout the procedure. A habit made all the more aggravating by the fact that he engaged in this one-sided conversation while he tended the worst of the damage, a badly torn upper lip. As he carefully sutured the gash, he politely chatted first about the injury and how he was planning to treat it, then about other matters of no more consequence than what he'd had for dinner the evening before. By the time her last hurt had been washed, disinfected, and bandaged, Winston was ready to kill him.

She and the unconscious Ryan had been carried in basket-stretchers to the *Truth*'s sick bay, while the body of the man called Lucas Penrose was taken to the ship's morgue. Perhaps the only useful bit of information the gabby pharmacist's mate had imparted to her was that Doctor Donati planned to do a post-mortem as soon as he finished working on Ryan. Winston grinned at the thought of Ryan's reaction should he find out that the same surgeon who'd patched him up was about to autopsy the man who shot him. The good Major's feelings would probably hover somewhere between revulsion and satisfaction. Her grin threatened to widen into a full blown smile, but the tug of the stitches holding the torn edges of her lip together reminded her, a bit painfully perhaps, that such an expression was not a good idea.

When Donati at last put in an appearance, his face was drawn. Dark smudges under his eyes told of the weariness he was fighting. Alain Beresick followed the doctor in, his own visage mirroring the stress painting Donati's face.

"I'm getting too old for these little excursions," Donati said, dropping into a chair beside Winston's bunk. Suddenly the fatigue left his face, and he became a medical man again. He took Winston's chin in his right hand, gently rotating her head from side to side as he inspected the pharmacist mate's handiwork.

"Ah, that's not too bad. Couple of weeks, and we'll take those stitches out. You'll be good as new. I doubt that will even scar."

"Doesn't matter if it does." Winston shrugged. "I wasn't all that much to look at in the first place."

"Humph," replied Donati. He plainly didn't like it when his patients said negative things about themselves. Winston wondered if he thought it had an adverse effect on the healing process. When he made no further comment, she didn't pursue the issue.

"Does this hurt?"

"Ow! Yes, it does!" Winston yelped as Donati explored her bruised ribs. "Why do you doctors always ask if something hurts when you know bloody well it does?"

The doctor ignored her outrage-tinged question. "Any ringing in the ears, blurry vision, dizziness?"

"No, no, and no. Except my right ear's a little sore where Penrose smacked me," Winston snapped. "Look, I've been all through this with your assistant."

"Yeah, I know. I just want to hear it for myself." He gently probed the back of her head and neck. "Any stiffness or pain here? No? How about numbness?" She shook her head.

"Okay, General, I think you're going to survive. You've got a couple of really nice bruises there, a broken tooth, a nasty split in your upper lip, and a mild concussion. Nothing that won't heal or that we can't fix."

"What about Ryan?"

"He'll be all right too." Donati sat back, crossing his legs. "He's got a deep, massive bruise on the right side of his chest, and some broken ribs. Good thing those DEST guys are a little paranoid. That armored jacket he always wears probably saved his life. He may have a concussion too. He's awake and complaining, as might be expected.

"We told him what you did, and I think he's trying to figure out whether he should yell at you for being incredibly stupid, or offer you a job with his team." Donati laughed as he pushed himself out of his chair. "I'm supposed to tell you, from him, and I quote, 'You ran an awful risk. If Penrose had really had some sort of detonator, maybe rigged to a heartbeat monitor, you could have gotten us all blown to kingdom come. Believe me, if that had happened, I'd never have spoken to you again.' "

"I take it, from the fact that everybody here is relaxed and smiling, that there was no detonator?"

"At least not any we could find." Beresick shook his head. "I've had the ordnance crews and some of Ryan's demolition experts crawling around the for'ard naval autocannon magazines for the past couple of hours looking for bombs. So far all the EOD experts have gotten for their trouble is really dirty."

"Well, that's not all, really. A couple of them have developed contact dermatitis," Donati corrected with a grin.

"What? How?"

"Seems one of the teams actually went so far as to inspect the feed track running from the magazines to the gun breaches." Beresick shook his head with an amused chuckle. "Those tracks are less than a meter square, so they had to crawl on their knees and elbows. The tracks are also coated with dust from the propellant blocks. Some of the components in those blocks are mildly toxic. So, we'll have a couple of itchy commandos on our hands for a few days."

"Don't they usually take precautions against things like that?" Winston asked, her question tinged with disbelief.

"Usually, but like I said, the tracks are less than a meter square. Crawling through that small a space in a protective suit would be difficult at best." Beresick shrugged.

"I take it they didn't find anything?"

"Not a thing. No bomb, nothing." Beresick was obviously relieved by the results of the search. "I've got them checking out all the other magazines, the fuel bunkers, power plants, anything else that Penrose might have tried to sabotage.

"I doubt we're going to find anything. I'd have to guess that your man Penrose was desperate, just buying time, trying to bluff his way out of a hole."

"To what end? He certainly knew we had him, that we certainly weren't going to give him a starship and send him on his merry way, with a General for a hostage."

"That's what worries me. If he *was* just buying time, who was he buying it for?" Beresick spread his hands in the universal gesture of confusion. "I suppose he might have known that we weren't going to let him get away, and was making some last-ditch effort to save himself, but that's just a little too pat. What really worries me is what if he had an accomplice? What if Julia Davis was his confederate? Or maybe someone else we haven't found yet? We could *still* be in really big trouble."

"I don't know," Winston said. "It just doesn't feel that way. My gut tells me that Penrose was our man, and that he acted alone."

"Well, General, I hope you're right."

"One more question, Commodore," Winston said. "Checking the ship for boobytraps isn't going to delay us any, is it? I'm afraid we're a bit behind schedule over this business as it is."

"No, General, it shouldn't," Beresick said. "As you know, we made our last jump into deep space, rather than a star system. Neither Agent Trent's charts nor the Explorer Corps maps listed a suitable star system in this area. There's got to be one. We just didn't have the stellar coordinates for it. We're recharging the ships off their fusion engines. It won't take any longer than using the sails. We'll be ready to jump out in about a week."

For several minutes, the officers sat in silence, each contemplating the repercussions of the past few days' events.

"I want to see the body." Winston flinched in surprise at her own request. She had no idea where the sudden desire to see the assassin's corpse came from, but she shuddered with distaste at the rather morbid idea.

"Uh-uh, General. Not a chance." Donati shook his head. He leaned on the rails, which tradition seemed to dictate as part of every hospital bed ever made. "Ryan asked me the same thing, and I'm going to tell you what I told him. 'Not until you've had at least eight hours sleep. Just because you aren't banged up all that seriously doesn't mean your body doesn't need time to rest and recuperate. Maybe tomorrow.' "

Alain Beresick laid a reassuring hand on Winston's shoulder. "We've got a couple of the DEST team members digging around in Penrose's quarters. I'm going to get some of my own people on the job, poking into his background, interviewing his cabinmates, co-workers, and so on. There's got to be something somewhere to tell us why he killed Morgan."

"We don't know for certain that he's the one who did it," Winston reminded him.

"Oh, come on, General," Beresick shot back. "Why else would he have done what he did? You don't murder a couple of guards, kidnap a senior officer, and try to steal a JumpShip for no reason. Who else could it have been?"

"I don't know." Winston shook her head. "For my money, I'd have to say it *was* Penrose, but what I say may not carry any weight with the brass-hats back home. They're going to want some more conclusive proof than what I think. That's why we've got to keep digging."

"No, that's why *they* have to keep digging," Donati said with a smile. "You aren't doing anything except lying down and going to sleep."

"Blast it." Winston allowed him to push her gently back into the bed. "I've got to do something about these bloody doctors. Always giving orders even when their patient outranks them."

"Down here, I outrank everybody, even you." Donati gave Winston the benefit of his best bedside smile. "Eight hours, then we'll see."

"Yessir." Winston tossed him a sarcastic salute, settled back against the pillows and closed her eyes. With a cry of alarm, she sat bolt upright.

"Doctor! What about the shuriken? Did you find out who threw it?"

The officers exchanged questioning glances. Donati shrugged. "What shuriken?"

"There was a shuriken, a black metal star, sticking out of Penrose's back when I rolled him off me." Winston couldn't believe he didn't know what she was talking about. "Don't tell me neither of you saw it."

Donati shrugged again, looking at Beresick in confusion.

"General, nobody saw any shuriken." Beresick spoke soothingly, reassuringly. "You took a couple of nasty cracks on the head. Are you sure you weren't imagining it?"

"Dammit, Alain!" she barked. "In all the time you've known me, have you *ever* known me to imagine *anything*?"

"No," Beresick said. "But a knock on the head and a concussion can have strange effects on a person's perceptions, can't they, Doctor?"

"Well . . . yes," Donati agreed, reluctance shading his reply.

"You examined Penrose." Winston turned her attention to the doctor. "Are you telling me you didn't find any wounds on his back?"

"No I'm not saying anything of the kind. In fact, I haven't had time to examine the body at all, other than a cursory examination to make sure he was really dead. All I saw at the time was a big gunshot wound in his chest, and a number of undeveloped bruises on his face. I'm assuming those are all your handiwork. But I'm certain that I didn't see any black throwing stars sticking out of his back." He broke off, holding his hands palm outward as though to ward off the vitriolic stream of curses forming on Winston's lips. "I'm not saying that there *wasn't* a shuriken. I'm saying I didn't see it.

"Remember, I was busy with Major Ryan when you and Penrose were having your little tango. Then I was busy examining you. The marines were the first ones to Penrose's body. Maybe one of them dislodged it."

"I didn't see it either." Beresick's voice had taken on a more thoughtful tone. "Give me a minute, I'll check."

As he crossed the deck to where an intercom sat bolted to the admitting desk, Donati leaned a little closer to Winston.

"General, are you absolutely sure of what you saw?"

"Of course I'm sure."

"Why don't you tell me exactly what happened. Start just before you shot Penrose."

"Okay. It's all a little fuzzy, but I'll try." Winston took a deep sighing breath and tried to focus her thoughts. "When I saw that Penrose didn't have any kind of detonator in his hand, I jumped him. We wrestled around a bit in the cabin, and he dropped one of his guns. We crashed through the door into the corridor. I remember head-butting him. I threw a kick, but he blocked it. I fell. He went for the other gun . . .

"Wait a minute. That's it! He went for his gun, but he dropped it. It didn't register at the time, but he went stiff all of a sudden. You know, like when you get hurt and sort of tense up against the pain? That's what it was like." Winston's words betrayed her excitement as the memory came flooding back. "He dropped the gun, but just stood there, all tensed up. It didn't register right away, 'cause I was grabbing for his gun. Next thing I knew he was on top of me, dead. I shoved him off me. That's when I saw the shuriken. Then you guys all came running up and stuffed me onto a stretcher."

"Did you see what happened to Penrose?"

"Yeah. He was lying on his side, facing me. A couple of Com Guard marines came running up, flipped him onto his face, and cuffed him. They gave him a quick patdown, looking for more weapons, or a detonator, or something, I guess. Then they let a couple of hospital orderlies take him away.

"You know, Doc?" Winston gazed intensely at Donati. There was a note of weary sickness in her voice. "I don't think I'll ever forget his eyes after I shot him. Bright blue, but just as cold and flat and dead as they could be.

"When you're fighting from a BattleMech, no matter how many enemies you knock out, 'nobody gets killed,' know what I mean? All you're doing is destroying great, big machines, like there's nobody inside them. I know I've killed people before, but that was on the battlefield. I saw their 'Mechs blow up or their fighters crash. I've even seen infantrymen go down. But I think this might be the first time I've ever actually *seen* someone die by my hand." Winston shivered in horror. "It was like I just *saw* the life drain out of him. I could almost see it in his eyes. It was like a light going out, just kind of fading away." She shivered a second time.

"Look, General . . . Ariana." Donati's tone was soft and sympathetic, indicating that he was speaking doctor-to-patient, rather than subordinate-to-superior. "I can't tell you what you saw in Penrose's eyes. That's one thing we doctors don't like to admit. We don't understand exactly what happens to a human being when they die. I guess a chaplain might tell you that you saw his soul leaving his body, I don't know. What I can tell you is that, from the location of the wound, and the probable bullet track, Penrose was probably dead before he hit the deck."

"And that's supposed to make me feel better?"

Donati sighed, with a slight shake of his head.

"General?" Beresick returned to her bedside. "I just talked to the marines who took charge of Penrose's body. None of them remember seeing anything like a shuriken. One, a private named Fitchell, says he remembers there being a little blood on the back of the man's tunic, just below the collar. He said he just assumed it got there when you rolled him off your legs."

"Did you check with my orderlies?" Donati asked.

"Uh-huh. Neither of the guys who carried Penrose to the morgue remember seeing anything like a shuriken, and neither mentioned seeing any blood on his back."

"Gentlemen, do you know what this means?" There was a note of fresh concern in Winston's voice. "This conspiracy may be a lot wider than we had feared."

10

***Battle Cruiser SLS* Invisible Truth**
Task Force Serpent
Deep Space, 150 Light Years from Huntress
24 January 3060

As much as Ariana Winston hated to admit it, Doctor Donati had been absolutely correct. The eight hours of sleep, enforced by the *Truth*'s chief medical officer, had done wonders. Though the various wounds, bruises, and scrapes hurt enough for her to know they were there, the pain had sufficiently diminished to allow her to function without wincing every time she moved. Only the gash in her lip continued to inhibit her in any way. She had developed a sort of temporary lisp when she spoke, and had to be very careful not to move her mouth any more than necessary or else the sutures closing the tear would pull, sending darts of pain through her face. Winston found it necessary to completely avoid Edwin Amis and Charles Antonescu. The customary by-play and verbal barbs between the Eridani Light Horse's two senior regimental commanders tended to bring a smile to her lips that would end in a yelp of pain as the grin tugged at the stitches.

As soon as Doctor Donati gave her permission to leave sick bay, Winston paid Major Ryan a visit.

"So, Major, I understand you're thinking of offering me a job."

At Winston's entrance, Ryan gingerly pushed himself into a

sitting position. He had recovered most of his color, but was still unable to move very quickly.

"I was, then I came to my senses." Ryan smiled, but the expression faded quickly. "For God's sake, General, what were you thinking? With all due respect, you violated every rule in the book. You gave in to the demands of a terrorist. You placed your own life in danger by going into a closed room with him. You endangered everyone else's life by attacking him. What if he'd had a detonator you didn't see? What if he'd had it rigged up to a heart monitor, or something like that? All you had to do was sit there, keep him isolated, and wait for the professionals to arrive, and what did you do? You went off half-cocked, playing *Immortal Warrior*. I tell you if one of *my* men ever tried such a stupid, grandstand stunt, he would consider himself lucky that I didn't have him shot."

Winston, who had secretly been proud of her handling of the situation, visibly bristled before Ryan's scathing reprimand.

"I didn't think I had the time to wait for your 'professionals' to arrive," she shot back, recovering some of her dignity. "Penrose was threatening to blow up the ship. I couldn't take the chance that he was serious. Besides it all turned out to be hogwash, didn't it?"

"Yes, it did," Ryan admitted. "This time."

"Well, let's hope there'll never be a next time."

"*Hai,* General."

For several moments there was silence between them.

"So, Donati tells me you're doing okay."

"Doctor Donati is a quack," Ryan grumbled. "He says I've got three broken ribs and a mild concussion. He's saying I've got to stay penned up here for three, maybe four more days. I tried to tell him I've had broken ribs before, but he won't listen. I can't just lie here in bed, and leave things to you amateurs." The last phrase was spoken with dry humor.

"Oh? Amateurs, is it? Maybe I'll tell Doctor Donati to keep you here for a few more days. Maybe I'll have him throw in a high colonic and put it on my tab." Winston placed her hands on her hips, trying desperately not to smile. "How do you feel, really?"

"Not too bad." Ryan became a bit more serious. "It feels like somebody smacked me in the side with a hammer, and I don't dare laugh. Otherwise, pretty good."

"All right, Major. You lie there and listen to the doctor. I don't want you bucking him, understand? After all, down here, he outranks everybody, even me."

"Hai, wakarimas," Ryan said, quietly agreeing with Winston's assessment of the chain of command in the sick bay. "Doctor Donati won't tell me anything, though. And, he has forbidden my men to do so either. How's the investigation going?"

"Well, Beresick has taken over the inquiries. Your boys are continuing the investigation. I'm sorry to say they haven't turned up a thing so far. He had your EOD experts crawling around in the ammo bins hunting for signs of sabotage. I'm glad to say they haven't found anything. I guess Penrose *was* bluffing after all."

"What about Penrose?"

"Nothing. So far, the guy's still a total blank."

"Well, keep looking."

"Oh, you can count on that."

As Winston was turning away from Ryan's bedside, the door hissed open behind her.

"General, I'm afraid I owe you an apology," Donati said without preamble as he entered the room.

"How's that?" Winston noticed Alain Beresick entering the sick bay right behind the surgeon. Obviously Donati had some new information for the investigation team, probably the results of the autopsy of Lucas Penrose. Holding up her right hand to stop his flow of words, she glanced suspiciously around the room before settling a pointed gaze on Donati.

"Don't worry, General," Beresick replied to her wary survey of the office. "I had one of Ryan's boys sweep the sick bay and Doctor Donati's office as well as my own shortly after we checked yours. There aren't any bugs here."

Winston nodded her acceptance. "Now, Doctor, you were saying?"

"Yes, I guess I owe you an apology." Donati handed her a printed form. When Winston scanned the paper, she realized it was a hardcopy of his preliminary autopsy report. Her only exposure to post-mortem examinations came from the detective holovids of which she was secretly so fond. From those dramas, she knew that a doctor performing an autopsy dictated his findings into a recording device, which, using voice-recognition software, stored the report electronically. The page she was reading was a printout of just such a file.

"I finished the post mortem on Penrose late last night." Donati activated his noteputer, and consulted the information displayed on the screen. "The man we knew as Lucas Penrose was a male Caucasian, one hundred seventy-five centimeters tall, weight, eighty-one kilograms. Blond hair, blue eyes.

"Preliminary examination revealed that the subject Penrose died of a single gunshot wound to the torso. The bullet entered the body at a steep angle, just below the lower end of the breast bone. There were no powder burns or residue stippling of the wound or clothing, indicating that the shot was fired from a distance greater than fifty centimeters. The bullet traversed the thorax, destroying the heart and shredding the ascending aorta as it went. It smashed, and was deflected by, the third thoracic vertebrae before coming to rest just beneath the skin of his right shoulder, seven centimeters from the spinal column. The projectile was badly deformed by its impact with the backbone, but otherwise remained mostly intact. The wound was non-survivable, and in my opinion, was probably instantly fatal."

"That's all well and good, Doctor," Winston said as she waded through the complex maze of esoteric medical terms. "What makes you think you owe me an apology?"

"Try this," Donati answered. "The preliminary, external examination of the subject's body revealed a single small wound in the subject's upper left dorsal quadrant, approximately three centimeters left of the spine. Corresponding tears were found in the subject's uniform tunic and shirt. At first I thought they might have been exit wounds, caused by bone fragments from the shattered vertebrae. Further examination of the site revealed that it was an entry wound, penetrating the subject's back to a depth of approximately two-and-a-half centimeters. The wound was caused by a single, sharp triangular blade, which was approximately five millimeters thick at the widest point. The wound showed little sign of bleeding, so I must assume that death intervened shortly after it was inflicted. The wound itself was in no way deep enough to cause death, nor did it impinge on any vital systems.

"Now, here's what's really interesting. Toxicological screens of the victim's blood revealed no traces of any foreign substances. Similar scans of the tissue surrounding the wound in the back revealed high concentrations of refined venom from an Eniffian gremlin viper.

"General, somehow a short, heavy blade entered that man's back, just missing his spine. The blade was coated with a very pure form of one of the most powerful, naturally occurring neurotoxins known to man. Whether you shot him or not, Penrose would have been dead in seconds."

Winston stared at Donati for what seemed like several minutes, trying to digest the information he had just given her.

"So you're saying there probably *was* a shuriken."

"I didn't say that. What I said was that the wound was made by a short, relatively thick blade, which was coated with a rather potent toxin." Donati shrugged. "If I had to make a guess, I'd have to say it *might* have been a shuriken."

"I knew it," Winston said with a mixture of satisfaction and relief. "I knew that was a star sticking out of his back. I knew I wasn't seeing things." Then, satisfaction turned to concern.

"Wait a second. If there *was* a shuriken, where is it now? Who threw it and why? Were they trying to silence Penrose, or stop him?"

"Good questions, General," Donati said. "I think we might begin by asking who might have access to that type of weapon."

"Practically anybody," Winston answered with a shake of her head. "Every city of any size has at least a dozen marital arts studios, and most of those sell throwing stars over the counter. You can get them for about a C-bill apiece."

"We're not talking about cheap junk here, General," Ryan interrupted. "From what Doctor Donati is telling us, Penrose got hit by a good, heavy, 'professional' model. Weapons like that are rather expensive. The average line soldier doesn't just buy them on a whim, even if he can find a place that sells them."

"So we're back to the original question: who in this task force might have access to that kind of star?"

"Offhand, I'd have to say the DEST teams," Beresick said. "We all know that shuriken are a traditional Japanese weapon, and DEST has used them in the past, especially coated with neurotoxins."

"That's true, the DEST teams are carrying shuriken. But by now, so are a lot of people." Winston's chuckle of amusement turned to a hiss of pain as her torn lip reminded her that laughter was not a good idea. "I've even got a couple of the bloody things. You know how soldiers are. 'What equipment are you carrying? How does it work? How is it different from mine?' Well, some of us have been trading little pieces of equipment back and forth for a couple of months now.

"It's the same old argument we've all been having about this. Theodore Kurita went through all the trouble of helping to organize this task force, assigned us a full DEST platoon and a brand-new *Kyushu* Class frigate. I really doubt that he'd be involved in trying to wax a commander he trusted with such important assets. No, I think the truth lies somewhere else."

"Were there any shuriken among Penrose's personal effects?" Donati asked.

"Not that we found," Beresick said, shaking his head. "Ryan's men impounded his belongings for examination. They gave me a detailed catalog of what they took. Most of the stuff was typical spacer's gear, uniforms, tool kits, and so on. It's kind of strange. They didn't find a whole lot of personal stuff. This is a big ship. We can give each crewman a good bit of personal space, or at least more than they get on most other ships. Most sailors will bring a small pile of personal effects aboard. Things like chip-readers, personal trid players, even small musical instruments. All Penrose had were a few hardcopy letters from a 'sister,' a music-chip player, and a few dozen music-chips, mostly classical and neoclassical stuff. I can tell you that there were no shuriken on the list, no vials of poison or lock-breakers either."

"So we're right back where we started?"

"Not exactly, General." It was Beresick's turn to consult his noteputer. "We did some discreet checking into Mister Penrose's activities over the last few weeks. He was off duty and unaccounted for during the time of the suspected break-in of the Marshal's flag suite. Now, on the face of it, this is not conclusive evidence, but coupled with the lack of a pre-ComStar background and Penrose's actions the other day, it's all pretty damning.

"A little further checking revealed that Penrose was seen entering the galley on Deck Sixteen a few hours after the murder. That's kind of unusual for several reasons. First of all, the timing is rather suspicious. Then, Penrose was quartered on Thirteen, so what was he doing on Sixteen? And, as a jump technician, he had no reason to enter the galley—the mess hall, yes, the galley itself, no."

"Does anybody know what he was doing there?" Winston's mind was busily churning through the information Beresick was presenting.

"As might be predicted, no," Beresick answered tightly. "It was between shifts, and the galley was empty. Maybe he was just a little hungry and was just going to make himself a snack, but somehow I doubt that."

"So what was he doing there?"

"This is only a guess, mind you, but I'd have to say he was destroying evidence." Beresick stroked his chin thoughtfully. "Waste aboard a starship is collected in injection-molded 'trash cans.' The cans are dumped out a hatch in the engineering sections and get incinerated by the ship's drive plume. Penrose could have timed his visit to coincide with the trash collection and incineration by checking the service logs or simply by asking someone on the galley staff."

Ryan, holding his side to ease the discomfort of his broken ribs, suggested that Beresick put some of the Fox Team to work checking the Deck Sixteen disposal units for traces of Penrose's fingerprints.

"Already taken care of," Beresick said, smiling. "Your Talon Sergeant Raiko hasn't got much hope of lifting anything too useful. He said with the number of people who use that unit, the best he can hope for is a partial match."

Winston shrugged. "Well, that'll have to do."

"There's something else. I'd say it was odd, but the way things are turning out on this mission, 'odd' is becoming a way of life.

"The day we jumped out of Trafalgar, after the battle with the Ghost Bears, the *Truth*'s sensors picked up an anomalous trace right before we jumped. The sensor operator on duty said it looked like an incoming JumpShip. But, being as how there's no way for one JumpShip to track another through hyperspace, Major

Karabin, my Fourth Officer, simply logged it as an anomalous EMP with inconclusive sensor scans, and then forgot about it.

"Now that was a major violation of regulations. I gave him a good dressing down about it, and almost forgot the incident myself. After all, we haven't seen any signs of ships other than our own since Trafalgar. Now, I'm not so certain."

"Pardon me, Commodore," Ryan said, an expression of concern mixed with confusion on his face. "Are you saying that there might be a JumpShip shadowing this task force? That maybe Penrose *wasn't* bluffing?"

"I don't believe anything of the sort, Major Ryan, and neither do you," Beresick snapped. "You know as well as I do that there is no way to shadow a fleet through hyperspace. Even the Clans can't do that. The only way they might have managed it is if they had a copy of our star charts and mission plans. And the only way they could have gotten that was from one of us, or from Prince Victor or the Precentor Martial, and I don't think any of that happened."

"So what are you saying, Commodore?" Winston asked. "What was this 'anomalous sighting'?"

"I'm saying I don't know," Beresick answered. "I looked at the sensor tapes. It might have been a starship, and it might not. If I had to hazard a guess, I'd say it wasn't. If it was a JumpShip shadowing this fleet, it would have jumped right into the middle of us while we were making repairs at Trafalgar."

"So why bring this up?"

"I brought it up, General, because so much else on this voyage has been so weird. And, in light of recent events, I'd suggest that we keep the fleet in a high state of readiness every time we jump into a new system, just in case."

"Very well." With a deep sigh, Winston got to her feet. "Is there anything else, gentlemen? If you'll excuse me, I'm going back to my office. I inherited a lot of headaches along with this task force, and I doubt that they've gone away just because I was in sick bay. If I had to guess, I'd say I've probably got twice as many problems to resolve as I had three days ago."

Fortunately for Ariana Winston, she was the sole passenger in the lift from the Deck Fifteen sick bay to Deck Four, where her office was located. She was tired, sore, and on the ragged edge of emotional exhaustion, all due to the traumatic events of the past few weeks, and really didn't want to see anybody for several hours.

My God, has it only been a few weeks? It seems like a couple of months, at least.

She marveled at how much had happened since Morgan was found dead in his bunk. The Marshal's sudden death was first suspected, then confirmed to have been the result of foul play. The subsequent investigation had turned up no hard evidence, only the circumstantial indication that several ComStar crew members might not be exactly what they seem. Then the man they knew as Lucas Penrose murdered two Com Guard marines, and under the threat of destroying the *Invisible Truth*, tried to extort the command staff into giving him a JumpShip in which to make his getaway.

As she punched in the access code that would open her office door, Winston gave the cryptolock's keypad a critical, suspicious look. If Penrose, or whatever his name was, had an accomplice, had that co-conspirator broken into her office, leaving her some kind of lethal surprise?

Stop it, Ria, she told herself. *You're getting just a little too paranoid.*

"Lights, low." In response to her command, the voice-activated systems brought a faint glow to the overhead illumination strips.

Winston made her way through the friendly shadows to her desk, where she collapsed into her chair. She immediately regretted the casual flop against the seat back as her bruised body spasmed in protest. She could see that a number of hard- and chip-copy reports that required her attention had been placed on her desk. Calling for full lighting, she skimmed through the six pages of status reports, originally sent to Morgan's attention and forwarded to her upon his death.

I don't want to deal with this. The tension of command was already beginning to make its presence felt. She leaned back in her chair, eyes closed, hoping to take a few minutes to collect her thoughts.

A sharp buzz prevented any such respite. For a moment, she considered not answering the incoming message, allowing the comm unit's recording device to take the call. Her sense of duty and responsibility prevented that all too human response. She reached across the desk, and pressed the Answer stud.

"Winston."

The screen flared brightly, but there was no image displayed on the unit's liquid-crystal monitor. A now-familiar series of twisting bands of color was overlaid with the legend "video portion blocked at source."

"General Winston." The caller's tone was soft, polite, bearing no trace of an accent. There was none of the distortion that had marked the earlier call, leading Winston to believe that she was hearing the caller's real voice. "My name is Talisen. I was a friend of Marshal Hasek-Davion's, and though you are not yet aware of it, a friend of yours as well."

Winston's heart leapt at the odd name the caller claimed. She recognized it as one of the many code-words on the list in Morgan's safe, the code-words to be used in communicating with the nekekami. The caller was one of the spirit cats, if not the team leader himself.

"I know that you are investigating the assassination of Marshal Hasek-Davion, and that you are suspicious of several persons now aboard the *Invisible Truth*. Let me assure you that there was only *one* assassin, and that man is, or was, rather, Lucas Penrose.

"Penrose—that is not his true name, as you might have surmised—was a high-level operative in the employ of the House Steiner agency known as Loki. I know this to be true because I have encountered him twice before, during the course of performing my own duties. I know for certain that Penrose was responsible for three previous unsolved assassinations, which he performed both within, and on behalf of the Lyran Commonwealth and later the Alliance. Two of these murders were committed against high-level operatives of the Draconis Combine's Internal Security Force. The third eliminated a Lyran military officer, whose superiors deemed him just a little too pro-Davion for their liking."

"That's easy to say," Winston began. "Can you prove . . ."

"I will prove every word I say, General," the mysterious voice cut in. "I will provide you with all the evidence you might desire, as soon as I can confirm it. In the meantime, you are holding a

ComStar crewman. I believe her name is Julia Davis. You may wish to release her from house arrest."

Before the baffled Winston had time to reply to this rather bold demand, the line went dead.

Battle Cruiser SLS **Invisible Truth**
Task Force Serpent
Waypoint Mulberry, 120 Light Years from
Huntress
Deep Space
19 February 3060

For several weeks following the dramatic, almost theatrical death of Lucas Penrose, the inquiry into the assassination of Morgan Hasek-Davion continued. The DEST team investigators ransacked Penrose's berthing space, with a total result of nothing. This, in and of itself, was of immense interest to Major Ryan.

"It's like Penrose never even existed," he told Winston during their first meeting since his discharge from sick bay. "We couldn't find a single person aboard the *Truth* or any of other ComStar ship in this task force who knew him before he was assigned to this operation. His bunkmates said he was kind of a quiet guy, that he was always more interested in his music and books than in being part of the gang.

"Funny thing, though, anytime there was a really heated discussion of any kind—politics, the Word of Blake, even the food in the mess hall—Penrose was always right there. He never said too much that anyone can remember, just kind of hung around on the edges of the discussion. Everybody my men talked to just figured Penrose was somewhat shy, or uncertain of himself. His bunkmates said he was a likable enough fellow, but he never seemed to really fit in.

"When my team swept his quarters they didn't find too much, just a lot of music chips, mostly classical and neoclassical. He had a dozen books on chip too, and a very expensive data unit to play them on. That's not unusual. We must have found a hundred chip players and readers when we searched the ship the first time. Some even the same make and model as Penrose's. I've got my men going over the chips and the reader now, just to make sure there are no messages hidden between the notes of Kachaturian's *Saber Dance*."

"That's not funny, Major." Winston glared at him. "We're only a couple of jumps from launching the biggest invasion this side of Tukayyid, and our original commander is dead. We've got a body down in sick bay that may or may not be our assassin, the rumors about who killed Morgan and why are getting more and more pervasive and more and more outrageous as time goes on, and the troops are starting to distrust each other. If it goes on much longer, this task force is going to launch the offensive against itself instead of the Smoke Jaguars. So, let's get this thing settled right away, and hold the jokes until *after* we take Huntress, all right?"

Ryan blinked in surprise at Winston's uncharacteristically harsh reprimand for what he considered to be a relatively minor offense.

Winston was astonished herself.

"I'm sorry, Major," she said, shaking her head with a sigh. "I guess I could put it down to the stress of the last couple of days, but I won't. I was out of line."

She sighed again.

"Let's just get this thing wrapped up as quickly as possible."

During the long weeks of the investigation, Task Force Serpent crawled its paradoxically slow way along a route that roughly approximated what the Clans called the Exodus Road, the semi-mythical path supposedly taken by the Star League armada, only lately revealed by a defector from the Smoke Jaguars. Ariana Winston was not exaggerating when she compared their mission to the battle of Tukayyid. Had the Com Guards failed in their bid to halt the Clan invasion of the Inner Sphere, mankind might well be facing another dark age more horrible than the one following the collapse of the original Star League. If this mission failed, the hope of a renewed Star League, now less than a year old, would die with the men and women of Task Force Serpent.

Winston did her best to impress this fact upon the command staff.

"Ladies and gentlemen, if you'll look at the mission status reports in front of you, you will see confirmation of what I know you've all been supposing ever since we jumped into this system." She paused while the officers crowded into the *Invisible Truth*'s briefing room opened the hardcopy reports that a Com Guard yeoman handed out as they entered. "We have reached Waypoint Mulberry. Our next jump will take us to within striking range of our objective. This is to be the final council of war before we begin Operation Serpent. I want to review each unit's assignment for the initial assault, and be certain that everyone is ready to go.

"We might as well begin at the beginning. So, Major Ryan?"

Michael Ryan rose and executed a proper, formal bow.

"The first phase of Operation Serpent is to be carried out by the Draconis Elite Strike Teams," Ryan began. As he spoke, a holographic projection of the world called Huntress appeared in the air above the conference table. The image was generated by a small laser-based projector, built into the table and controlled by a yeoman seated at a console in the back corner of the room. The map had become so familiar to the command staff that any one of them could have rendered a freehand drawing of Huntress, strictly from memory, and not have left out a single major detail.

"My teams will jump into the Huntress system aboard the *Haruna*, using IFF codes provided by Agent Trent. These codes, according to Trent, will designate the *Haruna* as a Jaguar *York* Class destroyer/carrier on a routine transfer mission. As you know, we have altered our original plan, which called for us to use the *Bisan* as team transport. The plan now is to use the *Stiletto*. We've transferred the *Bisan*'s crew over to her, so as to preserve the integrity of my team."

Ryan could almost feel Marshal Sharon Bryan trying to lase holes in his chest with her eyes. She had tried, unsuccessfully, to have the *Stiletto*, a Clan *Broadsword* Class DropShip, assigned to her forces, or at least kept out of the DEST teams' hands. The *Stiletto* was one of the prizes of the battle of Trafalgar.

"As you know," Ryan continued, ignoring Bryan's poisonous look, "the plan originally called for my teams to make an orbital drop, after which the *Bisan* would ground on Huntress' only moon, Sentinel. The *Bisan* is an *Achilles* Class ship; she cannot carry out atmospheric operations. We were never too happy about that plan. I didn't like being cut off from our ship, and the *Bisan*'s crew didn't like the idea of grounding on Sentinel. But, there was no way around it. No other ship in the fleet was as fast and as heavily armed and armored as the *Bisan*.

"Fortunately, we've got a genuine Clan *Broadsword* now. Even if the Jags don't believe our IFF codes, the *Stiletto* will at least pass visual muster."

"Major, is there something bothering you about the codes?" Winston had caught an odd note in Ryan's normally confident voice.

"*Hai,* General. Put it down to a deeply ingrained survival instinct," Ryan said. "That and a healthy respect for the native intelligence of our enemy. The *Haruna* is a *Kyushu* Class frigate with a mass of about six hundred twenty-five thousand tons. The ship we're masquerading as, the *Queen Lynx* I think she's called, masses only about five hundred ninety-five thousand tons. That's a thirty-five-thousand-ton difference. Add to that the fact that there's absolutely *no* visual resemblance between a *York* and a *Kyushu,* and the odds of the operation being blown before it even starts just keep getting better and better."

"We've been over this before, Major," Alain Beresick put in. "When you're dealing with something as large as a JumpShip, thirty thousand tons isn't all that much. Chances are the Jags won't notice the discrepancy in mass. If they don't, I doubt they'll want to do a flyby to check you out."

"*So ka?*" Ryan shot back. "Is that right? And what if they do check us out? Then what? It isn't going to be you, Commodore, sitting in a tin can thirty light years from the nearest help."

The command staff knew that Ryan's concerns were not voiced out of fear for his own safety, but out of concern for his men and the success of the overall operation.

"We've been over this before, Major," Winston reminded him. "You detach the *Stiletto* and make a run for the planet. The

Haruna will jump back outsystem on her lithium-fusion batteries, and return to the fleet. At that point, we all come in hot.

"But that's a worst-case scenario. The Precentor Martial and Agent Trent both seemed to think that those codes are still good, so let's not borrow trouble. Besides, Trent says that the Jags are so hidebound that if the Identify Friend and Foe codes say that a ship is a *York* destroyer/carrier, then it's a *York* destroyer/carrier, no matter what their instruments tell them. I guess the only thing that would convince them otherwise would be if you opened fire on them. And we both know you aren't going to do that, right?"

"Right." Ryan's tone made it quite clear that firing on any Smoke Jaguar ship the *Haruna* might encounter was the last thing he planned to do. "Well, to continue . . . assuming the Jags don't blast us to scrap, we'll detach the *Stiletto* and head insystem while the *Haruna* jumps out again.

"We're figuring an in-run of about two hundred-forty hours."

"Ten days?" Beresick made the conversion mentally, almost without thinking. "That's too long."

"Yes, it is," Ryan agreed. "That's one of the reasons I was so concerned about the IFF codes. We thought about making a high-speed in-run, at say two, two-and-a-half Gs, but that would only cut a couple of days off our time, and put a severe physical strain on my men. We've opted for the slower burn to help avoid detection, and that's why we're going to need the IFF codes to bluff our way through.

"Once we're insystem, we'll make a HALO jump into the Jaguar's Fangs, the mountain range that borders the capital city of Lootera. We'll drop from low orbit, using standard ablative capsules, penetrate the target airspace with a minimal chance of detection, and pop our 'chutes at the last minute.

"After we jump, the *Stiletto* will issue a false distress call, saying that it's about to crash in the Dhuan Swamp area. What they'll really do is drop under the Jag's radar and ground in the Lunar Range on the continent Abysmal. Once the *Stiletto* drops off their screens, they'll probably project her course along her last heading. Of course, Captain Ge, the *Stiletto*'s commander, will make sure his 'last heading' will be directly toward the swamp."

As Ryan detailed his operation, the terrain features he mentioned glowed faintly on the holographic map. Though Winston knew the map and the details of the operation as well as Ryan did, she leaned forward to study the laser-generated image.

Huntress was a forbidding planet. Having just two continents, Jaguar Prime and Abysmal, it was a bleak, stormy world of stark, jagged mountains, thick jungles, and scorching deserts. Much of the planet was uninhabited, with what population there was mainly centered around the world's five larger urban centers. Of the two continents, Jaguar Prime and Abysmal, only the former was inhabited. The latter was well named. The Hatya Desert was a huge expanse of blistering sand, while the Lunar Range was a jagged range of volcanic peaks. A few of these were still active.

The two large bodies of water, the Sangram and Dhundh Seas, were salty and had a high sulfur content.

Mount Szabo, she knew, was a monument to the colossal pride, or maybe it was hubris, of the Smoke Jaguars. The mountain lay on the northern edge of Lootera, overlooking the planetary capital. Carved into its southern face was a gigantic rendering of the smoke jaguar. Housed deep within that massive pile of granite was the planet's primary defense command center. Included in the command center was the control facility for Huntress' "Reagan" Space Defense System. This installation was the DEST teams' primary objective.

"I have a question about your 'dropping under the radar,' " Colonel Kingston put in. "From what I understand, most radar systems are pulse-doppler arrays, whatever that means. I was given to understand that you couldn't get 'under' pulse-doppler."

Ryan half-chuckled. "Dropping under radar is kind of a misnomer in the first place, Colonel. In theory, there's an area of several degrees above the horizon where surveillance radar is unable to get a clear return due to what they call 'ground clutter.' Ground clutter is that big lump of junk you always see in the center of a conventional radar screen. It comes from radar echoes reflected off things like hills, buildings, trees, and so on that are in the radar's so-called dead zone. It extends to a theoretical altitude of about forty-five meters. So, if you stay below that ceiling, you're fairly safe from radar detection. That's the ideal.

"In reality, well-sited radar installation won't leave that much of a dead space between the radar coverage and the ground. I certainly wouldn't want to be aboard anything so large as a Drop-Ship trying to skim the surface and still stay in the 'safe zone.'

"The way things really work is you get a region the sensor techs call 'anaprop'—that's anomalous propagation. It's a zone that, for whatever reason, weather, atmospheric conditions, and so on, produces poor signal propagation on ground-based radar. The result is a gap in the radar coverage. Anaprop usually occurs around one hundred thirty-five meters. It makes low-level flying a lot less dangerous. The problem is that the anaprop can change from hour to hour, so we can't guarantee a gap in a specific place at a specific time. Fortunately, our EW sensors are good enough that we can detect a dead zone and drop into it.

"Pulse-doppler radar is pretty good, but its primary function is to detect and track objects moving relative to the direction of the pulse. They work by sorting through the radar returns and eliminating what they call 'non-targets.' That means those objects that don't seem to be moving. Most fighters carry this type of radar now, and they sometimes call it 'look-down-shoot-down radar' because it lets you see and engage targets flying below you that would normally be hidden by ground returns.

"Now, with the Electronic Warfare equipment carried by most military DropShips, detecting surveillance and tracking radars is no problem, even if they're pulse-doppler. For constant wave or non-doppler pulses, we can drop into an anaprop, or even 'go below' the coverage. Doppler pulses are a little trickier. There we'd have to angle off, which means turn ninety degrees from the pulse axis, so we're traveling in conformity to the enemy pulse. That way, in theory at least, the radar computer will drop us from the screen because we're no longer a moving target.

"Once we're on the ground," Ryan continued, "we'll make our way to Mount Szabo, hit the command center in Lootera and take out the Reagan system control center. If we're lucky, we should have the advantage of surprise. According to Trent, the Jags are arrogant enough to believe a strike against their homeworld is impossible, so we should be lucky.

"There may be one additional benefit to hitting the Mount Szabo installation. According to the information provided by Trent, the mountain also houses a portion of the planetary defense force. If we're very lucky, we may be able to damage or destroy a significant portion of the units billeted there.

"After we accomplish our part of the mission, my teams will withdraw to the west and go to ground in the mountains. We are to wait for the follow-on forces to secure their landing zones before we attempt to make contact."

"That's right," Ariana Winston said. "Once the DEST teams begin their operation, they will be out of contact. Their phase of the operation is on a timetable. They will have fourteen days from the time they leave the fleet until the main invasion body arrives.

"The *Haruna* will recharge her drives and then jump out of the Huntress system and return to the fleet. She'll make another recharge and jump back to Huntress with the rest of the task force." Winston gestured to Commodore Beresick, indicating that he should take over his portion of the briefing.

"As soon as the *Haruna* is recharged, the whole fleet will jump into the Huntress system," Beresick said, picking up the thread. "The assault will be made in two waves. The WarShips will go in first, arriving at the zenith point. As soon as we arrive, we will engage and destroy any Clan WarShips we find in-system. According to our intelligence, we can expect some resistance. Trent says he saw a couple of corvettes and a larger combat vessel, possibly a cruiser. Unfortunately he was unable to determine if the WarShips comprised a permanent defense force or if they were only making a stop-over in the Huntress system. Our best guess is that they are a regular system defense force. Using a worst-case scenario, we're calling the cruiser a *Liberator* and the corvettes *Vincent*s. With that in mind, the *Invisible Truth* and the *Fire Fang* will engage the cruiser, while the *Emerald, Rostock, Antrim,* and *Ranger* will engage the corvettes. The *Starlight* took some heavy hits at Trafalgar, so we've assigned her to remain behind as a picket ship for the transports.

"Our objective will be to engage to destroy. That is *destroy,* not capture, because one hour after we jump in, the *Starlight* and the transports will follow. As soon as the transports are in system, they'll detach their DropShips and commence recharge operations. Each of the WarShips will have an assigned duty. The *Fire Fang* and the *Ranger* have been assigned to escort the DropShips on the in-run. They will then go on orbital station to provide support fire, if necessary."

Beresick's last words carried a note of emphasis directed at the ground-force commanders. The debate over using the fleet's combat ships to provide orbital support fire, or even a saturation bombardment, had been rather bitter. Some of the officers, Beresick among them, had supported the idea of "softening up" the Clan defenders with an orbital bombardment before the main troop landings.

Before his death, Morgan had passed judgment on the idea; there would be no planetary bombardment. The Smoke Jaguars had used that very tactic themselves during the now infamous Turtle Bay incident. In an act of unparalleled barbarism, the Jaguars had unleashed a hellstorm of naval gunfire on the helpless and officially surrendered city of Edo. Tens of thousands died. The heinous act was condemned by the other invading Clans, who resolved to bid away their WarShips in any future operations.

Morgan and some of the other commanders had seen holovids of the destruction of Edo and other major cities on Turtle Bay. He had been adamant that the WarShips of Task Force Serpent would not sink to that level of cruelty and barbarism. Though Winston had initially supported the idea of naval bombardment, she felt herself bound to obey Morgan's orders. The fact that he was gone played no part in her thinking. He had given the command, and she, as his successor, would see it carried out.

"Thank you, Commodore." Winston nodded her approval of Beresick's briefing. "The operational plan calls for simultaneous strikes at a number of targets. We know that there are only a limited number of troops on Huntress, and that they are mostly older, solahma warriors."

Though Winston used the Clan term for a warrior who was considered past his prime by rigid Clan doctrine, her tone carried no hint of the contempt a Clansman would have expressed with the same word. To Winston, and the vast majority of her Inner Sphere contemporaries, an older warrior was to be respected, if not feared, for his wisdom and hard-won experience.

"We know from Trent's intelligence report that there are only two organized Galaxies on Huntress, the Iron Guard and the Watchmen. Both solahma units," she continued. "There are also a number of training cadres and their sibkos. Now, if we hit the Jags in a number of different places at the same time, we'll stretch their resources pretty thin, hopefully to the breaking point. If we can stick halfway to the plan, and if we're lucky, this mass strike should help minimize the casualties taken by any one unit.

"Now, specific assignments. The Knights of the Inner Sphere and Kingston's Legionnaires are to hit the training bases at New Andery. According to our intelligence—and remember this is two years old—if you're engaged, it will be probably by members of a training sibko and their instructors. The Kathil Uhlans will go after the manufacturing centers, here at Myer."

As Winston spoke, the holographic map lit up, showing each objective in succession. "The Lyran Guards will attack and take out the training facility at Bagera. The Northwind Highlanders are to attack and destroy the factory complex northeast of Pahn City. Trent's report places the Watchmen in garrison at Myer, just to the north of there. We have to assume they're still there. Just remember that solahma doesn't mean stupid or incompetent. They'll still put up a fight. The St. Ives Lancers and the Fourth Drakøns are to destroy the training camp on Abysmal, and establish a landing zone there.

"Captain Montjar, your Fox Teams will drop into the mountains to the southeast of Lootera. Your job is to keep an eye on Falcon Eyrie."

Montjar leaned over the holomap to get a better view of his area of operations. Falcon Eyrie was a small compound set high among the peaks of the Eastern Mountains. He knew the mysterious Trent had promised that the other Clans would likely stay out of the fighting. But what troubled Montjar was the fact that Trent's intelligence regarding Falcon Eyrie was extremely limited, and would be two years old by the time his teams dropped into those mountains. The Rabid Foxes had no solid evidence regarding the quality, nor even the number of troops occupying the facility they were to surveil. And, given the Jade Falcon reputation for aggressiveness, Montjar couldn't bring himself to trust the Falcons to stay out of the fight. Neither could General Winston, nor Marshal Hasek-Davion before her. The original plan called for the Davion commando teams to surveil the Falcon base, just in case the tiny, but potentially hostile force garrisoned there decided to take a hand in the battle for Huntress.

"If it looks like the Falcons are about to get involved," Winston continued, "you call in the Lancers or the Drakøns to stop them.

"Colonel Grandi?" Winston looked at the Com Guard ground

forces commander. "You're on back-up. If the DEST teams get tangled up with the Jags at Mount Szabo, your troops will attack that facility, and relieve them. If Ryan's men *do* eliminate the command center, you'll ground at the base on Abysmal and remain in reserve.

"Now, the Eridani Light Horse has the toughest nut of all. We're going to ground to the northwest of Mount Szabo. From there the 21st and 151st Regiments will attack the big training base just outside of Lootera. The 71st, under Colonel Barclay, will attack and seize the Jaguars' genetic repository at Mount Szabo.

"If all goes well, we should be able to secure the whole planet in less than a week.

"But, let's not count on everything going according to plan. We've got to be prepared for one mother of a street fight. I want everyone from the greenest infantryman to your battalion commanders to know not only his own job, but that of his immediate superior. I don't want to take a single casualty more than we absolutely have to. You people are the closest thing to an elite strike force we could assemble. If we do this right the first time, we won't get bogged down in a war of attrition. If that happens, we'll probably lose this fight. Our job is to jump in, level the Jags' warmaking capability, and jump out. That's it.

"All right, let's go over each operational phase one more time. Colonel Masters?"

As the commander of the Knights of the Inner Sphere began to recite his strategy for seizing New Andery, Colonel Sandra Barclay, commander of the 71st Light Horse Regiment, breathed a silent sigh of relief. It wasn't because her regiment, which had been battered almost into oblivion by the Jade Falcons in the battle for Coventry, was slated to attack the genetic repository. She'd known that from the very beginning of Operation Serpent. Her relief came from hearing that her assignment to attack that lightly defended facility hadn't been changed.

It wasn't as though she was a coward. Far from it. Barclay had acquitted herself brilliantly during the bloody defense of Lietnerton, the last Inner Sphere stronghold on Coventry. No, it was something different. Ever since the task force made its first jump out of the familiar space of the Inner Sphere, she had been haunted by a growing sense of impending doom. At first she put this uneasy feeling down to her encounter with a Jade Falcon *Man o' War* during that last desperate battle. But the closer they got to actually launching the invasion of Huntress, the greater her fear became.

No, she told herself. *Fear is the wrong word. Call it a premonition, a premonition of death.* The feeling had been gnawing at her ever since she'd learned of this mission, a fear not of dying, but that she might malf up her part of the operation, get her regiment wiped out, and survive to live with the guilt. To Sandra Barclay's mind, living with the ghosts of those who died following her orders would be worse than dying at the enemy's hand.

***Battle Cruiser SLS* Invisible Truth**
Task Force Serpent
Unnamed Star System, 30 Light Years from
Huntress
Clan Space
19 February 3060

For Ariana Winston, the conclusion of the final strategy session was perhaps the single most important moment in her life. For most of her forty-seven years she had been aware of a manifest destiny that lay before the Eridani Light Horse like a golden road. Now, here, nearly fifteen hundred light years past the edge of the Inner Sphere, she was preparing to take the last fateful steps on that road.

As the various unit leaders returned to their own command ships, Winston and her regimental commanders embarked aboard a high-speed shuttle that would carry them back to the *Gettysburg,* the Eridani Light Horse command vessel. Colonels Edwin Amis and Charles Antonescu had much to say about the coming assault on Huntress, but Sandra Barclay kept her own counsel.

Winston noted the junior Colonel's silence. Though Barclay was never what any reasonable individual might call talkative, there seemed to be something more behind her stony silence and bowed head than her normal detachment. Had Ariana Winston been superstitious, she might have said Barclay was fey, under the spell of impending death. Briefly, she wondered if the younger woman might be losing her nerve.

Barclay must have sensed her stare. The dark blonde head came up, and her deep blue eyes burned back at Winston. There was a bright spark of defiance in their gaze.

No, Winston told herself. *She's not losing her nerve. But something is bothering her. Whatever it is, it will have to be rooted out before we go into Huntress. I can't take the risk of having one of my unit commanders at anything less than one hundred percent.*

As though reading Winston's thoughts, Barclay smiled. In that simple expression, Winston saw once again the confident young officer she'd once considered as a possible successor to the command of the Light Horse. The narrow grin was laced with weariness and apprehension, but that signified nothing. They were all tired, and anxiety was a natural enough reaction to what was about to happen.

Maybe I read her wrong, Winston thought, returning the smile. *Now what do I do? If I've misinterpreted Sandy's attitude, giving her a pep talk might make it seem like I don't trust her. But if I'm right, and I don't talk to her, I might be condemning the entire regiment.*

With a heavy sigh, Winston decided to defer judgment on the whole issue. After all, it would be a full week before the main invasion fleet jumped off for Huntress. That would be plenty of time to observe Barclay and determine what, if any, action was needed.

She had barely arrived at this decision when the shuttle pilot informed his passengers that they were about to dock with the *Gettysburg.* That brief message caused Winston to shift the focus of her thoughts. Though, with Morgan's death, she had ascended to command of the entire operation, she also retained command of the Eridani Light Horse. It had always been her policy to lay out the overall plan of battle for the whole unit, and leave the operational details to her regimental and battalion commanders. Despite the enormity of the task before them, she saw no reason to alter this long-standing custom.

"Thank you, Lieutenant," Winston replied to the pilot's report. "Contact the *Gettysburg's* command center, and have the battalion commanders standing by in the conference room. I want to give them a full mission briefing as soon as possible."

"Right away, General."

* * *

Just thirty-five minutes later, Winston was concluding her short explanation of the Light Horse's role in the coming operation. A holographic map, similar to the one used by the command staff aboard the *Invisible Truth*, hovered in the air a few centimeters above the *Gettysburg*'s conference table. The Light Horse's holograph generator was smaller and consequently less powerful than the one used on the *Truth*. As a result, the map was less detailed. That hardly mattered, though. Each battalion commander had a comprehensive hardcopy chart of his or her Area of Operation. Each company commander would have an electronic copy of the AO map loaded into his 'Mech's computer.

Every battalion commander knew his assignment, and would be able to complete it without direction from the Light Horse's upper-command echelon. Each had been fully briefed on the overall objectives assigned to their regiment, and would be able to step into their commanding Colonel's shoes if such action became necessary. Winston knew that the battalion commanders, Majors all, would in turn brief their company commanders, preparing them to take over the battalion if they were wounded or killed. Each officer knew the order of succession for his or her battalion or regiment. There would be no bickering over who was senior while the enemy closed in around them. This was the tradition of the Eridani Light Horse. It ensured both an unbroken chain of command and a steady supply of replacement officers.

When each of the ten battalion commanders had confirmed that the orders were clearly understood, Winston smiled in satisfaction. But, there was still one officer who had yet to speak. She thumbed a button on the table-top computer terminal. Instantly she was connected to the *Gettysburg*'s command center.

"Bridge, this is General Winston. Open a communication channel to the rest of the Light Horse."

"Channel open, General." The speed of the reply told her that the communications technician had been expecting the order. Looking across the briefing table, she nodded at the captain, who had remained silent throughout the briefing.

Captain D.C. Stockdale, the Light Horse's brigade chaplain, got carefully to his feet. Gripping the edge of the table to maintain his equilibrium against the zero-G environment, he bowed his head and intoned words almost as ancient as those he'd spoken at Morgan's funeral.

"Dominus noster Jesus Christus vos absolvat."

Though a Protestant minister, Stockdale was sensitive to the spiritual needs of all the troops under his pastorage. The words of general absolution came hard to him, but he knew the comfort they would bring to those troopers of the Catholic faith.

"Do your duty," Stockdale concluded. "And the Lord watch over you."

As he resumed his seat, Winston cleared her throat.

"Light Horsemen," she said in a strong, clear voice. "Today we stand on the brink of our destiny. We are fulfilling the hopes and dreams of all those who have worn the uniform of the Eridani Light Horse, from the days of the Star League until now. It has been my pleasure and my privilege to serve with you. Each one of you, from the rawest recruit to the most hardened veteran, all know what is expected of you. I have faith in your will to fight, your desire to live free, and your dedication to the dream of the Star League. I know you won't let me down.

"Good luck, and I'll see you on Huntress."

She severed the communication link with a sharp poke at the intercom.

"Ladies and gentlemen," she said to the officers in the briefing room. "You all know your jobs. I have to return to the *Invisible Truth* to oversee the operation. I'll rejoin you before we launch the assault. Good luck. Do 'em in."

Edwin Amis laughed under his breath at those last words, which were growled out like a tiger's snarl. To cover his amusement, he snapped his right hand up into the palm-outward salute used by the Light Horse, and his comrades followed suit.

With a satisfied grin, Winston returned the gesture, and left the room.

A few dozen kilometers away, a similar scene was being played out by the members of the Draconis Elite Strike teams. Following the final mission briefing, Michael Ryan and his staff returned to the *Haruna* to make what last-minute preparations remained.

During the briefing aboard the *Invisible Truth*, the captured Clan DropShip had docked at the *Haruna*'s number three docking collar. Her former owners, the Ghost Bears, had named her *Ice Dart,* but the Task Force was calling her *Stiletto.* In accordance with the revised mission plans, technical crews assigned the DEST teams had transferred the commandos' equipment from the *Bisan* to the *Stiletto.* The OmniMechs that were captured along with the DropShip had been transferred to the Kathil Uhlans' JumpShip, the *Ericsson.* Sharon Bryan hadn't been too pleased when she learned of the transfer, believing that Winston was assigning the captured Clan war machines to the FedCom troops. Winston had wearily explained to the staunch pro-Steiner officer that they had to do something with the captured Omnis, and it was simply easiest to move them aboard the JumpShip to which the *Stiletto* had been mated.

Ryan smiled thinly at the irony of the ship's new name. Though the DEST team members revered the warrior tradition of the Draconis Combine, they were more akin to ninja than to samurai. Now, the captured Clan DropShip, repainted in Smoke Jaguar colors, would become the slim knife of assassination aimed at the Clanners' throats.

In the *Stilleto*'s cavernous 'Mech bay, now empty of the armored giants it was intended to carry, the DEST warriors made ready to launch their phase of Operation Serpent. Each trooper carefully checked over his or her equipment. No item, from the Kage power armor suits to the small *shuriken* carried by the members of each team, went uninspected. As each warrior finished inspecting his own equipment, he turned to go over his partner's. In this way every piece of gear was examined twice, so that any tiny flaw which might otherwise endanger the mission would be detected and corrected.

Even Michael Ryan was not exempt from this ritual. Slowly, with infinite care, he ran his hands along each segment of his Kage suit's black, non-reflective surface, checking for any dings or dents in the armor, possible signs of hidden damage that might manifest itself at some inopportune moment. Satisfied that the armor and its "low-delectability" coating were intact, he moved around the rack-mounted suit to inspect the folding stub-wings attached to the unit's back. Again, a careful check revealed no flaws in the wings' airfoil. The power suit's internal mechanisms checked out flawlessly, as did the powerful blazer carbine Ryan favored for infiltration operations.

After checking his Kage suit, weapons, and other equipment, he traded places with Master Sergeant Raiko. Ryan knew that many officers outside of the DEST teams looked on the notion of an officer submitting himself to the inspection of an enlisted man to be beneath his station, even demeaning. Ryan himself had once held a similar view. But that was before hearing a training officer at the Internal Security College on New Samarkand tell of a *chu-i* who had refused to allow an enlisted man to check over his parachute before a practice jump. The officer's main 'chute later failed to open, and he barely had enough time to deploy his reserve. He hit the ground hard, sustaining compound fractures of both legs, injuries severe enough to disqualify him from further military service. Remembering that man's disaster, Ryan forced himself to submit his gear to the inspection of his subordinate.

As usual, the inspection was unnecessary. All of the equipment belonging to DEST Team Six was maintained in as close to perfect working order as possible. Ryan was an absolute fanatic when it came to maintaining the team's gear. When they weren't using it, they were cleaning, inspecting, or repairing it.

Once the last bit of gear had been checked and re-checked, he made the appropriate notations in his noteputer and signed it with an electronic stylus. Turning to the communicator mounted on the 'Mech bay's inner bulkhead, he tapped a button that opened the intercom system with the other bays.

"All teams report in when ready," he said into the wire-covered grille.

"Team Four, ready," Captain Kenyu Yosuke must have been standing next to the communicator, waiting to make his report. Captain William Culp, Team Five's leader, reported in a few moments later.

"*So ka,*" Ryan responded, and switched channels.

"Bridge, this is Major Ryan. All teams ready to begin operation. Standing by."

"*Hai,*" acknowledged Captain Randolph DeMoise, the *Haruna*'s commander. "Stand by for jump."

Aboard the *Invisible Truth,* Ariana Winston was just making her way onto the bridge when the call from the *Haruna*'s captain came through.

"General, *Haruna* reports that the DEST teams are ready to begin the operation."

"Thank you." Winston nodded to the commtech. "Tell Captain DeMoise to stand by. Then, open a channel to the fleet."

"Channel open."

Winston drew in a deep breath, held it for a moment, and let it out in a rush. Stepping into the center of the holotank, she began to speak.

"Attention all task force personnel, this is General Ariana Winston.

"My friends, we stand on the brink of a new day. In just a few short minutes, we will begin perhaps the most important military operation since the liberation of Terra from Stefan the Usurper in 2777. This is the moment we've spent nearly a year building up to. This is the moment that Morgan Hasek-Davion gave his life for.

"I know that I don't have to remind any of you to do your duty. You have been doing your duty since the day you arrived on Defiance. Now is the pay-off. Now, all the time and toil, sweat and blood, will suddenly become worth it. Now we are going to free our homes, our nations, our families from the threat of tyranny." Feeling the power and emotion of the moment, she hammered her clenched fist on the holotank's brass rail. "Now we go to take back what is ours!"

With those words ringing across the *Truth*'s bridge like an iron bell, Winston paused. For a moment, she felt vaguely foolish, like one of the politicians she so often despised for their high-sounding, but empty words. When she spoke again, it was with the business-like tone of a general officer.

"All commands, report when ready to jump."

A wave of her hand signaled the communications tech to close the channel.

One by one, in rapid succession, the ships of Task Force Serpent checked in. When the last vessel, the Knights' *Bernlad,* reported all in readiness, she nodded with satisfaction. A pointed finger told the commtech to re-open the channel.

Winston stood silently for a few breaths, gazing with a mixture of pride and apprehension at the holographic image of the fleet suspended in the air above the holotank.

"Dammit, Morgan," she whispered to herself. "Just when we need you the most . . ."

She took a final breath, and blew it out in an explosive puff.

"All commands, this is Dancer," she said, using her assigned codename. "The word is given. Commence Operation Serpent."

13

Frigate SLS **Haruna**
Task Force Serpent
Unnamed Star System, 30 Light Years from
Huntress
Clan Space
19 February 3060

Aboard the *Haruna* Captain Randolph DeMoise keyed open a communicator set into the arm of his command chair.

"Major Ryan? We just got the word. 'Commence Operation Serpent.' "

"*Hai,* Captain, whenever you're ready," Ryan replied. DeMoise could hear the pride in the DEST commander's voice. He felt it himself. After the Combine had lost almost a third of their worlds to the Clans, after nearly a decade of waiting, they were finally going to take revenge upon their tormentors. In the wake of the attempted assassination of the Coordinator, everyone even vaguely associated with the Draconis Elite Strike Teams and the Internal Security Force had been declared suspect. Those who survived the subsequent purges, like Ryan and DeMoise, felt a burning shame over the treachery of their comrades and their own failure to prevent the cowardly attack. Now, hundreds of light years from their homes, they stood on the brink of an operation that would simultaneously wipe out both shameful blots on their honor.

"Engineering officer," DeMoise barked out. "Charge the drives. Navigator, lock course into navigation computer."

The Captain's commands were repeated even as his men leapt to comply.

"Captain," the *Haruna*'s chief engineer called. "The ship is ready for jump."

"Very well. Jump."

In the blink of an eye, the universe turned itself inside out as the powerful Kearny-Fuchida drives buried deep inside the frigate's armored hull ripped a hole in the fabric of space, catapulted the WarShip and her fragile human cargo through the rent, then slammed the portal shut behind them. Lights, colors, and sounds, none of which had a name, assaulted the senses of everyone aboard. Time stretched out around them until it seemed that DeMoise could see the beginning of Creation, the end of Armageddon, and every possible future and past displayed at once in the space of a single heartbeat.

Then, just when it seemed that he might go mad from the sights and sounds before him, the universe snapped back into its proper order. Strange stars burned in the air above the vessel's small holotank.

"Navigator . . ." DeMoise began.

"Captain, we are right on target. Zenith point, Huntress."

"Communications, begin transmitting our Clan IFF code," DeMoise ordered. Even before he finished speaking, the technician manning the *Haruna*'s main communications panel replied that the ship was broadcasting the false Identify Friend and Foe signal provided by Trent.

"Run a full sensor sweep. Report all contacts. I want to know if there are any WarShips out there that aren't supposed to be here."

"*Hai*, commencing sensor sweep." Moments later the report came back. "Captain, my sensors show no WarShips, just a single *Merchant* Class JumpShip. Her sail is rigged out, but there are no DropShips attached to her docking collars." The tech paused.

"Captain, she is transmitting a different IFF code."

"What?" DeMoise snapped.

"Captain," the tech repeated. "The *Merchant* is transmitting an Identify Friend and Foe signal that is somewhat different from the one we were given."

"Show me."

In response to DeMoise's order, the tech punched a rapid series of commands into the holotank control system. Almost immediately the tiny graphic representation of the Huntress system was replaced by a larger-scale image of the area around its zenith jump point. The *Haruna,* displaying the false IFF code, hung in the air a few dozen centimeters away from the narrow, needle-like shape of a Clan *Merchant* Class JumpShip. Despite the graininess of the image, DeMoise could clearly see that the transport vessel's docking collars were empty. Of even more importance was the alphanumeric string hanging in the air beside her. Though Precentor Martial Anastasius Focht, who'd helped plan the overall mission to Huntress, had expressed his confidence in the code provided by his spy, DeMoise never could quite bring himself to trust it completely.

Now, alone and cut off in a system that was home to the worst enemy the Draconis Combine had ever faced, he'd just learned that the radio signal that was supposed to declare the *Haruna* to be a Smoke Jaguar *York* Class destroyer/carrier might not be functioning properly. If the IFF code was sufficiently out of date, or just plain wrong, the Jaguars might even now be scrambling fighters and combat DropShips. Worse, if Trent's information was correct, and there *was* a functioning space-defense system defending Huntress, a robot WarShip might already be vectoring to intercept and destroy the *Haruna.* "Repeat the sensor sweep," DeMoise ordered. "And report all contacts."

"Sir, my only contact is the Clan *Merchant.*" The results took less than a minute to obtain.

"Nothing from in-system? Nothing from Huntress?"

"No, sir. Just the *Merchant,* and she shows no signs of alarm."

DeMoise let slip an oath in Japanese that in polite society would have been cause for shock and outrage. But here, on the bridge of a WarShip in the middle of enemy territory, nobody really noticed.

"Could it be that the Clanners use different IFF codes for transports and combat vessels?" he wondered aloud.

"Possibly, Captain." The *Haruna*'s executive officer misread his superior's muttered speculation as a question requiring an answer. "That's how we do it. Even in the case of military transports, the codes are just a little different from those of WarShips. There's no reason to think the Clanners do it any differently."

"Huh," DeMoise snorted. "There's no reason to think the Clanners do anything the same as we do." He uttered another curse, and stabbed the intercom button.

"Major Ryan, we may have a problem here."

"What's wrong, Captain?" Ryan's brow furrowed at the concern tinging DeMoise's words.

In a few concise sentences, the *Haruna*'s captain laid out the situation.

"What concerns me most," he concluded, "is the fact that the Clanners have never been especially slow to react to any situation, good or bad.

"What if they're in the process of scrambling fighters right now? Or worse, what if they're activating their Reagan system? If you detach now, they might catch the *Stiletto* halfway to the planet and I might not be able to support you. All I could do is jump outsystem again and return to the fleet. If I do that, if we fail to cripple the space defense system, then the fleet will have only two options. They can scrub the whole mission and go home, or we can come in, guns blazing, and try to bull our way through.

"Either way, the whole thing is going to be pretty messy."

Ryan digested the other man's words for a few moments. If DeMoise's fears proved true, if the false IFF code had been seen as such by the Smoke Jaguars, they might even now be sending a counterstrike to rid their system of the intruder. If that were the case, the DEST teams hadn't much more in the way of options than flee, fight, or bluff. Though DeMoise outranked him, Ryan was in overall command of the mission, right up until the time the *Stiletto* detached from the *Haruna*. DeMoise could only override Ryan's commands if Ryan's orders placed the WarShip in unreasonable jeopardy. At this stage of the operation, the "go, no-go" decision was Ryan's.

If the Jaguars launched a counterstrike, the *Haruna* would probably be overwhelmed by sheer weight of fire. If the Inner Sphere ship jumped outsystem again, using her lithium-fusion batteries, the Jags would know something was up, and the task force would have to launch its assault against a prepared enemy. Despite DeMoise saying that they might have to scrub the mission, turning back was not really an option. That left bluffing.

"Captain," Ryan said at last. "We're staying. We're just going to have to brazen it out, and trust the Smoke Jaguars to be as hidebound as everyone says they are. We'll have to trust them to believe a ship transmitting an old Smoke Jaguar code is still a Smoke Jaguar vessel."

"*Hai, Sho-sa* Ryan-*san.*" DeMoise's tone revealed that he was less than thrilled at the prospect. "That is what I thought you'd say. Now, what do you want me to do, sir?"

Ryan chuckled at DeMoise's formal words.

"Rig out the sail and begin routine charging operations. My people will make final preparations for breakaway. When everything is ready down here, we'll detach and make our in-run."

"*Hai,*" came the reply. "Rigging out jump sail. Report when ready for breakaway."

Thirty minutes later, Ryan reported through the *Stiletto*'s commander, Maeda Ge, that all was in readiness. In response, a series of thick steel bolts slid back, freeing the massive clamps that locked the *Broadsword* Class DropShip to the *Haruna*'s armored spine. As the clamps retracted, a faint shudder was felt throughout both vessels.

"Clamps unlocked and retracted," a crewman reported. "*Stiletto* is free to maneuver."

"Roger. *Stiletto* copies free to maneuver," Ge answered. With a deft touch on the DropShip's controls, the pilot gave her just enough thrust to pull away from the *Haruna*. A dull, heavy clunk, more felt than heard, ran through the ship. The deck canted sharply as Ge aimed his ship at the faraway planet.

"Breakaway, breakaway," Ge called. "*Stiletto* is free of the docking collar. We are heading in-system."

"Copy, *Stiletto*," DeMoise said. "Good luck. We'll see you when this is over."

"*Arigato,*" Ge replied. "*Sayonara.*"

With that briefest, and most prosaic of messages, the invasion of Huntress began.

14

DropShip SLS Stiletto, *Approach Vector*
Huntress System
Kerensky Cluster, Clan Space
19 February 3060

"That's it, Major, we're on our way." Ge half turned in his seat to look at Ryan, who stood behind him watching over the captain's shoulder at the faint gleam that marked the *Stiletto*'s destination. At a distance of over a billion kilometers, the planet all but disappeared in the starfield filling the DropShip's narrow viewscreen.

"*Hai,* Captain," Ryan said. "Let's start up our own transponder."

Ge pressed a black plastic stud, which to Ryan's eye looked exactly the same as the score of similar buttons surrounding it.

"Transponder active," Ge said, casting a suspicious eye on the control he'd just touched. "Do you think that ComStar spy really knew what he was talking about, sir?"

"*Shirimasen.* Marshal Hasek-Davion thought so," Ryan answered. "So does General Winston. I'm willing to take their word."

In addition to the route of the Exodus Road, agent Trent had provided the task force with a wealth of intelligence on Clan Smoke Jaguar—their standard operating procedures, communication frequencies and codes, force compositions, transponder settings, and the like. Ryan knew from attending mission strategy sessions that the spy's report was long and somewhat unorganized, as though Trent had recorded it as he went along, rather than entering the data into a framework of categories and classes. As a result, one had to sift through a great deal of speculation and partial information to glean what Ryan would have classed as solid, reliable intelligence.

Based on Trent's report, the *Stiletto*'s Identify Friend and Foe transponder had been reprogrammed. Now, if any Smoke Jaguar pilot or ground-bound sensor operator interrogated that particular instrument, it would respond by transmitting an IFF code belonging to a Jaguar DropShip named *Tracker*.

"Humph." Ge shook his head. "If the Jaguars have changed their identity codes, we could land in a world of trouble in very short order."

"Things could be worse," Ryan reminded him. "We were originally supposed to make an orbital drop from the *Bisan, neh*? The Jags don't have anything that even vaguely resembles an *Achilles* Class DropShip. If we hadn't captured this Clan ship, imagine what would happen if some nosy Jaguar pilot decides to make a close visual inspection rather than relying on his electronics? This whole operation would be blown even before my teams made their drop.

"I am willing to die for the Dragon. It is my duty to do so if necessary, and it is the highest honor for a Combine warrior. But dying uselessly because a Clan fighter pilot showed some initiative is another thing altogether. This way, even if our code is wrong and they decide to make an inspection pass, at least we're in a Clan ship. The *Muen no Daineko* will probably think twice before shooting down a Clan ship just because it has an out-of-date IFF code."

"And if they shoot us down anyway?"

"Then it will have been our honor to serve the Dragon faithfully unto death."

Captain Maeda Ge didn't respond to Ryan's half-proud, half-cheerful statement. He merely shrugged and turned his attention back to the business of piloting the DropShip.

The in-run to Huntress turned out to be uneventful, even boring. Only two events broke the monotony of the long trip. The first came just three days before the *Stiletto* was due to begin its shallow entry into Huntress' stormy atmosphere. At about seventeen hundred hours, on 26 February, the *Stiletto*'s sensor tech reported that a large electromagnetic and tachyon flare had blossomed and faded at the system's zenith jump point. The emission profile was consistent with that of a departing *Kyushu* Class WarShip. When the word was passed, Ryan felt an unaccustomed chill. The *Haruna* had jumped outsystem. The DEST troopers were now truly on their own.

The second event came just twelve hours later, when a groundbased sensor sweep triggered the *Stiletto*'s transponder. A thrill of tension passed through the ship as the passengers and crew waited for the Jaguars' response. Here was the first, and most critical, test of Trent's intelligence. Was the code correct? Was there some vocal exchange in addition to the electronic password? If they were challenged, would their bluff hold up?

For several long minutes there was no sign of a response from the planet below. Ryan supposed to Maeda Ge that the Jaguars might be discussing what to do with the *Stiletto* né *Tracker* if the IFF code wasn't one hundred percent correct. All during that time the only sound heard on the DropShip's bridge was the mournful and irritatingly high-pitched beeping of the radar warning system. The unpleasant tone was a constant reminder that the ship had been detected and was now being "painted" by tracking radars.

Then, as suddenly as it began, the interrogation signal ceased. The tracking radar was switched off, and the Smoke Jaguars seemed to have lost interest in the *Stiletto*.

"What happened?" Ryan's voice was a fierce whisper, as though he were afraid to talk too loud, lest the Jaguars hear and take a renewed interest in the ship.

"I don't know," Ge replied, scowling at the *Stiletto*'s instruments. "It's not supposed to work this way. Once you're on radar, you're on radar until you land. Flight controllers don't just shut down tracking systems like that."

"Maybe they've got some sort of passive system?" Ge's copilot suggested.

"Maybe," Ge allowed. "But I wouldn't want to rely on it. Passive systems are far too unreliable when it comes to holding a good track on a moving object.

"I can only come up with two answers. One, they've got some kind of tracking system our electronic warfare suite cannot detect. Or, two, they've switched over to standby and will pick us up again once we enter the atmosphere. For now, we have to assume the former. We have to assume that we're still on some kind of sensor screen, though there isn't much we can do about it."

"So what do you suggest?" Though Ryan, like all DEST commandos, had received basic instruction in DropShip operations, he understood little of the more technical side of space flight.

"For now, we stick to the plan," Ge answered. "We go in just like we're supposed to. We're a nice friendly Smoke Jaguar DropShip carrying parts and supplies for the factory at Pahn City. If the Jaguars don't believe our story, we'll have to think of something else."

"Major? Atmospheric interface in one minute." Ge's voice crackled from the tiny headset speakers clamped over Ryan's ears. "Drop in five."

Fortunately for the DEST teams, the Smoke Jaguars seemed to have believed the story told by the *Stiletto*'s transponder, because the Clan surveillance and tracking sensor stations left the intruders alone until the DropShip reached the point where Huntress' atmosphere was replaced by the emptiness of space. The mission plan called for the teams to be inserted over their drop zone in the dead of night, around 0300 local time. The darkness would provide cover for the commandos, while the timing of the drop would ensure that those who were awake on the ground would be at their lowest ebb, physically and mentally. It was a long-used tactic, but one against which no human had ever developed a countermeasure.

Several hours earlier, Ryan and the members of DEST teams Four, Five, and Six had made their way down to the *Stiletto*'s number two 'Mech bay. There were no BattleMechs present in that huge, booming space. Instead, two dozen miniature versions of the multi-ton combat machines stood silently in their specially designed racks. These were Kage suits, powered battle armor similar to that worn by Elementals, the hulking, genetically engineered Clan armored infantrymen.

The greatest differences between Clan battle armor and the Kage suits were size and mission. Whereas Elemental armor was massive and clumsy-looking, the Kage suits were small, almost dainty by comparison. Elemental armor was intended for combat on the field of battle, and was armed and armored as befitted that intent. Kage armor, on the other hand, had been specifically designed as scout-suits, under the advice of the Draconis Elite Strike Teams. Instead of mounting powerful, 'Mech-killing weapons, Kage suits supported anti-personnel weapons, though the fully manipulative mechanical hands fitted to each suit allowed the trooper inside to operate any of a wide range of man-portable anti-armor weapons, including the fearsome Inferno incendiary missile launcher. In addition the Kage suits had a skin made of a mimetic polymer, commonly called sneak-coating. This high-tech camouflage allowed the Kage suit to blend in, chameleon-like, with its surroundings. The suits were fitted with high-tech sensors and electronic countermeasures, making them perfect for scouting and reconnaissance missions. A small but powerful jumppack and stub wings would even allow the armored troopers to bound across the battlefield like jumping mantises.

But, for all the military technology built into the Kage suits, most of the men and women who wore them considered their mission at least a partial failure if they had to rely on even the barest fraction of the suit's capabilities. Each DEST trooper considered his or her training the best camouflage and the most effective weapon in their vast inventory.

Ryan was firmly secured inside his Kage suit, lacking only his helmet, when Maeda Ge informed him of the approaching drop.

"Thank you, Captain," Ryan answered. Then, switching channels, he spoke to the troopers gathered around him. "Five minutes. Prepare for drop. And remember, you are the first Inner Sphere troops to carry the battle to the enemy. You are here to fight and to die for the glory of the Dragon, and to liberate those of our worlds now in the oppressor's grip. You all know your duty. I know that you will do it.

"Banzai! Banzai! Banzai!" The ancient shout of warriors about to go into battle rang through the 'Mech bay.

As Ryan settled the helmet over his head, a quartet of ship's crewmen scuttled around him, erecting a drop pod around him. This thick, heavy egg of ceramic and steel would protect him during his long fall through Huntress' upper atmosphere. To prevent their detection on enemy radar, the pods were given two layers of Radar Absorbent Material. In theory, the outer-layer RAM would protect the pods during their fall into Huntress's upper atmosphere. That thick coating of high-tech paint would be burned away by the entry heating, along with the pod's ablative shell. The inner layer of RAM would continue to hide the pod until it split apart deep inside Huntress' atmosphere. If things went according to plan, the DEST teams would be "below" the Jaguars' radar net by the time that happened. In some ways this was the ultimate in High-Altitude-Low-Operating drops.

The pods were larger than the ones the DEST commandos had previously used. The old model was so small that the warrior inside was forced to curl up into a fetal position for the drop. The additional bulk of the Kage suits required a larger capsule. Fortunately, the design team had built the pods so the warrior inside could at least kneel in an upright position, rather than being curled up into a ball.

To cover the disappearance of the DropShip, Captain Ge would broadcast a weak, purposely broken distress signal, claiming that his vessel was in trouble and was about to crash. The subterfuge had the added effect of explaining any faint radar traces the Jaguars might get off the descending pods. As small as their radar cross-section would be on the enemy's sensors, the pods would in all likelihood be mistaken for debris falling from a supposedly stricken ship.

At various places around the bay other techs were likewise cocooning the rest of his unit. This was the part of an orbital, or high-altitude, drop, that Ryan hated the most. In order to protect its occupant, the pod had to be made of thick, dense material. So thick were the sides of the capsule that normal radio communications were impossible. The larger versions used by BattleMechs were often fitted with a service umbilical, which allowed a MechWarrior to stay in touch with the outside world. The pods used by the DEST teams were so much smaller than the enormous 'Mech pods that a service umbilical was impractical. Thus, Ryan had ordered his techs to hold off closing up his pod until the last possible moment. Due to the time involved in locking the pod down and running diagnostics to ensure its safety, the order gave him only two more minutes of freedom than his team mates.

Ryan knew that each team would be accompanied by one unmanned pod, which was loaded with whatever equipment the troopers could not fit into their individual capsules. That pod would be controlled by a simple on-board computer system. Though the theory was sound, Ryan didn't have any great faith in the drone pod. During the DEST teams' training on Defiance, the pods had failed about one time in ten. In an operation as critical as this, he didn't dare rely on a system that had a ten-percent failure rate. Thus, he ordered his men to load themselves down with as much gear as they could cram into their pods. He himself was so heavily loaded as to make walking a chore, even in the strength-enhanced Kage suit.

As soon as the last drop pod panel had been bolted into place, the egg-like container rocked heavily. Ryan knew that the motion was caused by a crewman wearing a heavy industrial exoskeleton lifting the pod and placing it in the ship's drop chute. Locked inside the capsule, Ryan tried to anticipate the moment when Maeda Ge would give the command to eject the pods. He knew approximately how long it took to load the pods and to seal the chutes, and watched the chronometer set into the Kage suit's viewscreen, counting down the seconds until . . .

Unexpectedly, the world dropped out from underneath him. His count had been off by nearly ten seconds. For several long seconds, the pod fell free, buffeted by the wake of the *Stiletto*'s passing. Dimly, through the thick shell, Ryan began to hear the roar of the wind as his pod punched through the air like a rifle bullet. Despite the heavy insulation of the pod, and the environmental protection of his suit, heat began to creep up his legs and back. His pod, and, he prayed, those of his men, was entering Huntress' upper atmosphere, where air friction would heat the capsule's ablative covering to a hellish temperature. Ryan hoped that any Smoke Jaguar seeing the fiery streaks, which he knew the team's drop pods were scoring across the night sky, would assume they were shooting stars, and perhaps make a wish.

I know what I'd wish for. Ryan snorted a bitter laugh. *I'd wish that the Jaguars would just stay fat, dumb, and happy.*

Looking again at his chronometer, Ryan estimated the time remaining until the pod entered the lower atmosphere. This time he was right on the mark.

Just as his count reached zero, the pod split into six narrow sections and peeled away, leaving him falling through space. Arching his back as far as his armored suit permitted, Ryan fought to bring himself under control. As he settled into the spread-eagle position dictated for High Altitude, Low Opening jumps, he searched the sky for the rest of his team. At first, the black-armored troopers were invisible. Switching on his visor's built-in thermal imager allowed him to pick out the falling commandos as barely lighter patches against the cool darkness of the sky. Not far away was the robot-controlled cargo pod. For a wonder the blasted thing was working correctly.

With outstretched arms and legs, the troopers maneuvered into a rough aerial formation, falling into place behind their leader. Following the discretes generated by his suit's Heads-Up Display, Ryan angled off into the night sky, aiming for an unseen point on the planet below. Like a flock of silent predatory birds, the twenty-three men and women under his command followed his lead.

Making the drop itself wasn't particularly difficult. Finding the right drop zone was. With no navigation aids or drop beacon, the DEST commandos had to drop almost blind, trusting the data loaded into their suits' on-board computers to locate the out-of-the-way plateau in the mountains west of Lootera, the planetary capital. Ryan prayed that the spy's information was accurate. If it wasn't, the commandos might be in for a very hard landing indeed.

Ryan's altimeter clicked over to five hundred meters. A second later his drogue chute deployed, slowing his fall. At two hundred meters, the black nylon main canopy deployed with a muted pop. A careful look upward assured Ryan that the air-foil parachute had opened properly. With grim purpose, he aimed his chute toward the now-visible drop zone. The relatively level area designated as his insertion point was narrower than he had been led to believe, and appeared to be strewn with low, thorny bushes.

As the ground rushed up to meet him, Ryan wheeled into the wind, bringing himself to a gentle, upright landing. No sooner had he touched down than he slapped the quick-release harness, freeing himself from the now limply flapping parachute. All around him, the rest of his troopers were doing the same.

Silently, by means of hand signals, his team checked in. All had made the HALO drop safely.

High above, as the DEST troopers got themselves organized to begin their mission, the *Stiletto* swung away from the drop zone, turning her nose for her own landing zone on Abysmal.

* * *

"What do you mean they have disappeared?" Galaxy Commander Russou Howell hissed to the lower-caste sensor operator as he stalked into the command center.

Howell was unhappy at being awakened in the middle of the night by what he considered a routine matter, the unscheduled arrival of a DropShip. He had only gotten an hour or so's worth of fitful sleep when the officer of the deck awakened him. All the drink he'd consumed the evening before had yet to pass out of his system, leaving him with a sick, pounding headache. Of late, Howell felt the increasing need to bludgeon his senses and emotions into oblivion in order to sleep. It was bad enough that he had been sent back to Huntress to take command of the Iron Guard and the Watchmen, solahma warriors long past their prime. What made his age-imposed exile worse was the fact that the death of his one-time friend, Star Captain Trent, at Howell's own hands still haunted him. Sometimes, even a string of fusionnaires, his favorite concoction, could not bring sleep. Predictably, it was one of those nights when a trivial problem that demanded his personal attention arose.

When questioned, the sensor operator informed Howell that the ship, a *Broadsword* identified as the *Tracker,* had arrived in-system, claiming to carry parts and technical personnel for the 'Mech production complex at Pahn City. When the cargo was delivered, the *Tracker* was to take on a Star of OmniMechs for transport to the Occupation Zone. Though the arrival of an unscheduled flight was rare, it was by no means unheard of. The ship's captain would be reprimanded for breach of normal operating procedures, as would the merchant-caste administrator who had failed to arrange the proper scheduling.

No, it wasn't the arrival of an unexpected cargo that bothered him. It was the second part of the *Tracker*'s supposed mission, the transfer of a Star of 'Mechs to the Occupation Zone. He had believed himself familiar with the shipping schedule. To the best of his knowledge, there was no shipment of 'Mechs, or any other military asset, for that matter, due to leave Huntress for at least a month. If what the *Tracker*'s pilot said was correct, then someone would receive more than a reprimand for his failure to keep the proper records.

By the time Howell reached the command center, something new had developed.

"I am sorry, Galaxy Commander." The technician's reply was soft, and respectful. "One minute the *Tracker* was on my scopes, just as it should have been. The next it vanished."

"Confirm her cargo and destination."

"Yes, Galaxy Commander."

It took a few seconds for the technician to locate the proper section of the automatic communications log and play it back.

"Cargo and destination confirmed, Galaxy Commander. *Tracker*'s captain said he was carrying parts and technical crew for Pahn City, and that he was to take aboard a Star of heavy OmniMechs for transportation to the Occupation Zone."

For a few minutes Howell stared at the computer-generated map of Huntress hanging in the air at one end of the communications center. He knew that the sensor techs and aerospace controllers used the map to keep track of all traffic arriving or departing from the planet. High-speed computer links from similar tracking stations all over the planet kept the data current.

"Where did she disappear from your sensors?" Howell demanded. "Show me."

The tech manipulated the proper controls to draw a glowing line across the face of the map. The track began over the Dhundh Sea, just to the west of the Path of the Warrior Peninsula. From there it extended across the northwestern portion of the continent of Jaguar Prime, and ended abruptly just before reaching the edge of the Shikari Jungle.

Howell cupped his right elbow in his left hand and stroked his chin, gazing thoughtfully at the band of dark green rain forest that ran at a slight angle across the larger of the two continents making up Huntress' land mass. At the western end of the jungles was an expanse of fetid, water-logged marshes called the Dhuan Swamp. It was just to the north of these marshes that the *Tracker*'s flight path came to an abrupt end. If the ship's flight path were extended along its last known heading, the vessel must surely have crashed into those stinking fens.

"Did he send out any kind of distress call before he disappeared?" Howell asked.

"Yes, Galaxy Commander, but the message was so faint and broken up that we could barely read it. Sensor tracks suggest that she may have broken up in flight."

"This is most peculiar," Howell mused, tapping his right cheekbone with his right forefinger. "Most peculiar indeed.

"Very well." He arrived at a decision. "We can only assume that the *Tracker* has crashed, probably in the vicinity of the Dhuan Swamp. Initiate a search. When you find her, bring me the captain, the shipping manifests, and the flight-data recorders. Notify me if there are any further developments."

Howell barely heard the technician's acknowledgment. He felt an odd shiver along his spine, a sensation he had not felt since Tukayyid. Would his Jaguar pride permit it, he would have called the feeling a premonition of disaster.

Stop it, he chided himself. *You are beginning to think like a Nova Cat mystic instead of a Jaguar warrior.*

Russou Howell glanced at the chronometer fixed to the room's north wall.

Freebirth! he cursed silently. *I have to be up in less than three hours. It is hardly worth even trying to get back to sleep.*

With a wordless snort of disgust, he stalked out of the communications center, intending to return to his quarters anyway. Tomorrow was going to be a full day, and he'd need all the sleep he could manage.

15

Jaguar's Fangs Mountain Range
Huntress
Kerensky Cluster, Clan Space
02 March 3060

A low pop sounded in Ryan's headset, followed by a pause. A series of pops followed the first in a three, pause, two pattern. Clucking his tongue against his teeth, Ryan sent the countersign. Two, two, one. In response to his signal, a handful of shadows, deeper than the black of night, flitted into the small grove of scrubby thorn trees under which he and his men had been sheltering. The grove, a half dozen kilometers south of Team Six's drop zone, had been designated as the primary rendezvous point for the three Draconis Elite Strike Teams under his command.

Ryan was both proud of and impressed by his men. Though they had dropped into essentially unknown terrain, with little to no navigation aid, all twenty-four had made it to the ground safely. An additional source of amazement came when it was revealed that all three cargo pods had landed intact, and relatively on target, though two men of Team Five had to climb one of the low trees to free their pod from its upper branches.

By means of hand signals, Ryan indicated that his subordinates, Captain Yosuke and Culp, should open their helmets so they might hold a brief discussion of their situation without having their words go out over the radio.

"I think we landed a little farther west than we intended," Ryan began, speaking in a low whisper. "It's hard to tell, not having accurate maps. That means we've got to push hard to reach our objective on schedule."

The hushed voice was not really necessary. There probably weren't any Clanners within a dozen kilometers of their position. But, a near mania for stealth and secrecy had become so ingrained in the commandos that they spoke in low tones out of sheer habit.

"We'll move in three groups, using a traveling overwatch with a one-hundred-meter spread. Kenyu, your group will be on point. Mine next. Bill? You're on rear guard. I'm not expecting to run into the enemy, but it's possible, so keep your men alert. If you see anyone, avoid contact if at all possible. Pull back and we'll try to bypass them."

Yosuke and Culp nodded their understanding of Ryan's orders. The teams would move in a narrow column, with a wide gap between each individual unit. The tactic, called a traveling overwatch, would allow for a fast rate of travel, while providing the commandos with a great degree of tactical flexibility. Such formations were routinely used when contact with the enemy was possible but not likely. Had Ryan actually expected to run into the Jaguars, he would have ordered what was termed a bounding overwatch, in which one team moved while the other two covered it. This latter tactic afforded the moving, or bounding, team with a great degree of protection, but was painfully slow.

Ryan glanced at his chronometer.

"Time check. On my mark it will be oh-four-twenty-two. Ready . . . mark. Intelligence says local sunrise is at oh-six-thirty. That gives us an hour and a half of movement time. We'd better get moving. I want to be well away from the drop zone before daybreak."

Ryan knew he hadn't miscalculated the amount of time until sunrise. It was standard practice when making a night march to halt and lie up shortly before daybreak. The extra half-hour would be used in selecting a hiding place for the team, and in making that position secure before the sun rose enough to betray their presence.

Without another word, Yosuke and Culp returned to their teams to pass along his orders. Ryan called his own team to him and explained what he had just told the other team leaders. Moments later, DEST Team Four led off, fading silently into the night. The other teams followed as directed by Ryan, leaving almost no trace of their passage. Had anyone been present to see the hideous, black-armored shapes passing from shadow to shadow, they would have been tempted to call what they saw a legion of ghosts wandering the hills in search of some kind of supernatural vengeance.

"There it is," Ryan whispered in Talon Sergeant Raiko's ear.

Under normal circumstances, it would have taken the DEST teams less than a day to walk from the landing zone to their current position just north of Mount Szabo. But nothing the Draconis Elite Strike Teams did could be described as normal. Moving unseen through hostile territory was a painstaking, dangerous process. At Ryan's order, the rate of travel had been set at only a few kilometers a night. Every hundred meters or so, the commandos would hunker down in loose defensive formation, watching and listening for any signs of a potential threat to their mission's security.

The going was dreadfully slow, but the trade-off of stealth and secrecy was worth it. As a result it had taken the strike force three nights to reach their objective. Now, the need for a tight noise discipline was even greater. Not more than three hundred meters away loomed Mount Szabo, the huge granite block that housed the Smoke Jaguars' primary command communications and control installation, as well as Ryan's primary objective, the control center for Huntress' space-defense system.

"How do you read it, Sergeant?"

Raiko clapped a pair of electronic binoculars to his unvisored eyes. For a long time he studied the scene before him. Ryan knew from long association that though Raiko enjoyed the added protection and strength of the Kage suits, the senior noncom didn't trust them completely. Instead, he preferred to use older, more proven technology, especially when it came to reconnaissance. Thus, Raiko always insisted on packing along an old-fashioned pair of electronic binoculars.

After carefully surveying the mountain and the surrounding area, Raiko passed the binoculars to his commander.

"Take a look."

Pressing the eyepieces to his face, Ryan adjusted the instrument until he had a sharp, clear image. The mountain was exactly as Trent had described it, a bleak, almost forbidding sight. From their position, beneath a creeper-shrouded fallen tree northwest of Szabo, they could see little of the facility buried deep in the rock. A three-meter-high fence topped with razor wire, and broken by a single gate, surrounded what appeared to be the only entrance to the base. Two armored Elementals stood guard at the gate. It was too far to tell for certain, but Ryan suspected that the rest of the Point, and possibly a few more besides, were stationed just inside the massive, gray-painted steel doors set into the living rock of the mountain itself. Anyone trying to force his way into the command center would quickly find himself on the losing end of what promised to be a brief, but very bloody fight.

Beyond the bulk of the mountain, Ryan could see reflected on the undersides of the dark, sky-obscuring clouds the glare of the symbol of Clan Smoke Jaguar, which was carved into the mountain's southeast face. Just beyond the mountain, the ever-present, low-hanging storm clouds were lit with an orange glow. Ryan knew that the faint, ugly luminescence came from the streetlights of Lootera, the planetary capital and the seat of Smoke Jaguar power.

One last detail caught his attention. Lancing razor-straight up into the humid night sky was the argent streak of a laser beam. He knew what it was and considered it to be the height of foolish pride. It was the eternal laser of the Smoke Jaguars, a lasting tribute to the fallen warriors of the Clan, blazing forever into the sky. The location of the monument was horrible. Ryan and his men had been so thoroughly briefed on the Mount Szabo area that he could see it clearly in his mind's eye.

The immense laser generator had been erected at the foot of the pyramidal structure standing in front of Mount Szabo. The building faced onto the Field of Heroes, a parade ground of stone 'Mechs dedicated to great Jaguar warriors and battles fought by the Clan. It was the heart and soul of the Smoke Jaguars, the inheritance of their past and their legacy to the future, the Clan's genetic repository.

Ryan had initially asked to be allowed to attack the repository, but the request was denied. Such an act was essentially terrorism, and though he had no qualms about committing such an act, he knew that terrorism was a two-edged sword. The destruction of the repository, or worse, its capture by those the Clan called barbarians, would have a significant negative effect on the morale of the Jaguars. It was feared that the same action might enrage them to the point that they would stop at nothing to rescue their genetic heritage. No, any attempt on the repository would have to be left to the BattleMech-equipped follow-on forces.

"So what do you think?" Raiko's urgent whisper snapped Ryan back to the task at hand.

"Looks impossible, doesn't it?"

"Hai." Raiko nodded with a sly chuckle. "But the impossible just takes a little longer."

Ryan grinned back at his subordinate. He had never known Raiko to use such an expression before their training sessions with the Rabid Fox teams. Now, such aphorisms were becoming a common part of his vocabulary.

Before either man could speak again, a high-pitched whine pierced the night. All thoughts of witty sayings were forgotten as they slammed their visors shut and tried to burrow their way deeper into the soil beneath them.

Carefully turning his head, Ryan spotted the source of the racket. It was an unsightly, gray-painted hovertruck making its way up to the installation gates. Using the magnification systems built into his suit's visor, he was able to discern a pair of figures in the vehicle's cab. Neither was armored, and both seemed to treat the Elemental guards with a great deal of deference. One of the massive armored warriors examined something the truck driver handed him, and then gestured to his companion warrior. The gate rose with a rackety whir that was barely discernible to the commandos, and the truck passed into the facility.

"I think we just found our way in," Ryan whispered as he tapped his sergeant on the wrist. "You stay here and keep an eye on things. I'm going to let the others know what we've found."

"You are late," the huge Elemental said. "You were due here at twenty-four-hundred."

Michael Ryan had never spoken to an armored Elemental before. At a distance of less than two meters, the featureless V-shaped faceplate seemed to be a single eye, slitted in hate and suspicion. The metallic tone of the speaker set into the helmet's lower plate distorted the giant warrior's voice, making it sound as though he were really the demon the armor made him resemble.

"The *stravag* truck broke down," Ryan answered, passing the warrior a plastic identity card. To verify his story, he gunned the engine, eliciting not an even roar, but a rough, coughing bellow. "It took two hours and all we could do to get it to function again."

The truck's engine had been skillfully sabotaged by Private Kenichi Akida, the team's demolitions expert. The vehicle, along with the drab gray uniforms worn by Ryan and Talon Sergeant Raiko, had been hijacked by the DEST commandos. A fast, quiet ambush had been laid just a few kilometers to the east of the mountain fortress, netting the commandos a hovertruck full of supplies and a pair of scientist caste technicians. It was testimony to the speed and ruthless efficiency of the Draconis Elite Strike Teams that both the driver and his mate had been killed silently and bloodlessly within moments of their stopping to aid an "injured pedestrian," so artfully portrayed by Private Peter Wu. Of the twenty-four commandos in the strike group, only Ryan and his senior noncom could be said to even remotely resemble the dead technicians. Ryan smiled ruefully at the outcome of the ambush, and hoped aloud that the Clanners didn't have some sort of password system.

Looking closely at the hulking Elemental, he mentally expressed that hope again. If they did, there was no chance that they would be able to bluff their way past the guard. The warriors of Team Six, hidden among the crates occupying the truck's cargo deck, would burst out of their concealed positions and seize the guard post by force. Ryan knew that his team could easily defeat the guards, but that knowledge brought him little comfort, for he also knew that he and Raiko would probably be the first ones killed in the exchange.

"Next time notify us, and we will send someone out to repair the vehicle properly." The Elemental handed back Ryan's stolen identity card, then waved the truck into the narrow compound. As the heavy steel door closing off the mountain installation swung open, the hovertruck engine sputtered, the vehicle dipped sharply, then rose again as its forward blower fan slowed almost to a stop and then raced up to maximum revs.

Just as the truck cab drew even with the massive door jamb,

the truck stalled out completely, an event precipitated by the simple expedient of Ryan's killing the ignition. The vehicle slammed to the pavement with a hollow thud.

The Elementals turned to see what had happened. It was the last thing either of them did. A quartet of sharp, flat cracks split the air. One Elemental pitched over on his face. The other collapsed as though he were a marionette with its strings cut.

Black armored figures swarmed from the back of the truck. They swept past the grounded vehicle and into the cavernous space beyond. From the rocks and brambles lining the single, narrow access road came the rest of the strike force. Their Kage suits' electronic camouflage blurred their outlines to the point that it seemed that the night air had suddenly come to violent life. Ryan knew that four of these troopers, armed with Tsunami Gauss rifles, were the snipers who gunned down the Elemental guards. The weapons, though heavy and bulky, were powerful and relatively silent. The cracks Ryan heard were actually miniature sonic booms, caused by the hypersonic projectiles. Though the report seemed loud in the stillness of the night, he knew that the sound was no louder than ninety decibels, about the noise level of a busy street.

Ryan restarted the truck's fans, which were badly damaged in the intentional grounding. The vehicle lurched aloft on a cushion of air, but was terribly unsteady. Struggling with the controls, Ryan coasted the yawing vehicle through the doors, grounding it again just inside what looked like a massive loading dock.

The reason for crashing the truck in the middle of the doorway was an old one. If the sentries managed to get out an alarm, and/or tried to close off the fortress' only apparent entrance, the disabled truck would stop, or at least slow them long enough for the DEST teams to dart inside. Since the entry was taken quickly and quietly, the plan called for the truck to be removed so that the doors might be closed and sealed from the inside, thus securing the entrance against any possible reinforcements.

As the last armored trooper sprinted through the doorway, Captain Yosuke slammed his fist against the large, red "Close" button next to the portal. In a few seconds the door was shut, then locked by the press of a second stud labeled "Lock."

With the aid of two armored troopers, Ryan and his senior noncom struggled into their armored suits, which had been hidden in the back of the truck. Kage suits normally required the use of a complex ingress/egress module to don or doff. But, the designers had realized that there might be a reason the wearer would wish to take off the battle armor while in the field. Thus, a procedure was developed for one already-armored trooper to help another get into or out of his power suit without the aid of the module. Meanwhile, Private Akida permanently disabled the vehicle by tearing the internal combustion engine's fuel pump, a feat made possible by his Kage suit's enhanced strength.

"All right, you all know your targets," Ryan said over the team's tactical frequency, having at last sealed his helmet in place. "Split up. Head for your objectives. As soon as you're done, rally back here. If anything goes wrong, evade out of here and head for the alternate rally point. Now move."

The DEST teams had been assigned three vital installations within the command center. Team Four had been tasked with destroying the planet's main sensor control room. Team Five was to attack the primary command, communication, and control center, while Team Six was charged with the job of disabling the Reagan Defense Grid.

Though the scant descriptions provided by Trent gave the teams a vague idea where each of their targets were located, wall-mounted maps and directories, so thoughtfully provided by the Smoke Jaguars, were even more useful. At first, Ryan thought the idea of displaying floor plans of a supposedly secure facility was rather foolish. But he gradually realized that the only persons who were intended to see the maps were the people allowed inside the facility in the first place. Any installation of sufficient size was easy to get lost in, and according to Trent, the Mount Szabo installation was large indeed.

Quickly the armored commandos of Team Six slipped along the corridors and stairways of the Jaguar control center. Their intelligence suggested that though external security was rather tight, there were no internal patrols to be dealt with. Normally, Ryan regarded anything an intelligence officer told him with a great degree of skepticism. He was, however, coming to have a great deal of respect for agent Trent, even if the man was a Clanner, and a renegade Clanner at that. The spy's information was almost perfectly accurate. Save for a bit of confusion over the location of a stairway that Trent had reported was in one place and the wall-hung floor plans indicated in another, the team located the Space Defense System control center with no difficulty.

Seconds later, the facility was in DEST hands. Ryan's team crashed through the room's single door, killing five unarmored guards as they went. A half dozen scientist-caste technicians were also killed in the brief bloody engagement. Not a single DEST commando was injured.

"Sa," Ryan barked. "Line those techs up against the far wall, search them for weapons, and keep them quiet. Akida, Nakamura, get to work on the charges. Wu, Tanabe, watch the corridor. Carter, Sior, drag those bodies out of the way."

"You," Talon Sergeant Raiko growled at the surviving Clan technicians. "You heard what he said, over against the wall, and no heroics, *wakarimasu-ka?*"

One of the technicians must have thought he understood all too well the commandos' intentions toward the prisoners. He began to meekly comply with Raiko's command, then, before any of the stunned troopers could react, he darted back to the control panel. His fist came down hard on a large red button just as he was cut down by a blast of laser fire. The crack of Raiko's Blazer rifle was lost in the screeching clamor of an alarm siren.

"Chicksho!" Ryan cursed as he threw the still twitching corpse aside. Vainly he searched the panel for a way to cancel the alarm, but, as he expected, found none.

"We're torqued," he snarled. "Hurry it up with those charges. We don't have time for finesse now. Just make sure they'll destroy this equipment, and get out of here."

"Sho-sa." In the excitement of the moment, Raiko lapsed back into calling Ryan by his DCMS rank, rather than his new SLDF title. "What about the techs? We can't leave them here and we can't take them with us."

"Hai," Ryan said. "That's right, we can't." He jerked his armored head at the line of cowering technicians.

In response to Ryan's short nod, Raiko sent a single well-aimed bolt of laser energy through each technician's head. To some the execution of the helpless prisoners might have seemed a pointless act of barbarism, but in the dark and bloodstained arena in which the Draconis Elite Strike Teams routinely operated, there was no room for mercy or compassion. In other words the only laws were kill or be killed, and there were no noncombatants.

"Tengu to group," Ryan said, sending a broad-band transmission to each DEST team member in the complex. "An alarm has been sounded. We can expect enemy reinforcements any time now. Complete your missions and head for the rendezvous point. Tengu out."

"All done here, sir," Akida called as he planted the last of his five-kilo demolition charges.

"*So ka.* Set the timers and let's get moving."

Quickly, with no wasted words or motions, the commandos of DEST Team Six filed out into the rock-hewn corridor. Private Kenichi Akida, the team's demolition expert, was the last man out of the SDS control center. Before closing the door, he booby-trapped it with a small, tandem charge. Fitted with an anti-handling detonator, the device was made up of a two-kilo block of pentaglycerine, coupled to a standard anti-personnel grenade. If anyone tried to open the door, the grenade would drop free and go off three seconds later. The pentaglycerine charge would explode at the same time, detonating all the other charges in the control center by means of sympathetic detonation. If no one tampered with the door, the main charges would go off in twenty minutes.

Even if the Jaguars managed to pass the booby-trap without setting it off, the demolition charges rigged to the SDS controls were fitted with anti-handling devices. Anyone careless enough to treat the charges with other than the utmost care would trigger the devices. As a last measure of redundancy, Akida also rigged a remote command detonator to each bomb. Michael Ryan could set off the charges anytime he liked by means of the radio trigger built into his Kage suit.

Suddenly his radio flared to life.

"Tengu, Hammer group is taking fire!"

"Copy, Hammer. Give me a sitrep."

"Hammer is under heavy enemy fire. Enemy is ten, that is one-zero, Echoes," Captain Yosuke of Team Four, Hammer group, responded. Ryan knew that "Echoes" were the brevity code designation for Elementals. "We are in the corridor leading to the loading bay. We are taking casualties. Request immediate assistance."

"Hang on, Hammer. Tengu is almost there." Ryan paused to indicate that he had finished his message to Captain Yosuke. "Ronin, what is your status?"

"Tengu, this is Ronin." Captain Culp's voice bellowed from Ryan's headset. "Mission accomplished. Charges set. We are about three levels above Hammer. We're heading his location now."

"Understood, Ronin. Hammer, did you copy Ronin?"

"*Hai, Sho-sa.* I copied Ronin." A burst of automatic weapons fire interrupted Yosuke's message. "Suggest you hurry. I've taken four casualties, including my second in command and weapons specialist. If you don't get here soon, there won't be any of us left."

"*Wakarimas.*" Ryan noticed how uneven his voice sounded. Trying to talk while running, even allowing for his superb physical condition and the enhancements of the Kage suit, was always difficult. Add to that the excitement of the moment, and his words came out in short, disjointed bursts. "We're almost there."

Seconds later, Ryan could see the harsh glare of laser fire reflecting off the dull stone walls, and hear the rattle and snap of the firefight in the loading bay.

"Contact!" Peter Wu's report was a shout full of the joy of battle.

The DEST troopers swept into the loading bay with a precision born of long practice. Some broke left, others to the right. Ryan, as commander, stepped a few meters to the right of their line of approach, but remained in the center of the formation. Lifting the small laser he had chosen for this mission, he sent a bolt of coherent light across the bay, where it dug a deep crater into an Elemental's breastplate. The armored warrior staggered but did not fall until Ryan pumped two more shots into his massive chest. Carlotta Sior, as coldly precise as ever, felled another armored giant with a single Gauss rifle round.

Then, as Corporal Frank Hollis, Ryan's communications specialist, was moving to a better firing position, an Elemental launched a single anti-armor missile. The rocket, intended to penetrate 'Mech armor, slammed into the commando's right side and detonated. The explosion rocked the loading bay and literally tore Hollis in two.

The Elemental paid dearly for his kill. Weapons specialist Teji Nakamura hammered the Clan warrior with a long rolling burst from his Kage suit's heavy machine gun. The impact of the heavy slugs rocked the massive warrior. The Elemental turned and unleashed a blast of laser fire that shattered the rock wall behind Nakamura. The commando showed no sign that he even noticed the attack, but kept his stuttering weapon firmly centered on the Elemental's armored chest. Finally, the monstrous infantryman crumpled and fell, his breastplate a bullet-riddled ruin of composite and steel.

A volley of laser fire announced the arrival of Team Five and the doom of the defending Jaguars.

"That's it," Ryan bellowed as the last Elemental dropped to the stone floor of the bay. "Move out. Head for the rally point."

Fifteen minutes later Ryan heard a low rumble, like that of distant thunder. The demolition charges his team had planted in the command center had gone off right on schedule. Though his mission, the first engagement of the invasion of Huntress, had technically been a success, his victory was far from complete. The Jaguars had been alerted to the presence of the invaders. Though the Jags, in their arrogance, might never have conceived of an Inner Sphere attack on their homeworld, the DEST teams had to leave behind the bodies of six of their men. Even the Jaguars were not so stupidly prideful as to ignore the evidence of six dead commandos.

Bitterly, Major Michael Ryan cursed the fickle luck that took the lives of a fourth of his men and would bring the balance of the task force into a system already alerted to danger.

=== 16 ===

Battle Cruiser SLS Invisible Truth
Unnamed Star System, 30 Light Years from
Huntress
Kerensky Cluster, Clan Space
05 March 3060

At the very same moment that the last of Ryan's men were creeping into the rally point, General Ariana Winston looked, for perhaps the hundredth time since arriving on the *Invisible Truth*'s control deck, at the digital mission clock bolted to her starboard bulkhead. The glowing red numbers stubbornly read zero-six-thirty. If the DEST Teams were on schedule, Ryan's men would by now have crippled the Huntress Space Defense System.

Pride and apprehension swelled in her breast. This was the moment for which she had been born. The Eridani Light Horse's first telling blow in the restoration of a dream most men considered long dead, the return of the Star League. With the fulfillment of that destiny came the greatest risk the task force would take in their long, dangerous mission. It was time to start the invasion.

She glanced across the holotank, to where Andrew Redburn leaned against the waist-high brass rail surrounding the tank's raised platform. Just as she had done while Morgan was still alive, Redburn, as the task force's second in command, made every effort to be on the *Truth*'s bridge whenever the task force began a new phase of the operation. There was still a bit of weary grief in the way he carried himself, but that was rapidly being replaced by a coiled-spring readiness familiar to all soldiers on the eve of a major offensive.

Redburn caught her gaze and flashed her a smile. The grin was made of equal parts pride and eagerness, but was tainted with a bit of lingering sorrow. Though his smile was a ghost of its former self, Winston took his returning good humor as an omen of hope.

Winston asked a communications technician to open a channel to the rest of the fleet.

"Dancer to all commands," she began. "It's time. The signal is 'Pyrite.' Begin jump sequence. Good luck. And godspeed."

Turning to Commodore Beresick, she nodded once.

Without a moment's hesitation, Beresick began calling out the commands that had become so familiar.

"Lock course into the navigation computer. Secure all fittings." Beresick's voice cracked with excitement. His tone and his face told Winston that he too was feeling the awful enormity of what they were about to do. "Charge the drives."

Scant moments later a deep, harsh tone sounded throughout the ship, telling everyone aboard that the *Invisible Truth* was about to hurl herself through the netherworld of hyperspace, across thirty light years, and into a system filled with hostile Clan warriors. Though there may have been apprehension, if not fear, in every heart, no one protested or complained. Each man and woman aboard the massive battle cruiser was prepared to carry out his or her duty to the fullest.

"Sir, the ship is ready to jump," the *Truth*'s chief engineer called across the bridge.

"Very well." Beresick stared straight ahead as he spoke, as though looking across the long kilometers to their destination. There was both pride and awe in his voice as he said, "Jump."

A simple press of a control caused what had been described as "the single greatest physical anomaly ever" to take place. The powerful charge that had been built up in the *Truth*'s massive engines flooded through her Kearny-Fuchida drive. The physics-defying system sent a field of unbelievable energies coruscating their way along the ship's outer hull. The field expanded to encompass the DropShips *Honor* and *Integrity* mated to her docking collars. As the field completely enveloped the huge vessel, a hole was torn in the very fabric of space, an impossible hole in reality through which the *Invisible Truth* and the four hundred souls within her steel and composite hide were hurled.

For Ariana Winston the world turned ninety degrees from itself. The sickening feeling of a sudden drop seized her, as a wave of light and sound so intense as to be a tangible thing slammed into her. Seconds seemed to stretch into hours. For a moment she feared she might scream, not in pain or fear, but from sensory overload. Then everything was still. The *Invisible Truth* slid back into rational space, thirty light years from its starting point. There, above and behind the miniature, laser-generated image of the battle cruiser gleamed the bright yellow ball of the Huntress system's main star. Other bright red sparks flared and faded in the *Truth*'s holotank as the rest of the invasion fleet phased in at the zenith jump point.

"Blake's blood!"

"What is it?" Beresick barked at the sensor technician, whose startled cry broke the quiet of the bridge.

"Commodore, I have multiple contacts at zero-two-five, mark eight-zero. Distance, seven hundred kilometers."

Even as the young man spoke, the *Truth*'s holotank was creating a number of new images, somewhat separated from those of Task Force Serpent.

"Can you identify?"

"No, Commodore. They're too far away for positive ID." The tech broke off as a new bit of information crossed his instruments. "Sir, now detecting drive flares. The bogies are inbound to our position."

"Blast it," Beresick said. "Send to all commands. Clear for battle, launch all Combat Air Patrol fighters. Message to *Starlight. Starlight* is to remain with and protect the transports. We're here, and no Clan buggers are going to make us leave."

Turning to his executive officer, Beresick allowed a grim smile to crease his lips. "Sound General Quarters."

"General Quarters, General Quarters. All hands man your battle stations." The ancient cry rang throughout the *Invisible Truth* like a bugle call. Unnecessarily, the exec added, "This is not a drill."

"Commodore, this is your bailiwick. Where do you want me?" Winston asked.

Beresick threw her a quick glance. "If you want to stay on the bridge, that's fine. Morgan seemed to like the holotank. It'll give you some idea of what's going on. Just stay out of the way. Otherwise, clear the bridge. General Redburn, that goes for you too."

"Whatever you say, Commodore." Winston saluted and leapt up the short flight of stairs leading to the holotank.

Standing in the midst of the floating images, the largest of which was no longer than her hand, Winston began to grasp what was happening. To her left, the WarShips of Task Force Serpent were initiating a high-G burn toward the Clan vessels. Smaller images indicated the position of DropShips as they separated from their parent vessels. The DropShips either took up stations alongside the larger combat starships as they bore down on the Clan WarShips, or hung back to defend Serpent's transports, depending upon the task assigned to them. Even smaller icons flickered into existence, representing squadrons of fighters launched to screen the larger vessels from enemy fighter attacks.

At first the long alphanumeric strings hovering in the air next to each image confused her. But, as she watched the opening moves of the battle unfold, she rapidly came to understand the codes. The image tagged CG-1957-INTR represented Com Guard battle cruiser *Invisible Truth,* identification number 1957. Once she understood the jumble of letters and numbers, it was easy to keep track of the larger WarShips of the task force.

Moving in from her front right, from a position slightly above her head, came three Clan WarShips. These icons lacked the complete identification codes of the task force vessels. The largest ship, now in the lead and bearing directly for the *Truth,* bore the letters CC-SVSZ. Her consorts, much smaller in size, but much faster, seemed to be aimed at the FedCom corvette *Rostock* and the Com Guard destroyer *Emerald.* These smaller Jaguar vessels were identified as PL 01 VNCT and PL 02 VNCT.

Winston was able to dope out the identity of the large vessel from the information displayed next to her icon; she was a *Sovetskii Soyuz* Class heavy cruiser, an old Star League design mounting an unbelievable array of ship-killing weapons. The others were such a puzzle that she had to ask the holotank technician to clarify the meaning of the identification code.

"PL," he explained, "is an old code for 'patrol corvette.' The computer identifies the targets as *Vincents,* probably the Clan Mk

42 variant. Since there are two of them, we tagged them PL 01 and PL 02, just to keep track of which is which."

As Winston listened to the tech's explanation, she saw a series of new contacts pop into existence around the Clan vessels. This time she understood the codes, which identified the new images as DropShips and OmniFighters.

Morgan had once confided in her his fascination for the lilliputian world of the holotank and his sense of extreme frustration at being nothing more than a spectator during the task force's battle with the Ghost Bears. Winston was coming to share his feelings. She could watch the battle unfold around her through the technological miracle of the holotank, but lacked knowledge of fleet combat tactics to make even the most basic suggestions.

With a sigh she resigned herself to riding out the battle in Beresick's capable hands, and settled back to watch the show.

"Range to nearest target?" Beresick demanded of the weapons sensor operator.

"Four-zero-three kilometers and closing," came the reply.

"Can we get a weapon lock?"

"Yessir. Bow and forward NPPC and missile batteries have target lock," the *Truth*'s chief gunnery officer replied. "We're just waiting for your permission to fire."

Beresick glanced at the holotank, surveying the situation. He knew that *Soyuz* had much lighter armor than the *Invisible Truth* but heavier weapons. If he could cripple her before she closed range enough to turn the battle into a slugging match, there was a good chance for a relatively bloodless victory, at least for Task Force Serpent.

"Guns," he said. "Lock missiles onto the *Soyuz* and launch. Weapons will be free at three hundred-sixty kilometers."

"Aye, sir," the weapons officer replied. Like many shipboard traditions, the practice of calling the chief weapons officer "Guns" survived in the Com Guards. "Krakens locked on target. And . . . Shoot! Missiles away!"

The *Invisible Truth* trembled slightly as a pair of monstrous anti-ship missiles blasted free of her hull. Beresick watched the tracking station follow the course of the black-painted weapons as they homed on the Clan cruiser. Twice the technician seated at the tracking console made a tiny adjustment to a small joystick set into his console. The big "Kraken" missiles were of a new type issued to the task force just before they left Defiance. Fitted with a two-way communication link, the powerful weapons could be remotely guided to their target by the *Truth*'s tracking and communications systems. The fleet had a limited number of the big missiles, and Beresick had ordered them held back in the fight at Trafalgar.

"The missiles have acquired the target and are homing," the missile gunner sang out. "Closing on target. Five . . . four . . . three . . . two . . . one . . . impact!"

In the holotank a match-bright explosion flared and faded in the space of a heartbeat.

"Sensors indicate damage to the Clanner's armor, but no penetration."

"Very well." Beresick's acknowledgement was curt. "Reload and hit him again. Range to target?"

"Range now three-niner-zero."

"Weapons free. Fire at will!" Turning to the communications tech, he barked, "Message to the fleet: Break and engage."

"Launch, launch, launch!" a sensor tech bellowed, the hint of panic tinging his voice. "Sensors detect launch flares from all three enemy vessels."

Beresick looked up sharply. A small repeater screen set into his command console showed the narrow spike of a missile track in the wide bands of light illuminating the "waterfall" display. Unlike the graphic displays supposed by the entertainment media, the battle cruiser's sensor readings were computer-converted into bright bands on a screen to show where a contact had occurred. The larger the band, the larger the contact. A moment's study of the razor-edge line revealed that the incoming missile was headed for the *Invisible Truth*.

"Counter measures."

Though no match for Clan advancements in technology, all WarShips still carried signal-jammers and decoys as part of their standard electronic warfare suites. The equipment rarely worked as advertised, but even the slim hope of affecting the guidance system of an incoming missile was better than sitting passively waiting for the impact.

When it came, the impact was less than devastating. The *Truth*'s heavy armor shrugged off the Killer Whale's explosive punch without a shiver.

"Come right three-five degrees, down ten." Beresick knew the course change would bring the *Truth* onto a collision heading with the *Soyuz*. He also knew that the Smoke Jaguar commander probably didn't understand the game of "chicken," but he would understand courage and pride, and that was what Beresick was counting on.

"Zero-three-five, sir."

"Ease your helm, and level off."

"Ease and level, aye, sir." The man at the helm fairly sang the words.

The *Truth*'s helm could have been handled through a small joystick, or even a series of push-buttons. Her original designers had a different idea. Just as sailors, be they wet navy or black-water types, as starship crews were sometimes called, were a tradition-bound lot, so were ship designers. The men who drew up the original plans for the *Cameron* Class battle cruiser had stipulated that helm functions should be carried out by means of a control yoke, similar to that found in a large conventional air-craft. A relatively simple computer program translated movement of this yoke into the desired movement of the ship. The designers even allowed for an increasing degree of resistance in the yoke's movement, the farther the helmsman moved it.

"Sir, we are on a collision course with the *Soyuz*." The sensor operator's voice held a note of confusion.

"That's right." Beresick was self-assured, almost calm.

"Commodore, don't you think we should sheer off?"

"No," Beresick snapped. "Hold your course. What is the Clan-ner's reaction?"

"Sir, he's holding course and speed."

"Good." Beresick smiled. It was working just as he hoped it would. He believed his headlong drive toward the Clan ship would be seen as a challenge to the Clan captain, one he could not ignore. So far Beresick was right. It seemed as though the Jaguar would continue to drive forward, even if it meant ram-ming the *Truth* head-on.

"Range to the *Soyuz*?"

"Range now one-nine-zero kilometers, closing awful fast."

"Target his nose and fire, all forward weapons." Beresick seemed so calm that the order was almost a suggestion.

"Firing."

"Hard to port." This time the order sounded like one. "All engines ahead full. All starboard batteries fire as you bear."

As the massive battle cruiser swung sharply to the left, she shuddered under the impact of heavy naval autocannon shells and a trio of anti-ship missiles.

The *Soyuz* fared worse. The raking broadside shattered most of her remaining nose armor. Steaming rents in her thick hide showed in a number of places. Energy leaking from torn power feeds created a miniature actinic lightning storm in the gap where her port bow naval laser battery had once been.

Despite the appearance of having taken a crippling wound, the Clan cruiser was far from out of the fight. As the *Truth* sought to reverse her turn, the *Rostock* darted in from above to worry the staggering WarShip. Cannon and laser fire slashed into the *Soyuz*'s hull, inflicting no great damage to her armored spine. By way of retribution, the damaged cruiser rolled onto her starboard side, blasting the *Fox* Class corvette's vulnerable belly with a devastating broadside.

The thimble-shaped WarShip shook violently under the impact of the Clanner's hellish blast. As she staggered under that fearsome assault, Beresick could see nothing but a gaping hole where her port fore-quarter had once been. The sullen glow of superheated metal, rapidly cooling in the iciness of space, showed like dull orange eyes in the dark cavern of twisted metal.

"Commodore, Captain Floriano is on the line."

"Put him on," Beresick ordered the commtech.

When the *Rostock*'s captain appeared on the viewscreen, Beresick barely recognized him. Floriano's face was covered in blood from a deep gash over his left temple. A hand-sized blister showed through a rent in the shoulder of his khaki Star League uniform. Behind him, the *Rostock*'s bridge was a scene of carnage. Wires dangled from the overhead. Thin blue smoke filled the air. Worst of all were the number of huddled shapes, which might have been bundles of paint-stained rags, but weren't.

"Commodore." Floriano's voice was thick and his speech slurred, the result of a cut mouth and several broken and missing teeth. "*Rostock* is out of it. We've lost most of our port-side weapons and armor. Most of my crew is either dead or wounded. The bridge is smashed, and we've got plant damage. We're going to try to withdraw. Can you cover us?"

"Affirmative." Beresick struggled to control his revulsion. The fight at Trafalgar, while not bloodless, had been relatively clean. In most cases a naval officer never saw human casualties, merely the wreckage of destroyed ships and the gaunt, hollow faces of survivors rescued from escape pods and life boats. Seeing, for the first time in his career, the human cost of a naval engagement left Beresick feeling stunned and slightly sick. "Come left to two-seven-zero, relative. We'll swing around between you and the *Soyuz*."

"Copy *Invisible Truth*. Will comply." The relief in Floriano's voice was a tangible thing. "Thanks." He signed off.

"Helm, come about," Beresick called. "Run us between the *Rostock* and the Clanner."

"Too late!" Beresick couldn't tell who had uttered the appalled shout, but the report was accurate.

The *Soyuz,* seemingly bent on having the *Rostock* as its lawful prey, swung to follow the smaller *Fox* Class corvette. Running under her port quarter, the Jaguar WarShip fired another lethal volley into the *Rostock*'s side.

As the *Truth*'s bridge crew watched in horror, the shattered hulk that had once been a combat vessel began to break up. The Jaguar ship's full broadside had apparently clawed its way deep into the *Rostock*'s vitals, snapping the spine of her keel like a rust-eaten bar of iron.

"Floriano, abandon ship!" Beresick shouted at the disintegrating vessel. "Abandon ship!"

Ariana Winston, all but forgotten in the heat of battle, couldn't help but call out from the holotank. "C'mon you guys, get outta there."

A single lifeboat rocketed away from the stricken vessel. Barely had the tiny craft cleared the *Rostock*'s hull than a mammoth explosion ripped the corvette apart.

For a long moment, there was a deathly silence on the *Truth*'s bridge. Beresick was the first to recover.

"Helmsman, reverse your turn. Close with the *Soyuz*. Air Boss, launch our shuttles to search for survivors. Gunnery officer, all weapons target the *Soyuz*. I want that Clan bastard's hide to nail up in my stateroom."

A chorus of "Aye-ayes" greeted his orders.

In following the *Rostock* as the disabled corvette tried to limp out of the battle area, the *Soyuz* had inadvertently given the *Truth* enough time to swing into position to once again run across the Clan cruiser's bow. As the *Invisible Truth* ran past the enemy's much-abused nose, she let loose with a full broadside that made the assault against the *Rostock* seem like a pop from a child's cap-gun.

The *Truth*'s attack dug deep into the *Soyuz*'s armor, sending steaming chunks of metal spinning off into the void. Internal systems were obliterated in clouds of shrapnel and lightless explosions. Crew compartments were breached, leaving pale, glittering streamers of ice and vapor trailing like soft, frozen feathers from the deep wounds in the Clan ship's side.

"Hit him again!" Beresick shouted, his lust for revenge not yet sated.

A pair of PPC blasts savaged the reeling cruiser, followed by a volley of cannon shells and two anti-ship missiles. By the time the explosions faded, the *Soyuz* was listing heavily to the starboard, and down by her head. Clearly, she was disabled and out of the fight.

"Where are the *Vincent*s?" Beresick demanded.

"Commodore, *Emerald* reports *Vincent One* destroyed," a comm-tech replied. "*Starlight* reports *Vincent Two* ran past the fleet and attacked the transports. Several JumpShips have sustained damage. *Starlight* says the *Vincent Two* is adrift and burning. There are still a couple of Clan DropShips and a handful of fighters pressing the attack, but *Starlight* says they can handle them."

"Wshoow," Beresick sighed deeply, blowing out the breath all in a single rush. "Damage reports?"

"None of the transports were hit too badly. *Emerald* reports damage to her main bridge, radar, and jump sail array. Captain Kole says he can make running repairs in about four hours. It'll take two days to fix his sail. *Starlight* got hammered pretty badly. She's lost most of her port weapon bays, and her grav deck. Captain O'Malley thinks he can be operational again in about ten hours. And . . ." The tech hesitated as though his uttering the words would fix the events in history. "The *Rostock* is gone.

Shuttle One reports picking up five survivors in a lifeboat, all from *Rostock*'s flight division. They couldn't find any more lifeboats."

Beresick shook his head sadly. "All right. Recall the Drop-Ships. Let the fighters hunt down the last enemy ships. I don't want to delay the landings any more than necessary. Have *Fire Fang* and *Ranger* stand by. They'll be moving in-system with the invasion force." He looked up at Winston and Redburn for the first time since the naval engagement began.

"General, do you have anything to add?"

"Yeah. I want all unit commanders to give me a report on the readiness state of their troops, and I want it inside of one hour." Winston paused to rub her eyes. "The Jags already know we're coming, and I don't want to give them any more time to prepare a defense."

Many hundreds of millions of kilometers away, another commander was being informed of the naval battle's outcome.

"Do not lie to me, you *surat!*" he railed at the communications technician. "How could Inner Sphere barbarians engage and defeat three of our WarShips? They do not have that many combat vessels. Those they do have are dedicated to protecting their own filthy capital worlds."

"Galaxy Commander, the Watch reports that the Successor States have been building WarShips for some time now, and we know that ComStar has preserved a number of Star League-era vessels. The Watch says it *is* possible that the Inner Sphere could mount such an invasion fleet."

Russou Howell glared at the man who had dared contradict him. Though the other officer wore the quartered red and gold insignia of a Star Captain, Howell could not bring himself to regard him as a warrior. He considered agents of the Watch to be little more than bandits, lacking honor and any real claim to legitimacy within Smoke Jaguar society.

This was almost more than he could bear. First came the cowardly attack on Mount Szabo that had damaged the planet's main command, control, and communications center and destroyed the space defense grid that might have repelled the Inner Sphere *surats* once and for all. Though the deaths of the technicians assigned to those facilities hardly signified, the loss of three full

Points of Elementals angered Howell. Then the arrival of an Inner Sphere invasion fleet and the defeat of three WarShips, here at Huntress, the Jaguar's lair itself, put an even greater strain on his rapidly fraying temper.

As if that weren't enough, the filthy Inner Sphere *surats* had the unmitigated gall to claim that they were acting under the sacred banner of the Star League. Though Howell initially refused to believe the reports coming in from the WarShips defending the Huntress system, he finally had to admit that the barbarians did indeed have the colossal affrontery to paint the Cameron Star and the crest of the Star League Defense Force on their WarShips and fighters. As a final insult, he was being lectured on the naval capabilities of the Inner Sphere by a *stravag* agent of the Watch. He wheeled on the Star Captain and began shouting invective at the man, who weathered the storm impassively.

"Galaxy Commander?"

"What?" Howell bellowed at the tech who had dared interrupt him.

"G-Galaxy Commander," the man stuttered. "The Inner Sphere fleet is regrouping and is moving insystem. I believe they mean to invade Huntress."

With a howl of fury more befitting a wolf than a jaguar, Russou Howell balled up his fist and smashed the unfortunate tech to the floor. Standing over the unconscious lower-casteman, his hands still clenched in fury, Howell glared at the prostrate man's fellow techs.

In that one flame-hot moment of rage, all the depression, all the self-condemnation, all the madness and the overwhelming need to drown his despair in a bottle burned to a cinder. In their place Russou Howell felt something he had not known for a long time. Pride, and the joy of impending battle. He was a Jaguar warrior once again.

"Sound the alert," he growled. "Not one of those freebirth vermin will leave Huntress alive."

17

DropShip SLS Long Knife
Approaching Eridani Light Horse Landing Zone
Three Kilometers Northwest of Mount Szabo,
Huntress
Kerensky Cluster, Clan Space
12 March 3060

It's been a long time since I had to do this.

General Ariana Winston sat at the controls of her modified *Cyclops,* gazing at a large secondary monitor set into the left side of the front cockpit. Unlike the normal CP-11-A, her 'Mech had been refitted, at her request, to mount a command console. The 'Mech's short-range missile launcher and its ammunition magazine had to be sacrificed to shoehorn the second cockpit into the already-jammed interior, but the trade-off was worth it. Having a highly skilled communication and sensor operator behind her relieved some of the pressure on Winston, allowing her to concentrate on the job of running the battle and piloting the rather cumbersome 90-ton machine.

The monitor she was so studiously watching was tied into the DropShip *Long Knife*'s tactical computer system. According to the feed she was receiving, the *Overlord* Class ship was just coming to a slow coast over Mount Szabo. The feed was necessary, because Winston's *Cyclops* was bolted down tight in a ceramic and steel drop pod, similar to the ones used by the DEST teams when they'd made their initial drop onto the Smoke Jaguars' homeworld.

As the commanding officer of the mercenary Eridani Light Horse, it had been quite some time since she'd had to make a combat drop from orbit into an enemy-controlled area—what was called a "hot landing" in the warrior vernacular. But, given the large number of targets the task force had elected to attack, every MechWarrior was needed, and that included commanding officers.

It had taken only a matter of hours for the DropShips carrying Task Force Serpent's ground forces to detach from the Jump-Ships once the last enemy fighters had been run down. Getting to the planet was another matter. Huntress lay just over a billion kilometers from the jump point, requiring an in-run of seven and a half days at one G's worth of acceleration. The Light Horse, and their companion units in Task Force Serpent, had been opposed during the final few hours of their burn to Huntress by what appeared to be the last flights of Clan Omnifighters the Jaguars could muster. Like OmniMechs, Clan fighters could be easily modified to suit a particular mission or a particular pilot's fighting style.

Though the Jaguar pilots fought bravely, there was little doubt as to the outcome of the attack. The Clan fighters were battered aside by the inbound DropShips and harried to death by Serpent's own aerospace fighters. Still, they managed to inflict some damage. The *Avenger*, a *Union* Class DropShip belonging to the Kathil Uhlans, took heavy autocannon fire from a mottled gray *Jagatai-A* that jammed one of her 'Mech bay doors. Though the *Avenger* was still operational, some of the Uhlans would be forced to queue up to use the remaining door in that bay.

"General Winston?" A voice sounded in her ears.

"Winston. Go."

"General, we are over the drop zone. Request permission to deploy the brigade."

Having three combat regiments, as well as a headquarters company and support battalions, not to mention its own aerospace and starship transport sections, the Eridani Light Horse actually qualified as a light division, but was commonly referred to as "the brigade."

With a nod made of equal parts satisfaction and apprehension, Winston said, "Permission granted. Deploy the brigade."

"Very well." The *Long Knife*'s captain, one Jeremiah Lynch, sounded relieved. As soon as the ground forces were deployed, the DropShips could pull back and await the message signaling that the landing zone was secure. "*Long Knife* to all Light Horse commands, commence drop in five . . . four . . . three . . . two . . . one . . . Drop, now, now, now!"

The very second Lynch's third "now" blared from her headset, the remote feed to Winston's 'Mech was cut off. Faintly, through the huge, egg-shaped drop capsule and the thick legs of her *Cyclops,* Winston felt the trembling of the big spheroid DropShip as the first of thirty-six BattleMechs dropped free of her armored hull. Though she hated the waiting, cooped up inside the blind, silver-gray world of the drop pod, she would have to take her turn. As the Light Horse commander, and the overall leader of Serpent, her place was in the middle of the second "stick" of twelve 'Mechs to be dropped. With each barely perceived shudder of the huge vessel, her turn drew ever closer.

"Hang on, Kip," she called to her CSO. "By my count, we're next."

Warrant Officer Ian "Kip" Douglass, Winston's communication and sensor operator, didn't reply. She knew that he wasn't being purposely rude. Kip simply hated dropping out of a perfectly good spacecraft.

Winston barked a short laugh at the image of her battle-tested CSO gripping the arm-rests of his ejection seat so hard that his knuckles showed white. The laugh turned into an odd hiccough of surprise as the bottom dropped out of the world.

Making an orbital drop was in some ways a study in contrasts. MechWarriors experienced a sudden switch from the sensation of motionlessness aboard the coasting DropShip to the stomach-churning acceleration of being punted out the ship's drop tube, and then back to the feeling of floating in space. Winston, of course, knew better. Though she couldn't see the cloud-shrouded bulk of Huntress rushing up to meet her plummeting 'Mech, she was well aware of the fact that she was encased in over a hundred tons of armored BattleMech and protective drop-pod, falling at an increasing rate of about ten meters per second.

Then there was the contrast in noise level. Inside the *Long*

Knife's 'Mech bay, it was relatively quiet, save for the tactical feeds coming in through her pod's service umbilical. When the umbilical was detached, it became deathly silent, save for Winston's short conversation with Kip Douglass and the beating of her own heart. As soon as the *Cyclops* and its protective pod were launched into space, the quiet was broken by a faint hissing sound that soon became a high keening, then a basso roar. The sound was generated by the massive, egg-shaped capsule slicing its way through Huntress' upper atmosphere. Winston knew that the outer ceramic covering of the pod was heating rapidly due to friction with the air. Were it not for the pod, her 'Mech would burn up in the atmosphere long before ever reaching the planet below. If some small, hidden fault in the capsule's outer surface should suddenly manifest itself, the result would be the same.

Winston glanced at a multifunction display that bore a series of rapidly decreasing numbers. She knew that the figure represented her *estimated* height in meters above the planet's surface. Estimated, because her 'Mech's sensors were unable to penetrate the pod's thick skin and give her *actual* altitude.

Maybe this is why Kip hates orbital drops.

As the pod fell, and the roaring sound grew even louder, Winston thought she could feel the temperature inside her cockpit begin to rise as air friction began to heat and wear away the drop pod's outer, ablative surface. The pump set into her command couch kicked on with a loud thump, sending a wave of coolant flooding through her vest. Prior to the discovery of the Gray Death memory core and the release of advanced technology by the previously secretive ComStar, MechWarriors had been forced to wear bulky cooling vests, thick felt booties, a heavy neurohelmet, and little else when piloting their machines. The incredible amounts of waste heat generated by the 'Mech's power plant and weapons could fry a warrior in very short order. To combat that unpleasant occurrence, 'Mech designers installed a number of heat sinks to bleed off the high temperatures that would otherwise cause the machine to shut down, its ammunition to explode, render its electronic control and targeting packages balky, and incapacitate or even kill its pilot.

Even so, the temperatures inside a 'Mech's cockpit during a pitched battle could rise as high as forty-six degrees Celsius. To fight this oppressive heat, MechWarriors wore cooling vests that circulated the same ethylene glycol-based solution as their 'Mech's heat sinks.

With the technological advancements over the past few years came the introduction of the MechWarrior combat suit. This garment was made of ballistic cloth and contained the same type of tubing as a cooling vest, but a more efficient heat-exchange system and better coolant liquids allowed the designers to make the tubing smaller and less bulky. The suits also boasted a semi-autonomous medical pack, similar to those mounted in Clan elemental armor, which could inject the wearer with pain-killers, stimulants, and similar medical compounds. A lighter, more efficient neurohelmet completed the outfit. Though the systems were still rare, Winston had managed to procure a small number of the expensive suits, which she issued to her regimental commanders, keeping a couple for Kip Douglass and herself.

Winston felt the rush of fresh coolant flowing through the suit's tubing. This was followed by a wave of gratitude to Com-Star, which had provided the combat suits, as she watched the cockpit's internal temperature continue to rise on a secondary display screen.

A high tone sounded in her ears.

"Hang in there, Kip," she called. "That's the one-minute warning."

Sixty seconds later, the huge gray ceramic and steel egg split apart, leaving Winston's huge, boxy 'Mech falling toward the ground below. Now, her sensors worked, and she could tell exactly how far above the surface they were. Eighteen kilometers, still a long way above the ground, but at the rate the *Cyclops* was falling, it wouldn't take long to cover that distance, unless . . .

With a massive snap, a five-petaled blossom of parachutes bloomed into existence overhead. The dropping 'Mech suddenly slowed, its feet orienting violently downward. The chutes weren't intended to bring the massive war machine gently down on the landing zone. It was falling far too fast and weighed far too much for that. The quintuple nylon canopy was merely intended to slow the 'Mech's fall and orient it feet-downward. In that way, the strap-on retrorockets built into the drop pack would provide enough braking power to bring the *Cyclops* down safely. Such measures were necessary in all BattleMechs that lacked integral jump jets.

For the first time since entering the drop pod, Winston looked around with her own eyes. As far as she could see, there were bright red-orange streaks blazing against the night sky. It looked like a massive meteor shower, but she knew that the blazing fire-trails were not tipped by rapidly eroding chunks of nickel-iron, but by multiple-ton mechanisms of ceramic and steel and death. Other, smaller streaks, not as bright, but just as significant, laced the dark sky. These were the trails of drop pods, already split open to deliver their cargo of death into Huntress' atmosphere. Every four of these dull red strands meant another Eridant Light Horse 'Mech on its way to Huntress.

"General, I have the beacon," Douglass reported with a calm voice that belied his admitted and extreme anxiety. "Altitude now, eight kilometers."

A guidance discrete flashed into life on Winston's head's up display. The small green circle indicated the point toward which she was supposed to steer her dropping 'Mech. A gentle tap on the retro pack control swung her massive *Cyclops* onto a course for what Douglass called "the beacon." In reality, their landing zone was a broad, relatively flat expanse of ground three kilometers to the northwest of Mount Szabo and well outside the planetary capital of Lootera.

The small flashing light on her *Cyclops'* HUD gave Winston a mark toward which to steer her descending 'Mech. In theory, if she stayed on target, according to the guidance discrete, she would hit her assigned LZ with no trouble. The theory also stated that a fixed landing beacon increased the chances for hitting the correct landing zone. In this case the theory would probably be correct. On the northern edge of Lootera stood Mount Szabo and the Jaguars' genetic repository. Surrounding the repository's low, pyramidal bulk was the Field of Heroes, a wide parade ground lined with statues honoring the valiant warriors of the Clan. There the Smoke Jaguars had erected a monument to their own glory. The Clanners called this monument the eternal laser. Winston called it stupid.

It was the height of insane hubris to erect a powerful beacon that would burn straight up into the clouds overhead as a means to honor one's fallen comrades, especially when that same monument could be seen from orbit by any invading force that might happen along. The laser monument provided a perfect landing beacon for the Eridani Light Horse. Though the Field of Heroes could never serve as a landing zone for the entire brigade, their 'Mechs' sophisticated computer systems were able to key in on the beacon and determine the actual location of their landing zones.

"Sixty seconds," Winston called, as the altimeter clicked over to read four thousand meters. Clamping down hard on the retro-pack control, she fired the jets for a long, twenty-second burst, slowing the *Cyclops*. If she did hit the ground hard, at least now she was moving at a more or less survivable rate of descent.

At two thousand meters, Winston gave the jets another long burn, taking even more speed off her fall. Then, a scant five hundred meters off the ground, she closed the retro pack's nozzles to their narrowest settings, and lit off the powerful liquid-fuel rockets in a final braking burn. The ninety-ton, humanoid 'Mech shuddered with the incredible amount of kinetic energy being spent to bring it to a safe landing. The whining roar of the jets tortured Winston's ears as she struggled to keep the decidedly top-heavy machine in an upright landing position.

With a heavy, jolting thud, the *Cyclops* touched down. Winston bent the 'Mech's thick, armored knees to absorb the last of the machine's downward energy. Bringing the 'Mech upright again, she flicked a cover-locked control, and was rewarded with a firecracker series of sharp, flat cracks as a dozen explosive bolts fired, dropping the drogue chute and retro pack to the ground.

"ELH, this is Dancer. Check in," she snapped into her communicator.

"Dancer, this is Magyar." Colonel Charles Antonescu was, almost predictably, the first of her commanders to respond. "The 151st has landed and is moving on its objective."

"Dancer, Stonewall. We're down and safe." Colonel Edwin Amis, the 21st Striker Regiment's veteran commander, was far less formal than his more spit-and-polish counterpart. "We're heading out for the target."

Winston checked a secondary monitor, this one programmed to display a map of the Eridani Light Horse's area of operation. The 151st and 21st's objective, a large MechWarrior training facility, was a few kilometers west of the landing zone. Amis and Antonescu were tasked with attacking and obliterating the training base. Sandra Barclay's 71st Light Horse Regiment was dropping in just to the north of Lootera. From there Barclay's 'Mechs would swarm onto the Field of Heroes. There they would attack and secure what agent Trent had called the heart and soul of the Clan Smoke Jaguar, the low, pyramidal stone edifice housing the Clan's genetic repository. Winston made certain that Barclay understood that her forces were not to engage in a street-to-street battle for Lootera unless such a fight was absolutely unavoidable. But now, fate had dealt the Light Horse a wild card. Barclay was not checking in with brigade command.

"Phantom, this is Dancer, over?"

Winston got no reply from the Light Horse's junior Colonel.

"Phantom, this is Dancer, over. Phantom, this is Dancer. Respond please."

Still the hail went unanswered. Winston knew that a hundred relatively minor things could be at fault, a bad landing that crippled Barclay's communications gear, a flawed drop that scattered the 71st all across and beyond their assigned landing zone. Just because Barclay didn't answer there was no reason to suspect the worst

"Phantom, this is Dancer, respond please." General Winston's voice crackled in Colonel Sandra Barclay's ears as her senses slowly came back into proper focus. Her *Cerberus* had landed rather heavily, tossing her about in the cockpit like a die in a gambler's cup. For what had seemed like a long time she sat staring blankly at the colored lights flashing in front of her eyes. At the time she had taken the blinking patches of color for the after-effects of a blow to the side of her head, the added effect of a rough landing. Gradually her vision cleared enough for Barclay to realize that what she was seeing were the various controls and sensors of her BattleMech's cockpit.

"Phantom, this . . ."

"Dancer, Phantom," Barclay cut in. "Sorry, General. I made kind of a rough landing and I was out of it for a while. Hang on for a second."

Checking her displays, Barclay saw that her regiment was intact, though it had been somewhat dispersed during the drop. She relayed this fact to Winston.

"The 71st is all down, but we got kinda scattered during the drop. We're dispersed all along the northern edge of Lootera. I think some of my troops might have actually landed inside the city. Unless you say otherwise, I'm going to have my outfit rally on my location before we move against the repository. No sense in committing the regiment piecemeal."

"All right, Colonel." Barclay caught a note of concern in Winston's voice. It was a tone the younger officer didn't like. Not because it indicated a concern that Barclay couldn't handle the job, but because Barclay herself had been feeling something of the same concern.

Ever since the bloody fighting on Coventry, Sandra Barclay could not escape an overriding sense of doom. No matter what she did to prevent it, her hands shook uncontrollably every time she climbed into the cockpit of a 'Mech.

"ELH, this is Dancer. Move out and hit your objectives." Winston's clear voice carried the joy of battle to Barclay's ears, a joy she wished she could share. "Remember, our intel says the Jags have been importing captured Inner Sphere 'Mechs to Huntress. So check your IFFs before engaging."

Gripping the *Cerberus'* control joysticks with a white-knuckled ferocity, Barclay called out to the rest of her unit.

"Attention all Phantoms, this is Phantom Actual." The use of the term Actual told the 71st that their regimental commander was speaking. "I am lighting off my beacon. Form up on me and make it quick. I want to hit the repository before the Jags have a chance to reinforce it. Now move."

"Incoming!"

The age-old warning shout cut across the 71st Light Horse's communication channel like a laser through paper. In response, Barclay activated her 'Mech's anti-missile system. The radar-directed chain-gun, located in a low, flat turret above and behind the *Cerberus'* jutting cockpit, began searching the sky for targets. The system didn't have long to wait. A flight of long-range missiles streaked through the rain-laden air. There were so many inbounds that Barclay's anti-missile system wavered for a moment trying to decide which missile to engage first. Then with a roar muted by the 'Mech's thick ferro-fibrous armor, the weapon fired.

A flight of missiles was clawed from the air by the dense metal slugs. The self-aimed weapon switched targets and fired again, this time with less success. Only a few of the anti-armor weapons were intercepted by the anti-missile system. The rest slammed into the *Cerberus'* barrel chest and exploded.

The impact rocked the big machine slightly, but the damage was far from fatal. With a conscious act of will, Barclay pushed down the feeling of panic rising in her gut, and flicked on the targeting system's infrared sensors. Immediately the gray, rain-streaked semi-gloom was replaced by a vista as unearthly as any imagined by Dante Alighieri. At least ten, large, man-shaped forms glowed white in the dark green and black of the heat-sensitive IR display. The onboard computer's warbook sub-routine identified the nearest enemy as a *Vindicator*.

"What the . . ." Barclay began, confused over the computer's apparent mistake. Then Winston's reminder came back to her. According to the intelligence gathered by the Clan spy, the Jags had been bringing captured Inner Sphere 'Mechs back to Huntress for use by the second-line and solahma warriors populating the two Galaxies defending the planet.

It seemed strange to Barclay that the Jags would use anything other than their best warriors to guard the greatest treasure they possessed, the genetic legacy of all warriors who had died honorably in the past. But the 'Mechs that had swarmed out to meet the 71st Light Horse as the mercenary regiment entered the Field of Heroes were exactly the second-line and Inner Sphere designs reported by Trent.

A blast of PPC fire slashed into her 'Mech, driving all thoughts out of her mind, save one, and that one was born of long hours of training and drill—eliminate the enemy.

Dropping a red-glowing cross hairs over the enemy 'Mech's center of mass, Barclay waited a heartbeat for the targeting reticle to flash gold before she stroked the triggers for her machine's paired Gauss rifles. A bright streak flashed across her HUD, followed a fraction of a second later by another. Air friction had so heated the outside of the nickel-iron slugs fired by her Gauss rifles that they burned a laser-like trail across the infrared sensor image.

Down-range, the effects were more spectacular, and far more deadly. The paired, basket-ball size projectiles smashed into the enemy's torso. Through sheer luck, they landed less than a meter apart. Shattered armor flew in all directions, leaving faint white trails in their wake. The 'Mech staggered heavily under the impact, and its heat signature flared even brighter than before.

Engine hit. Barclay assessed the damage she had inflicted on the enemy 'Mech.

The reeling Jaguar 'Mech recovered its balance enough to loose a volley of missiles. The deadly steel wasps, with their high-explosive stingers, ripped through the dripping air with a sound like tearing sail-cloth. Barclay's anti-missile system seemed to be losing efficiency with each flight of missiles it engaged. Only one of the inbound rockets fell to the chain gun's screaming blast, the rest peppering the *Cerberus'* legs and torso.

Though the *Vindicator* had to be close to shutdown because of the excess heat caused by damage to its engine, the Clan pilot extended the big PPC replacing the spindly 'Mech's right forearm. The azure bolt of charged particles lit the battlefield like a stroke of lightning. Barclay's 'Mech Status Display told of damage to her machine's right arm, from which the PPC had flayed nearly two-thirds of a ton of armor.

Barclay returned the *Vindicator*'s fire with another pair of hypersonic Gauss slugs, backed up by a stuttering blast of laser fire from her 'Mech's pulse lasers. The vicious attack savaged the smaller 'Mech, leaving huge, glowing craters in the machine's right torso and right arm. Incredibly, the smaller machine stayed on its feet. Barclay gaped at the sight of the shot-riddled *Vindicator,* seemingly defiant in the face of her superior firepower. Hot anger welled up inside her.

If this Clan bugger wants to die gloriously in battle, I'll oblige him.

Carefully, she trained her 'Mech's powerful Gauss rifles on the *Vindicator*'s shattered torso, and tapped the triggers. The dense, nickle-iron projectiles blasted into the enemy's battered and useless armor. The spindly machine staggered and fell, a miniature lightning storm playing across the gaping hole where its chest armor had once been. The Clan pilot made no attempt to escape from his stricken mount. Whether he was dead, wounded, or merely too stubborn and prideful to abandon his 'Mech, Barclay didn't care. The *Vindicator* was down, and she had other things to worry about.

Though the fighting on the Field of Heroes was still raging, the

lead elements of her regiment's 17th Recon Battalion were reporting that they had reached the Smoke Jaguar genetic repository.

"The place might as well have been unguarded," Lieutenant
Ronald Boice reported. "We hit the guards and rolled right over
them. Didn't take too many casualties. Detailed butcher's bill to
follow. Lousy Elementals. My guys want to move in and trash the
place. What are your orders?"

"Negative!" Barclay fairly shouted over the commline. "Do
not, I repeat, do not destroy the repository. The Clanners are kind
of touchy as far as their gene pools are concerned. We start destroying the repository, and every Jaguar Kerensky ever spawned
will be down on us, looking for vengeance.

"Just secure the facility, dig in, and prepare to hold your
ground. I don't think the Jags are done with us, not by a long
chalk."

"Roger, Colonel," came Boice's reply. "Secure and hold. Will
comply."

"Good," Barclay said to herself as she switched communications channels.

"Dancer, this is Phantom," she said into her headset mike, surprised at the steadiness in her voice. "Seventy-first Light Horse is
down and safe. Primary objective is secure, casualties light.
Phantom is awaiting orders."

"Phantom, Dancer." General Winston's voice seemed to carry
a note of relief. "Establish perimeter and call in your DropShips.
Begin field repairs, but maintain security. Recon elements suggest the Jags may be massing for a counterattack. I want you to
be ready for them."

"Roger, Dancer, Wilco." As Sandra Barclay relayed Ariana
Winston's orders to her subordinates, she looked down at her
hands. All through the relatively minor scrap with the Smoke
Jaguars, she hadn't experienced so much as a twitch. Now, with
the battle done, and the objective secure, her hands began to
tremble like leaves in an autumn gale.

A dozen kilometers to the southwest, General Ariana Winston
leaned back in the cockpit of her command 'Mech. Though the
Smoke Jaguars must have had several hours to prepare a defensive strategy, the Light Horse as a whole had landed virtually

unopposed. Only a few Trinaries of 'Mechs had moved to oppose the landings.

What had surprised her was the composition of those Trinaries. The bulk of the defending machines had not been the advanced OmniMechs the Light Horse might have expected. Most of the defending 'Mechs were captured Combine machines that had apparently been shipped back to Huntress. She'd seen all the reports concerning the Jags' use of Inner Sphere 'Mechs, but she hadn't been prepared to see so many "friendly" designs.

"General, we're picking up some coded radio traffic here, on the special ops frequency."

The rather casual call from Kip Douglass interrupted her train of thought.

"Let me hear it."

A moment later Winston heard the now decrypted message.

"Dancer, this is Cobra, over."

"Cobra," according to her 'Mech's computer, was the codename assigned to the DEST teams' pre-invasion strike mission.

"Cobra, this is Dancer, go ahead."

"Dancer, Cobra is one hundred meters northeast of your location. Request clearance to enter your perimeter."

One hundred meters? Blast, those boys are good. Our pickets should have spotted them half a klick out. Winston made a mental note to have a quiet talk with her brigade's security element.

"You know what to do, Cobra."

"Roger, Dancer, Cobra has thrown smoke."

Winston turned her 'Mech's head to see a cloud of green smoke billow up out of the sedge-grass covering the gently rolling hills west of Lootera. According to the prearranged security procedures, when the DEST teams linked up with the Eridani Light Horse following the initial landing, Major Ryan was to identify himself both by codename and by tossing a colored smoke grenade as a visual recognition signal. The color of the smoke was dictated by the time of day. Winston glanced at the chart taped to the inside of her *Cyclops'* armored cockpit. Green smoke was specified for late afternoon. Her chronometer read seventeen hundred.

"All right, Cobra, I see green smoke," she said by way of confirmation. "Come on in."

As the DEST troopers filtered through the command company's inner perimeter, they switched off the stealth features of their Kage suits, revealing their locations.

Taking a deep, cleansing breath, Winston nodded in satisfaction. The Light Horse was safely onplanet and had linked up with the Draconis Elite Strike Teams. Their objectives had been secured, and the brigade's DropShips were inbound to their assigned landing zones. Phase one of Operation Serpent was well under way.

18

Fox Team Landing Zone
Near Falcon Eyrie, Eastern Mountains
Huntress
Kerensky Cluster, Clan Space
12 March 3060

At roughly the same time as Ariana Winston's *Cyclops* was being ejected from the *Long Knife's* drop bay, the *Claymore* Class DropShip *Marcinko* was beginning a long, shallow arc that would eventually take her through the lowermost levels of Huntress' upper atmosphere. The graceful lines of the vessel belied the deadly purpose for which she had been built. Designed as an assault ship, her heavy armor and weapons bays would have made her a formidable opponent to any Clan fighter that rose to intercept her, but none did. There had been some opposition during the long burn in from the fleet, now stationed at the system's zenith jump point, but even that had been dispersed like smoke in a gale.

Now the swan-like craft was shedding speed and heat as she coasted to a subsonic speed over the eastern half of the continent called Jaguar Prime. Secure in her belly were two squads of elite warriors. Though each was capable of piloting a BattleMech, there were none of the massive war machines in evidence. Instead, each warrior wore a light scout power suit, similar to the Kage suits used by the Draconis Elite Strike Teams. These armored infantrymen were not being sent into the heat of battle. Their mission was more strategic, one of containment and surveillance.

High in the Eastern Mountains, less than a day's march from the capital city of Lootera, was an installation that had not been slated for attack by the heavy 'Mech forces of Task Force Serpent. This was the base known as Falcon's Eyrie, an enclave belonging to Clan Jade Falcon.

According to the information provided by Agent Trent, the Jade Falcons were unlikely to interfere with Serpent's crusade to wipe out the Smoke Jaguars. The theory that the Falcons would be reluctant to involve themselves in a matter affecting only a single Clan baffled Captain Roger Montjar. But, as the officer in charge of the Rabid Fox Teams assigned to Task Force Serpent, it fell to him to lead his special forces troopers in a mission to "isolate and observe the Jade Falcons present on Huntress." In plain language, that meant his mission was to keep a close eye on the Falcons and make sure they didn't try to take an active part in the defense of the Jaguar homeworld.

To that end, his teams had been equipped with the best equipment the Federated Commonwealth had to offer. Jammed into a dozen cylindrical drop canisters was a staggering array of manned and remote sensors, digital surveillance equipment, and the latest infantry weapons systems the AFFC had to offer. In addition, each man was equipped with the latest in powered scout armor to come out of the New Avalon Institute of Science. The light scout armor was fitted with an integral jump pack and a full suite of sensor and communication equipment. The combination of standard and light powered armor would afford Montjar's teams the maximum amount of flexibility in the conduct of their mission.

That flexibility isn't going to do me a whole lot of good unless I can get my men on the ground. Montjar swore as he gazed at the monitor set into the assault bay's thick steel bulkhead.

As uneventful as the *Marcinko*'s in-run to Huntress had been, her long arc through that planet's stormy atmosphere was quite another story. No sooner had the graceful DropShip entered Huntress' upper atmosphere than she ran into a heavy storm system that seemed to be centered directly over the Jade Falcons' mountain base. The *Claymore*'s captain tried to circumvent the worst of the storm, but the gale-force winds battered and shook the ship so fiercely that Montjar would almost have rather faced a flight of heavy Omnifighters than the storm's fury, displayed in its fulminous glory on the monitor screen.

"Major, we need a decision here." The message from the *Marcinko*'s captain betrayed a level of tension that belied the man's fifteen years of experience shuttling the special forces teams into and out of hot landing zones. The DropShip pilot had not made a mistake in addressing Montjar by a higher rank than he actually held. Tradition dictated that there be only one captain aboard ship at any one time. Thus, everyone else who held that particular rank, especially ground-pounders, were given the honorary and very temporary rank of Major.

"Stand by, Captain," Montjar said as he turned to the jump-suited woman standing next to him. Her expression was one of deep concentration. "What do you think, Sal?"

"It's not good, Major," Sally Royale, the *Marcinko*'s drop-master answered. "We can push you out according to plan. That's not the problem. The mission profile calls for a covert HALO drop. But, with the weather outside, I don't recommend it. If you try to HALO, there's a more than even chance that you're going to catch a package, either on the way down, or on landing. A low-altitude drop would be a whole lot safer."

"Uh-huh," Montjar agreed. "Safer, but a lot more likely to compromise security. We take this ship in low, and I don't think the Falcons will mistake us for a big bird, do you?"

"Well, sensors says the secondary zone's clear," Royale said, switching the monitor to display a computer-animated image based on the DropShip's sensor sweeps. "We could divert to the alternate and make the HALO drop, but that means you'd have to yomp your gear in overland through some pretty rough terrain. The initial assault would be winding down before you even got within sensor range of Falcon Eyrie."

"Yeaah," Montjar stretched the word into a curse. Shaking his head, clearly not happy with any of his alternatives, he made a decision. "All right, we'll go with the primary drop zone and a low-level insertion. Captain?"

"Right here," the *Marcinko*'s pilot responded.

"Take us in under the cloud cover. We're going in low."

"Right." Montjar felt the DropShip canting forward even before the single-word response crackled from the intercom.

"Radar says the cloud deck is three hundred meters. I'll get you as low as I can. That'll give the Falcons the least amount of time to shoot at you on the way down."

"Thanks a lot." Montjar looked at Royale, who grinned ruefully at his sarcastic reply to her commanding officer.

Minutes later, the *Claymore* Class DropShip was skimming through the thick gray clouds less than half a kilometer above the rocky spine of the Eastern Mountains.

"Stand up!" Royale bellowed at the armored commandos.

In response the twenty men and women, indistinguishable in their powered scout suits, rose and faced the *Marcinko*'s drop bay door. Each grasped a steel snap hook in his suit's manipulative hand. Trailing from this spring-loaded double claw was a heavy nylon strap, which in turn led to a heavy nylon parachute pack strapped to the trooper's back.

"Hook up!" Royale shouted, and twenty snap hooks were attached to a steel cable running the width of the drop bay. "Check static line."

Each commando knew the drill as well as did dropmaster Royale. Though the sequence of bellowed command and programmed response might seem silly to an outsider, there was a serious and potentially deadly reason for each process. The Fox teams would be jumping into the dark, stormy skies over hostile territory, from an altitude of three hundred meters. No one could afford to make a mistake. Thus the ancient rituals, dating far back to the wars on Terra, were scrupulously observed.

"Check equipment."

Each man ran his hands along the nylon static line that attached his parachute to the overhead cable, ensuring that it was properly connected. Then he checked his release assembly and reserve chute to make sure each would function properly when the time came. Then, he looked over the gear of the trooper in front of him, inspecting his static line and parachute pack. A tap on the thigh indicated that all was well, then each man turned about and repeated the process for the man behind him.

"Sound off for equipment check," Royale barked.

"Twenty okay," the last man in line bellowed at the top of his lungs.

"Nineteen okay."

"Eighteen okay."

And so the count went until at last Captain Montjar, who, in defiance of military tradition, had insisted upon taking the first place in line shouted out, "One okay!"

"Stand in the door."

Montjar shuffled forward as the drop bay door slid upward to the accompaniment of a thin hydraulic whine. Instantly, the bay was filled with the deep-throated roar of the wind, generated by equal parts of the DropShip's speed and the storm. The bay door was too wide for him to place his hands on either jamb, as he would have when jumping from a conventional aircraft, so he rested them on his armored thighs. With knees bent and eyes staring straight ahead into the rain-lashed darkness, he was the very picture of coiled readiness. Behind him, the rest of his team shuffled into position, ready to hurl themselves, in turn, into the night.

"Ready." Sally Royale's glance jumped between the bulkhead-mounted screen, Montjar, and the traditional paired lights above the bay door. One burned a dull red, easily visible in the dimly illuminated drop bay. The other remained stubbornly dark.

Then, as the *Marcinko* arrived over the drop zone, it flared to life, a steady, blazing green.

"Green on. Go!"

Montjar didn't wait to hear Royale complete the command. As soon as the word "green" sounded in his ears, he launched himself out into Huntress' stormy sky.

Plummeting toward the ground below, he folded his arms across his reserve parachute, and began counting aloud, "One thousand one. One thousand two. One thousand three. One thousand four."

There was a sudden jerk that seemed to snap Montjar to a halt. Looking up, he checked his canopy. The black nylon airfoil had deployed perfectly and was slowing his descent to the prescribed six meters per second. Another look around assured him that the rest of his team had exited the DropShip and that their chutes had deployed properly.

Montjar had dropped almost one hundred meters before his chute deployed. At a release altitude of less than three hundred meters, that left him just thirty-four seconds before he hit the ground. Maybe Royale was right; the Falcons might spot the ship, but they certainly wouldn't have enough time to react before the commandos reached the ground.

In the unearthly world of Montjar's night-vision gear, the ground below him was a hellish, negative-image landscape of green, gray, and white. The ground, holding more of the day's heat, appeared as an expanse of pale green. The trees that lined the small clearing selected as the Fox team's drop zone appeared as black shadows on the edge of the grassy field because the trees retained less heat. Here and there were darker patches revealing small bushes or cool rock outcroppings. As he dropped, Montjar could pick out more details of the drop zone. The scrubby bushes dotting the clearing began to look like leafy plants rather than dark blobs. He could see the ripple of the grass as the storm's winds blew across the unmown clearing.

Montjar looked at his wrist-strapped altimeter. The device showed that he was about twenty meters above the ground. Acting on the basis of long and intensive training, he pulled the airfoil parachute into the wind, so as to slow his rate of descent and make his landing softer. Extending his suit's mechanical hands straight above his armored head, he grasped the parachute risers. Montjar pulled his feet and knees together, slightly bending the latter, and gently pointing his toes at the ground. He knew from training that the enhanced strength and rigidity of the power suit was not absolute proof against injury on a parachute drop. He knew that several men wearing the identical powered armor he and his team were now using had been injured while testing the system. Therefore, he insisted that his Fox teams follow the standard parachute-landing procedures.

As the commando's toes contacted the up-rushing ground, he twisted his body to the right. He dropped his chin, formerly held erect to his armored chest, as much as the helmet-breastplate interlock would permit, and pulled his hands and elbows in front of his body. In one fluid roll, Montjar broke his own fall. Leaping to his feet, he yanked on the risers to deflate the now fluttering parachute, which threatened to reinflate in the stiff wind. All around him, the men and women of his teams were touching down safely, just as he had.

Then, a sharp cry of pain cut across the team's tactical frequency.

"SITREP!" Montjar barked, demanding a situation report.

"Captain, this is Leftenant Fuentes." The report was a moment or two in coming. "Corporal Nye is down. He landed in some loose shale. It looks like his suit's ankle joint locked up on impact. The corpsman thinks he's got a bad sprain."

"Don't worry about me, sir." A new voice tight with pain cut across Fuentes' report. "If the doc here straps me up tight enough, I can make it."

Montjar took a few seconds to digest the information. Nye, as Team Three's heavy weapons specialist, had been tapped to carry a bulky man-pack PPC. Because of that weapon's size and weight, it was not considered to be suitable for an assault team, but the enhanced strength of the power suits made the weapon useful in a surveillance and containment situation.

"Corpsman," Montjar said at last, "tape him up as best you can, and keep an eye on him. I want to know if that injury's going to be any hindrance, and I want to know at the first sign of any trouble. Got it?

"Now, squad leaders, check in. Any other problems?"

"Captain, this is Sergeant Kramer. Half my squad got blown out of the zone. We're all okay, but Private Daltezze got hung up in a tree and had to abseil down." The usually jovial sergeant had a serious tone to his voice. "Problem is, some of our equipment canisters got scattered. We found three of 'em, and one of those got smashed up. About half our surveillance gear is busted. Number four canister is still missing. That's the one with all our rations in it."

"Dammit," Montjar hissed. "All right. All teams, spread out. Make a quick sweep for that canister. If we don't find it in fifteen minutes, we're going to have to abandon it. We'll make do with what rations we have, and whatever we can steal from the Jags. Now move."

Fifteen minutes later the team leaders clustered around Captain Montjar to report that the missing canister was nowhere to be found.

"That can't be helped," Montjar told them. "We're pushing our time table as it is.

"Okay, mission review. Team One, that's my group, will push out west and anchor our picket line at the far edge of the Falcon base. Two, that's Sergeant Burkas, you'll set up your OP about here." Montjar tapped the electronic map box to indicate the position selected for Team Two's Observation Post, a rocky promontory overlooking the Jade Falcon installation. "Three, Leftenant Fuentes, you're about a klick farther east. And Four, Sergeant Kramer, you're the eastern anchor, here against this ridge line.

"Remember, we're only here to observe. Intel says that the Falcons, as a matter of Clan honor, probably won't get involved. Now, remember, the intelligence is sketchy, at best, and two years old into the bargain. And we just can't exactly rely on the Clan honor thing to keep them out. If they *do* decide to take a hand in the fighting, it's our job to call in the 'Mech jocks and to slow the Falcons up until cavalry gets here.

"Everybody got it?"

The squad leaders indicated their understanding with a series of nods and affirmatives.

"Good. Now, get back to your squads. Run an equipment check. We're outta here in five minutes."

"There have been reports all night about incoming DropShips," Star Colonel Nikolai Icaza snapped at the technician manning Falcon Eyrie's small primary console. As a research station, the Eyrie had been fitted with many "scientific instruments" that could double as military scanners. "Thus far, all of those contacts have been aimed at the Smoke Jaguars. Why do you trouble me with this one?"

"Because, Star Colonel, this contact passed directly over the Eyrie, at low altitude," the tech answered. "Scanners suggest that a body of troops may have been dropped from the ship as it passed."

"Freebirth!" Icaza snarled. "What type of troops?"

"Sensors suggest infantry, Star Colonel, possibly armored infantry."

"But no 'Mechs?"

"No, Star Colonel."

Icaza stepped away from the sensor operator's station, folding his thickly muscled Elemental's arms across his equally powerful chest. His thick black eyebrows crept toward each other as his brow crinkled in thought.

Following the troubling events of the previous year, which had culminated in the crippling and recall of Falcon Eyrie's former commander, Icaza had been ordered to take command of the station. His orders also stipulated that he bring two Stars of Elementals to Huntress. It seemed that Khan Marthe Pryde had finally gotten wind of the virtually non-existent discipline plaguing the research station. His mission was to re-instill a measure of pride and self-respect in the warriors assigned to the Eyrie.

When he arrived and learned the true state of discipline among the troops at the station, he nearly ordered the entire garrison shot, so that he might start over from scratch. His Falcon pride would not, however, permit such an extreme, and easy measure. That very day he had made a vow to himself, and to the Jade Falcon, that he would whip, drive, coerce, and if necessary, beat, the lackadaisical freebirths into fighting shape.

In just over a year, he had molded a unit of worthless scum into a cohesive, if not particularly effective, fighting force. His warriors still lacked BattleMechs. Despite several strongly worded requests by Icaza, the Khan had yet to send any of the multi-ton war machines to his tiny garrison.

Now, in the midst of a storm of invading ships and 'Mechs, his troops were next to helpless. Granted, he still had two Stars of well-trained Elementals under his command, but ten of the hulking armored warriors would not last long against a determined assault by the attacking forces.

"Very well," Icaza said at last. "We will make no move against the invaders so long as they make no move against us." Turning to another technician, he snapped, "Prepare the HPG. I want to get an urgent message off to Strana Mechty. Khan Marthe Pryde must be informed of the situation immediately."

19

Knights of the Inner Sphere Operational Area
Smoke Jaguar Training Base, Shikari Jungle
Near New Andery, Huntress
Kerensky Cluster, Clan Space
12 March 3060

"Paladin, I have incoming 'Mechs. Grid five-five-four, three-seven-two. Engaging."

"Roger, Red One," Colonel Paul Masters replied to Dame Marie Yanika's concisely spoken message. "I am detaching Gold Two and Blue Two to support. Blue One, you'll have to thin out your line to take up the slack. I'll do the same."

"Roger, Paladin," came the reply from Sir Clovis Gainard.

The Knights of the Inner Sphere had made a successful landing at the Smoke Jaguar cadet training facility a few kilometers to the east of the city labeled New Andery on the maps provided by Trent. As lightly opposed as the task force's in-run to Huntress had been, the Knights' landing had been virtually uncontested. A single pass by two aging *Avar* OmniFighters had been the Jags' only attempt to slow down the Marik troops. The light aerospace craft were easily destroyed by the superior firepower massed by the Knights' DropShips.

With no other opposition in evidence, Masters made the decision to forego the risky high-altitude drop originally called for in his mission plan and to ground his DropShips, as well as those transporting Kingston's Legionnaires, the Capellan troops also assigned to the New Andery operation. As a landing zone Masters had selected a jungle clearing a few kilometers east of their objective.

The combined Knights/Legionnaires battle group moved swiftly from the landing zone to striking distance of their target, despite the thick equatorial jungle shrouding the Jaguar training camp. A pair of heavy *Galahad* fire-support 'Mechs, backed up by a trio of lighter machines, had been posted to guard duty outside the Clan installation. Unfortunately for the Jaguar warriors piloting those machines, the Inner Sphere force quickly overran their position without a single loss of its own.

The Knights and their Capellan allies didn't enjoy that level of success for long. Only three minutes after they hit the Jaguar base, the young Jaguar cadets had powered up their own 'Mechs and given as good as they got. Fifteen second-line Clan 'Mechs were destroyed in a short, sharp battle fought mostly at close quarters. Nine task force machines were put out of action, whether permanently or not, Masters didn't yet know. Another five got crippled so seriously that Masters, who had been assigned overall command of this particular phase of the operation, had to order them back to the DropShips for repair.

The combined battle group had little time for rest or repairs. Only thirty minutes after the last Jaguar cadet had been taken out of the fight, a sharp call from a Legionnaire picket rang from Masters' communicator. The Capellan warrior's initial report had been one of a large mixed force of light OmniMechs and Elementals. The Jaguar force was said to be closing rapidly on the Inner Sphere position from the west.

In response, Masters ordered the Legionnaires to pull back into readily defensible positions between the Jaguar relief force and the training base. His plan, as he laid it out for his subordinates, was for the smaller Capellan force to lay in wait for the Clan forces. Masters hoped to dupe them into believing that the Inner Sphere force was going to hang back and fight from static positions. At the same time, the Knights of the Inner Sphere would push out into the jungle flanking the Legionnaires' revetments. The thick log and earthen berms hastily thrown together after the base was initially secured would protect the Capellan troops, and hopefully cause the Jaguar commander to overextend his reach.

Masters smiled in satisfaction as he envisioned the Jaguar warriors, eager to come to grips with the foe who dared profane Huntress, leaping forward as fast as their 'Mechs could move. The lighter, faster, and consequently more thinly armored Omni-Mechs would be chewed to pieces by the Legionnaires' massed fire. As the incoming force got more strung out, the Knights would swing in on their flanks, to engage and destroy the enemy's heavier, slower machines.

Masters knew the ploy would work. It had been beautifully employed by the Eridani Light Horse against the Jade Falcons during the battle of Coventry. The difference here was that the Light Horse had had its positions in the outskirts of a city, with only scattered woods and low rolling hills to contend with. Here at New Andery, Masters was faced with detecting an incoming enemy through a thick, muddy jungle. Sensor ranges were so limited by the rain forest that Masters had to send out infantry pickets. Stationed just over a kilometer ahead of the Knights/Legionnaires' improved positions, the ground-pounders would watch and listen for the approach of the counterattack Masters knew was coming.

He felt little compunction about using deception against his enemies or borrowing a battle plan from the mercenary Light Horse. The Light Horse, though paid soldiers, had a proud and wily commander who was worthy of emulation. On the other hand, the Smoke Jaguars had proven themselves to be barbaric, unchivalrous foes, who seemed to take delight in exterminating their enemies to the last man. As a result Masters viewed the warriors of Clan Smoke Jaguar as a blight to be exterminated.

Despite his opposition to the wholesale destruction of the Jaguar Clan, he saw no contradiction in his stand. For him, the leaders of this militocracy, a society ruled by warriors, were to blame for the Clan invasion of the Inner Sphere and all of the suffering that accompanied it. If the ruling caste, the workers of evil, were destroyed, then the surviving Jaguars would be relatively harmless.

But before the Knights could accomplish this goal, they had to survive.

As the main body of the Jaguar relief force leapt forward to engage the Legionnaires, Masters' carefully laid battle plan was shattered by a report from his own pickets that another, larger Jaguar force was closing on the Knights' position. The commander of his Third Battalion, covering the Knights' right flank, reported a large number of Jaguars, mostly second-line 'Mechs and Elementals, approaching his position. As a result, Masters had to pull one company away from each of his other two battalions to reinforce the third.

"Paladin, this is Red One," came Yanika's voice from the communicator. "It looks like two full Trinaries of troops. I count at least thirty BattleMechs and as many Elementals. It's hard to tell because the blasted jungle is malfing up my sensors. I read mostly heavies, with a scattering of medium and light 'Mechs thrown in for good measure."

"Sit tight, Red One." Masters kept his voice level in spite of the apprehension rising in his gut. If the Jaguars had committed two full Trinaries, where was the rest of the Cluster? And where was the parent Galaxy? "Blue Two and Gold Two are on their way."

"Thanks, sir." Yanika's voice was tension-filled, and the transmission scratchy with static. "Tell 'em not to take too long, huh?"

"Will do, Red One." Masters switched channels. "Prefect, this is Paladin. Report please."

"Paladin, Prefect." Colonel Kingston shouted so loudly that Masters thought the Capellan commander almost didn't need a radio. "My First Battalion is under heavy attack. They report many Omnis and second-line 'Mechs, and many Elementals. Stand by."

Masters spared a glance at his *Anvil*'s tactical display. He studied the shallow arc in which the forces under his command were deployed. With the Knights on the right and the Legionnaires on the left, they half-encircled the southwest edge of New Andery and the nearby training base. According to the reports being steadily fed into his tactical computer, the Jaguars were split into two groups. One was attacking his right flank, as though to pin it in place, while a second, and apparently larger, unit was hitting the Legionnaires all along their front.

"Paladin, Prefect. You'd better come up and help us, Masters. We've got some real problems here!" Kingston's bellow carried a note of panic. "We're under heavy attack all along our lines. We're facing front-line OmniMechs. I say again front-line Omni-Mechs. Three full Trinaries or more." The message decayed into static as Kingston discharged his *Cataphract*'s extended-range PPC. "We aren't going to be able to hold out against this kind of pressure." Again the static-blanketed pause. "For God's sake, hurry!"

Masters glared at the tactical display for only the briefest of seconds.

"Red One, this is Paladin. Can you hold with the reinforcements I'm sending you?"

"I reckon I can," came the laconic reply.

"Good." Masters formed a hasty plan of battle and relayed it to his troops. "Third Battalion will stay in place. Beta Companies of First and Second Battalions are moving up to support him. The remainder of Gold and Blue Battalions will move to support Colonel Kingston. We will execute a left oblique and attack the Jaguars en echelon.

"I'm sorry, Knights, but we're out of time. This is the best we can do with what we've got. Now move!"

With a wave of his 'Mech's left hand, a gesture as old as organized warfare itself, Masters signaled his command lance to follow him.

It was slow going. The Shikari Jungle was thick with vines and creeper-enshrouded trees. The Knights' carefully formed ranks broke up in the dense rain forest. Warriors were separated from their lancemates. Lances lost contact with their company commanders. What Masters had envisioned as an elegant sweeping charge by two short battalions turned into a slow, clumsy overland hike by small groups of BattleMechs. All along the muddy, difficult, tree-cluttered way, Masters heard the crackle and roar of battle underlying Colonel Kingston's increasingly strident calls for help.

Suddenly a new voice broke from his radio earpieces.

"Contact! Contact! Blue Three-Five has contact with the enemy. Grid . . . Where the devil am I? Grid, eight-four-seven, six-five-five. I have three OmniMechs. One *Vulture* and two *Black Hawk*s. Holy crow! What the heck is that?"

The bright blue dot that represented Sir Jarvis Muto's *Thorn* winked out.

"Paladin, Paladin, this is Blue Three." Muto's company commander took up the call for help. "Colonel, we're meeting heavy resistance. Omnis and Elementals. And there's something else. Something the warbook can't identify." Static. "You've got to hurry."

"Masters to all Knights." No longer any need for codewords. The Jaguars knew who they were by now. "Everybody head straight in. Nobody waits. We all go in."

"Kingston?" No reply. "Kingston!"

"Yeah, Masters, I'm here." Despite his words, Kingston sounded like he was only partly there, as though the biggest part of his mind was drifting away on waves of shock and pain.

"Kingston, squawk your transponders," Masters barked. "We need to get a good fix on your positions."

In response, his tactical display lit up with a series of bright green flashes. Some detached, professional part of Masters' brain noted that there were far fewer of the transponder blips than when the New Andery operation had begun. Each missing signal meant a disabled 'Mech and possibly a dead MechWarrior.

"I've got it!" Masters shouted into his communicator. "All Knights, anything not squawking a friendly code is a Jaguar. Wipe 'em out."

With no warning whatsoever, a light and dark gray-mottled 'Mech appeared out of the steaming jungle. Masters pivoted his *Anvil*'s torso and lashed the enemy machine with a double, stuttering blast of laser fire. The target 'Mech staggered under the assault as Masters' pulse lasers burned more than a ton of armor from the Jaguar 'Mech's torso and legs. Recovering his balance, the Clan pilot savaged the *Anvil* with a blast of autocannon fire.

The *Anvil*'s computer finally identified the aggressor as a *Grendel,* one of the Smoke Jaguars' newer and less commonly seen designs. The big, dual-purpose gun mounted in the 'Mech's right arm told Masters that he was facing one of the variants, as the primary configuration of that 'Mech carried no such weapon. The *Anvil*'s warbook program sorted through Trent's intelligence report before determining that the crest was that of the Golden Fang sibko.

Masters leapt forward, again hammering the lighter Clan 'Mech with his heavy pulse lasers. The *Grendel,* as vicious and as tough as the Norse monster for which it was named, absorbed the punishment and replied with a savage blast of laser and cannon fire. Lowering the *Anvil*'s shoulder, he drove straight for his attacker. Then, at the last moment, he straightened and threw the *Anvil* into a twisting turn away from the *Grendel*.

The Jag pilot was fooled by his feint. Bracing his 'Mech to meet the onrushing enemy, he turned the *Grendel*'s torso slightly in an effort to deflect the impact of the attack that never came. Masters' impossibly graceful pirouette left him to the left of, and slightly behind, his opponent. Despite the heat that already made it hard to breathe in the *Anvil*'s sweltering cockpit, Masters punched his target interlock and fired his full weapons complement. The massive burst of laser energy clawed its way through the lightly armored 'Mech's torso. A stuttering flash lit the *Grendel*'s spine as ammunition exploded, blowing out its CASE panels.

Undaunted, the Jaguar pilot tried to turn his suddenly balky machine to face his assailant. Masters gave him no chance. Lifting the *Anvil*'s boxy forearms high overhead, he then brought them crashing down on the Jaguar's cockpit. The *Grendel* collapsed like a string-cut marionette.

Panting against the stifling heat of his cockpit, Masters searched the area for another target.

There. What was that? An Elemental?

The stunning dual impact of Clan lasers dispelled any illusion that Masters was facing one of the Clan's genetically engineered armored infantrymen. The gray-painted shape flitted through a mangrove thicket, moving more quickly than any Elemental Masters had ever seen. Four more of the six-meter-tall machines followed the first. The fast-moving gray shapes reminded him of half-scale BattleMechs.

Masters tried to bring his *Anvil*'s weapons to bear on the lead figure, but the red targeting pipper stubbornly refused to settle over the small, fast-moving target.

Blast it. It's like trying to target Elementals. Masters cursed bitterly as he wrestled with his controls, trying to lock on to the target. *All right, best guess.*

Bringing the crimson holographic dot as close as he could to the darting enemy, he jerked the triggers.

Two laser bursts, flashing a ghostly scarlet where they crossed the faint curtains of steam and smoke created by his fight with the *Grendel,* reached out for the enemy machine. Muddy soil exploded as the water-soaked ground suddenly flashed into vapor under the intense energy of Masters' attack. The lead enemy tumbled head over armored heels, blown off his feet by the steam explosion. Quickly, the Jaguar scrambled to his feet, ignoring the brown, gooey mud clinging to his armor.

A volley of laser and missile fire slammed into Masters' *Anvil*. He was stunned both by the ferocity of the attack and the fact that all five enemy machines had attacked him at once. He knew that the Clan code of honor forbade more than one MechWarrior from engaging any single enemy at the same time, and that the Jaguars were known as among the strictest adherents of the tradition. Elementals seemed to observe a modified version of this rule. No more than five of the hulking armored infantrymen could attack a single 'Mech, vehicle, or infantry platoon. Such conventions were one of the elements of Clan warfare that seemed to give an essentially ugly business a game-like atmosphere among them. It was part of the reason Task Force Serpent had come to Huntress, to convince the Clans that war was not a game. And to teach them the price of it.

Again Masters leveled his weapons at a single target and loosed the hellish blast. This time, he had more luck. One strobing lance of coherent light ripped into the lead target's chest. The machine staggered, but did not fall.

God in Heaven. Masters could not believe what he was seeing. *That blast would have killed an Elemental, and that thing shakes it off like it got hit with a bean bag.*

Again the enemy machines fired a volley. Lasers, autocannon fire, and missiles ripped into his 'Mech's armor. Amber warning lights on his console told of a damaged actuator package in his *Anvil*'s left knee and of a shattered heat sink. If he couldn't do something to stop the miniature BattleMechs, they'd quickly bring him down, like a pack of hyenas worrying at a lion.

Faintly, through the noise baffles shielding his ears, Masters heard the deep-throated roar of a heavy autocannon. A stream of orange-glowing tracers flashed past his cockpit to rip into the enemy's ranks. Exploding shells showered mud and death across the tiny jungle clearing. Still spewing autocannon fire, an oddly shaped *Champion* stepped up beside him. The 'Mech's mud-spattered gold-on-black paint job told him it belonged to one of his Knights. The sword-wielding lion painted beneath the outthrust cockpit identified the pilot as Sir Gavin Ellis, one of the original Knights of the Inner Sphere.

"Thought you could use some help, Colonel."

Ellis didn't wait for a reply, but hit the miniature 'Mechs with another burst of autocannon fire. The relatively tiny submunitions packed into each autocannon shell scattered across the now-depleted ranks of Clan war machines. Masters added his heavy pulse lasers to the hellstorm lashing the enemy position. When the steam and smoke cleared, Masters saw nothing but the broken hulks of wrecked Jaguar 'Mechs.

"What in Blake's name were those things?" Ellis called across the comm channel.

"I don't know," Masters returned. "Trent reported that the Smoke Jaguars were developing some new weapon systems. I assumed he meant new guns or new OmniMechs like the ones we've seen in the past. But this?" Masters waved toward the shattered Clan machines, though there was no way Ellis could have seen the gesture. "We had no idea the Jags were working on some kind of super Elemental."

Ellis didn't reply.

"All right, Ellis." Masters waved his 'Mech's right arm in the direction of the enemy's last reported position. "We'd better get going and pull Kingston's fat out of the fire."

Pulling Colonel Kingston's fat out of the fire proved far more difficult than Paul Masters could have anticipated. The sudden flank attack by the Knights broke the impetus of the Jaguars' attack, allowing Kingston to disengage from the Clan spearhead elements and withdraw his battered troops to a prepared fall-back position. The Knights took advantage of the confusion their attack had caused in the Jaguar ranks, and drove a wedge of death and destruction into their midst.

But, the advantage didn't last for long. The Jaguar relief force had been comprised of a mixture of second-line BattleMechs and Elementals, accompanied by a full Trinary of the "super Elementals," which Masters had taken to calling "Ocelots" because they were smaller versions of standard Jaguar 'Mechs. Despite the combined weight of the Knights and the Legionnaires, the Inner Sphere force was pushed relentlessly back through the thick jungle. Masters and Kingston put up a determined struggle, selling every meter of ground dearly, but the hard-to-hit Ocelots and the superior hitting power of their larger cousins took a deadly toll on the invaders-turned-defenders.

At 1830 hours, after four hours of hit-and-run fighting, the

Jaguars retook the training base. But even then, they weren't satisfied. The Clan relief force kept pushing the Knights and Legionnaires until the Inner Sphere force was driven back to the outskirts of New Andery.

The Knights' Third Battalion, which had been left in place to pin down the Jaguars' northern column, had fared better, forcing the bulk of the second-line 'Mechs to retire in disorder, and destroying those who tried to stay and fight it out. But Masters had to order the surviving Knights to pull back into New Andery to avoid having them cut off and destroyed.

As darkness began to settle over the jungle, a lull in the fighting occurred, as though by mutual consent between the Jaguars and the invaders. Taking advantage of the momentary and undeclared truce, Masters held a radio council of war with his battalion commanders and Colonel Kingston. With the three Knight battalion commanders, Kingston, his two surviving majors, and Masters all present, not to mention a yeoman and a communications operator, the small command van was hot, stuffy, and cramped.

"We're down below half strength, gentlemen," Master said. "The Legionnaires have taken nearly sixty-eight percent casualties. We can call for the DropShips and attempt a dust-off under fire, we can retreat into the jungle and wage a guerrilla campaign until General Winston can spare some troops to relieve us, or we can stay and fight it out."

"Stay and fight," Kingston snarled. "I'm not giving up, not after losing so many of my men. We can fall back into the city, throw up barricades, fight street to street. If we have to, we can call in an air strike, or even naval bombardment, but I'm not leaving."

"I'd have to agree with Colonel Kingston, sir," Sir Gainard chimed in. "All but that part about fighting street to street. If we pull back, it'll have to be into the jungle, not the city. If we make this a street-fight, a whole lot of civilians are going to get killed."

"So what? They're Jags," Kingston barked.

"They're people, Mister Kingston." Gainard's voice came out in a low growl.

"Sir Gainard is right. I will not order the Knights to engage in a street-fight." Masters, seeing that Kingston was about to launch into a blistering attack on Gainard, waved both men to silence.

"And I don't think we'll be able to call in accurate naval gun fire. The jungle is far too thick, and our spotters would have to be far too close."

"Then the only thing left is to withdraw into the jungle," Sir Gainard said.

"Not so," Dame Yanika interrupted. "There's another alternative. We can contact Dancer and ask for reinforcements."

"I agree." Masters nodded. "We can't leave, and we can't hold out by ourselves. We have to ask for help."

Without waiting for agreement from the others, he turned to the commo tech and requested a direct line to General Winston.

"Dancer, this is Paladin." The codenames had been assigned even before the task force left Defiance, nearly a year ago. "Paladin Group and Lorica Group have met with heavy resistance. We have taken very heavy casualties and are in danger of being driven off objective. Request immediate reinforcement. Over."

For a moment, Masters was not sure his encrypted, time-compressed message had gotten through. Then Winston's deep, contralto voice broke from the communicator.

"Paladin? Dancer. Sword One and Two are en route, and should be arriving your position any hour. Can you hold? Over."

"Dancer, we can hold, but tell Sword not to take too long. If the Jags launch another determined assault, we will have to withdraw. Over."

"Roger, Paladin. I understand." Masters could almost see Winston giving that slow, thoughtful nod she often used to indicate her comprehension of a grave situation. "I'll tell them not to pick up any hitchhikers. Dancer is clear."

"That's it then, gentlemen." Masters sighed as he stood up from the tiny conference table, being careful not to bang his head on the command van's steel top. "We wait for the Com Guards. Meanwhile see to your troops. Make whatever repairs you can. I understand we have some supplies, mostly ammunition looted from the training base. So top off your magazines. If you can, try to get your cooks going and get some hot food into your people. They probably need it.

"I also want you to post pickets two hundred meters in advance of your positions and two hundred meters off your flanks. That'll give us just about one minute's warning if the Jags come calling again, and I'm sure they will."

Paul Masters' belief that the Smoke Jaguars would pay yet another visit to the battered forces under his command was correct. Less than an hour after receiving Ariana Winston's promise of reinforcements, before most of his troops had reloaded their depleted ammunition loads or had eaten more than a few mouthfuls of their quickly heated field rations, an observation/listening post stationed in front of the Knights' sorely abused First Battalion shouted the alarm.

Masters dropped the brown plastic bag filled with barely warm chicken and rice, and sprinted toward his 'Mech. The *Anvil* still showed the blackened, pitted scars where the Ocelots had savaged his armor. In a few places, the hardened steel was so deeply scored that a single, heavy attack would pierce the 'Mech's skin, reaching the delicate inner components. But he gave the damage as little thought as he did his spilled dinner. The enemy was coming, and the Knights' chivalric oath dictated that he ride out to meet them.

Through the gathering gloom of evening, Masters picked out the faint thermal traces of three infantrymen running hard through the thick jungle. These had to be the pickets who'd shouted the alarm, pulling back to the relative safety of the Inner Sphere line.

"Paladin to all commands," Masters said over the broad band. "Remember, if we are forced to withdraw, do not, I say again, do not withdraw through the city. If at all possible, move around to the east and west. We will reform at the predesignated rally point.

"Now, let's go get 'em."

Shoving his controls fully forward, Masters urged his sixty-ton mount into a lumbering run. A small knot of bright heat sources glimmered at him through the trees. Pulling up short, he leveled his weapons at the thermal trace, held the bead for a split second, and then fired.

Instantly, the glowing targets disappeared, hidden from his infrared detectors by the superheated steam of muddy earth flash-heated by a missed laser shot. When the cloud dissipated, one of the small targets lay on the jungle floor, cooling rapidly. The others turned and unleashed a volley of short-range missiles at his 'Mech. The anti-armor warheads peppered the *Anvil*'s legs and lower torso, causing another warning light to flare on the 'Mech Status Display.

Another heat sink gone. I'll really have to watch the temp now.

Masters picked off another of the little targets, now revealed to be Elementals in the ghostly black and green world of his infrared sensors. Machine gun and laser fire snapped and rattled in reply. From his right side, a flight of missiles hammered into the remaining trio of Elementals, silencing their attacks forever.

Before Masters could thank the pilot of the red and white-crested *Trebuchet,* a Jaguar *Hunchback IIc* stepped from the trees and blasted the Knights' missile platform into scrap.

Masters screamed his inarticulate rage at the Jaguar warrior, and poured twin streams of pulsing laser fire into the barrel-chested 'Mech. The ugly machine barely seemed to notice the attack as it pivoted to bring its huge, 'Mech-eating autocannons to bear on the already-damaged *Anvil.* Desperately, ignoring his already soaring heat indicators, Masters poured laser fire into the Clan *Hunchback,* hoping against hope to cripple the armored monster before it brought the gaping maws of its twin guns to bear on his 'Mech.

Too late! The thought flashed across Masters' mind as the boxy, Class 20 autocannons were obscured by twin muzzle flashes. Each gout of smoke and flame was at least three meters across. The *Hunchback* seemed to rock backward under the tremendous recoil of the paired weapons. With a crack, audible over the thundering roar of the exploding shells, the *Anvil*'s right leg snapped off at the knee. Masters braced himself for the shattering impact as the sixty-ton 'Mech crashed to the ground. The shock of hitting the muddy earth slammed his neurohelmeted head into the right-side instrument panel. His vision clouded over with red and gold stars. His entire body screamed with pain.

When he could see again, Masters noted with horror that every warning light in his cockpit was lit up. In the center of the main console a seven-centimeter bar flared the scarlet word FIRE. Painfully, Masters reached out and slapped the button that activated the *Anvil*'s fire-suppression system. The warning bar remained stubbornly lit. Again, he hammered the mushroom-shaped button. Again, nothing happened. Fighting a rising tide of panic, he tried a third time, smashing the base of his fist down on the control with enough force to snap off one edge of the large plastic stud. This time he was rewarded with the faint hissing of compressed fire-fighting gas as it flooded into the 'Mech's engine compartment.

Fighting the pain and shock that threatened to drag him into unconsciousness, Masters heaved himself out of his command couch. Tearing at the latches securing the heavy neurohelmet to the padded collar of his cooling vest, he lifted the device from his shoulders. The action seemed to drain away what little strength was left to him. For a few seconds he gazed in dumb amazement at the deep crease in the helmet's thick metal shell. A corresponding dent in the main weapons panel showed where his head had slammed into the steel console. It was a wonder he was still conscious.

Fighting his own body, which wanted nothing more than to lie down and rest, Masters unlocked the *Anvil*'s cockpit hatch, but hadn't the strength to swing the heavy, armored door open. Too exhausted and in too much pain to wrestle with the hatch, he simply slapped the emergency egress button and blew the door off its hinges.

Through the open hatch, Masters heard the deafening roar and crackle of gunfire. Dropping heavily to the ground, he turned to what he thought was the north and began a slow, staggering run. He had to make it back to his command post, not because he was afraid of being taken prisoner, but because his sense of duty demanded that he take control of the bitter struggle of his Knights against the Jaguars.

I'm never going to make it. Masters rebuked the thought the moment it sprang into his head. *I have to make it,* he told himself. *I have to.*

A dull throbbing rumble blanketed the battlefield, drowning out even the clamor of battle. Masters looked up, trying to locate the source of the prolonged thunder. A few hundred meters to the southeast hovered a huge, spherical shadow, lit from beneath by the blazing drive flares of its massive engines. Smaller jets of flame showed where dropping BattleMechs were descending onto the battlefield, some of them landing almost on top of the Jaguar positions.

The Com Guards had arrived.

* * *

Forty-five minutes later, it was all over. The Smoke Jaguar resistance collapsed under the weight of the attack by fresh Com Guard troops, augmented by the battle-weary Knights and Legionnaires.

Paul Masters was picked up by a Legionnaire infantry platoon and hustled back to his command post. There, while medics treated him for shock, exhaustion, and a knot on his head the size of a child's fist, Precentor-cum-Colonel Regis Grandi filled him in on the outcome of the battle.

"When we arrived and started our drop, I thought the Jaguars were going to stick around and fight it out. And they did, at least for a while. But someone must have gotten their coordinates torqued up, 'cause my Second Battalion dropped right on top of the Jags' front lines. Blake's blood, wasn't that a mess. For the first few minutes it was hand-to-hand. We were so closely engaged that everybody was afraid to fire for fear of hitting a friend. It took a while to get things sorted out, but we managed to form a sort of half-baked battle line and start pushing the Jags. First Battalion landed more or less where they were supposed to, and came in on the Clanners' left flank.

"After that they folded up pretty quickly. Your Knights and the Legionnaires swung down on the Jags' right and kinda closed the door on them. The only way they had to retreat was south, toward the river. We chased them about two klicks before we figured enough was enough. I doubt more than a dozen of 'em made it to the river alive."

"Casualties?" Masters asked, fighting the grogginess of the mild concussion the medics said he'd sustained when his head hit the weapons console.

"Bad," Sir Gainard told him. "We're down by fifty percent. That's non-recoverable losses, including your *Anvil* and Dame Yanika. She lost both legs when her *Bombardier* exploded. The medics say she'll probably live, but she'll never pilot a 'Mech again." Gainard swallowed hard against the emotion of losing a comrade in arms, then continued. "Colonel Kingston is alive. He's wounded, but he can still fight. His *Guillotine* is pretty shot up, but the techs tell me it can be fixed, given enough time and access to enough spare parts. His regiment is another story. They're down to about thirty percent, maybe thirty-five, if his recovery crews work a couple of miracles."

"What about the Com Guards?"

"Don't worry about us, Colonel." Grandi smiled thinly. "We took about half a dozen non-recoverables. We have a handful of damaged, but repairable 'Mechs, and most of those should be on-line in an hour or so. Two of my pilots are dead, and five are wounded. We'll be able to hold.

"The good news is we chased the Jags clean off the training base before they had a chance to sabotage or destroy anything. I've infantrymen going over the place now, looking for any stay-behind forces, but I think we're all clear. There aren't enough Jags left in New Andery to put up any kind of a scrap."

Masters sighed in exhaustion. "Sir Gainard, please contact General Winston. Tell her New Andery is secure."

20

Northwind Highlanders Operational Area
Factory Complex near Pahn City
Huntress
Kerensky Cluster, Clan Space
12 March 3060

"What is that sound?" Star Colonel Cara's voice was a snarl of anger as she slammed her hand down on her *Stormcrow-B*'s communications panel, shutting off the unearthly wail that had been boring into her ears. Whatever it was, it was not electronic interference. Her OmniMech's computer had been programmed to recognize and overcome just about every type of jamming signal that either the Inner Sphere or the Clans could generate. Nor was the painful squeal the result of any natural phenomenon. The noise had enough variation in pitch, cadence, and volume to suggest that it was man-made. Cara supposed that the sound could even be music, but the musician, as well as his listeners, would have to be stark, staring mad, and completely tone-deaf to enjoy the tortured-cat howl that was cutting across all of her Cluster's communications frequencies.

The screeching had begun over an hour before local dawn, just as the sensor operators at Pahn City's small spaceport detected the radar tracks of incoming DropShips. The lunatic wail had continued, even increased in volume, until her troops were forced to communicate by hand-signals and line-of-sight, laser-based communication links. The invaders seemed to be taking no pains to conceal their presence, or their course, which put them on a direct line-of-approach to the Pahn City factory complex, so the jamming of the communications channels made no practical sense.

The primary effect of the nerve-scraping howl was to set the Jaguar warriors' teeth and humor on edge.

"Somebody tell me what that *stravag* noise is!"

"Star Colonel, this is Scout Star One-one." The message had to be relayed through several short-range lasercom links before it reached the Cluster command center. "We have reached the enemy's landing zone. He is off-loading his 'Mechs.

"Freebirth! The enemy is showing the crest of the Star League and the Roy . . ."

The message ended in mid-word to the accompaniment of a crash of static.

"Scout One-one, this is Star Colonel Cara, repeat your message."

There was no reply.

"Scout One-one. Repeat your message."

The silence on the lasercom channel only served to mock her angry, frustrated attempts to contact her scout section leader.

"Star Colonel, this is Striker Star Three, Point Commander Rurik." A different voice broke from her helmet-mounted speakers, a voice tight with barely controlled rage. "We have contact with the enemy. My computer says that they are the Northwind Highlanders, but there is something else. All of the attackers are wearing the Cameron Star and the insignia of the Star League Defense Force."

"What?"

"Aff, Star Colonel, the attackers are claiming to be the Star League Defense Force."

The insult was almost more than Cara could bear. She had heard rumors that an Inner Sphere force had managed to drive into Clan space, all the way to Huntress, and that some of those forces had crept into Mount Szabo and destroyed the planet's main C3 center. Not that it mattered much. The back-up facility in the heart of Lootera, Huntress' largest and capital city, was more than adequate to coordinate the defense of the Smoke Jaguar homeworld.

Other tales claimed that enemy forces, probably belonging to the Inner Sphere, had attacked and seized the Field of Heroes, as well as the genetic repository. Such a tale was too horrible in its implications to consider. Not even the filthy, honorless barbarians of the Inner Sphere could be so depraved as to threaten the future of Jaguar warrior bloodlines. Then, just when Cara thought she had heard the final insult, the invaders descended to a lower, even greater abomination. The lucrewarriors of the Northwind Highlanders were claiming to represent the Star League.

"Attention, all commands." Cara's voice dropped to a low, threatening growl. "Converge on Striker Star One's position. Engage and destroy the invaders. I do not want even one of the *surats* to survive. Command Star, on me."

With a degree of force that seemed to threaten to rip the instrument from its armrest mounting, Cara shoved her joystick straight forward, launching her fifty-five ton machine into a jolting run. Having a top speed of nearly one hundred kilometers per hour, the odd-looking OmniMech ate up the ground in ten-meter strides. Behind her ran four second-line 'Mechs. Unfortunately, each of the pilots driving those machines were also "second-line." They had either tested out so near the bottom of their sibkos that they did not merit postings to the Inner Sphere, even as garrison troops, or they were solahma.

Cara had always believed the name of her Galaxy to be a bad joke. "The Watchmen," they were called. But here on Huntress, who was there to watch for? And now it seemed the joke was on the front-line warriors of her Clan. The barbarians had somehow made their way here from the Inner Sphere to strike at the Jaguar homeworld, and now it was up to the solahma troops of The Watchmen and their brother Galaxy, the Iron Guard, to defend Huntress.

Still, whether her troops were untested, bottom-of-their-sibko misfits or worn-out has-beens, they were all she had. Cara knew that each would fight to the best of his or her ability, and perhaps even beyond, to drive the invaders from Huntress.

As her forces crashed through the thick foliage of the forest surrounding Pahn City, she began to hear the rattle and thunder of a 'Mech battle in progress. Glancing at her tactical display, she realized that the Highlanders had not bothered to make any attempt at jamming their enemy's sensors. The only interference that remained was that raucous, screeching wail that clogged every communication channel.

Suddenly, a short, angular-chested BattleMech painted in an eye-twisting green and blue plaid loomed up before her. The Highlander machine leveled its right arm at her *Stormcrow,* an arm that ended not in a hand, but in the gaping maw of a heavy autocannon. The cylindrical gun vomited smoke and flame, as high-explosive, armor-piercing shells slammed into her Omni-Mech's back-canting knee.

Cara fought her reeling 'Mech, and recovered her balance only a few dozen meters from her assailant. The computer-generated label identified the Highlander machine as a *Centurion,* an Inner Sphere design somewhat lighter than her *Stormcrow,* but possessed of a rapid-fire, dual-purpose autocannon and hyper-accurate guided missiles. Those facts barely registered in Cara's mind. Acting on reflex, she dropped a targeting pipper over the *Centurion*'s center of mass and thumbed the trigger.

Cara's odd-looking mount trembled like a man with a fever as the stubby-barreled autocannon replacing its left forearm belched out a plume of flame and steel. The massive projectiles slammed into the *Centurion*'s right arm, just above the gun mount. Armor shattered under the hammer blows of the armor-piercing shells. For good measure, Cara added a trio of laser bolts from the hexagonal cluster of weapons set into her 'Mech's right wrist. She didn't want to risk firing all her extended-range medium lasers. The waste heat generated by such a blast might have been enough to send her 'Mech into immediate shutdown. As it was, the wave of heat that flooded the cockpit of the suddenly sluggish *Stormcrow* brought beads of sweat out on her forehead.

For the Highlander *Centurion* the effect of the volley was even more devastating. One of the powerful beams of coherent light slashed into the invader 'Mech's right arm, melting the last intact slivers of the endo-steel bone exposed and savaged by the cannon blast. The plaid machine's big autocannon dropped to the ground with an audible thud.

As the *Stormcrow*'s highly efficient heat sinks brought the 'Mech's unbelievable internal temperature down to a more bearable level, Cara stepped in closer to the crippled enemy machine. Fire bloomed out of the *Centurion*'s chest-mounted long-range missile launcher. Most of the anti-armor missiles flew wide. Those that found their mark merely broke up on impact with her OmniMech's armored hide. The lucrewarrior at the *Centurion*'s controls had gambled and lost that his missiles would arm themselves inside their 180-meter minimum range. Still, the impact of a volley of unarmed eight-kilo rockets slamming into the *Stormcrow*'s torso was enough to cause Cara's 'Mech to stumble.

Recovering her balance, she loosed a close-range blast of autocannon fire, which tore into the invader machine's laser-damaged torso. The long-range missile launcher exploded under the impact of the heavy shells, leaving the *Centurion* only a pair of medium lasers with which to continue the fight. Brave though the Highlander might have been, he was no fool. Cara saw the 'Mech's head split open, followed by a bright gout of flame as the lucrewarrior ejected from his disabled mount.

Before the Highlander's escape parachute had fully deployed, a hammer blow to the right side of her *Stormcrow*'s head left Cara with a throbbing ringing in her ears. Spinning to face the new threat, she was confronted with a sight verging on obscenity of the vilest degree. A round-shouldered *Wyvern,* painted in the same garish green and blue plaid as the recently slain *Centurion,* leveled its arm-mounted lasers at her 'Mech. Just as her scouts had reported, all of the lucrewarriors bore the sacred Cameron Star and the insignia of the Star League Defense Force, emblems which no Clan warrior, however proud, would have dared to paint on his 'Mech. Unlike the *Centurion,* the *Wyvern* was an old Star League design, recently revived by the Inner Sphere.

Still, as arrogant as the display of those crests might be, displayed as they were on a barbaric lucrewarrior's machine, there was yet a third insignia brazenly carried on the *Wyvern*'s left breast that fanned the flame of Cara's righteous anger into a blaze of fury. The battle machine in front of her, and several others now rushing in upon her position, all bore the crest of the Royal Black Watch, the very unit charged with protecting the First Lord of the Star League.

Is there no end to their effrontery?

Spitting a stream of the vilest curses she could summon, Cara flung her fifty-five ton machine to the left, causing the mercenary pilot to pivot in a vain attempt to maintain his targeting lock. Green darts of light energy flashed past her 'Mech's cockpit.

Seething with unutterable fury, she locked the *Stormcrow*'s massive autocannon onto the center of the invader 'Mech. A squeeze of the trigger sent a volley of high-explosive shells ripping into the *Wyvern*'s thinner armor. The smaller 'Mech staggered under the thundering impact.

Cara gave the lucrewarrior no time to recover. She leapt forward, snarling like her Clan's enraged totem. Though her *Stormcrow*'s arms were thin, almost spindly, they were possessed of great strength. Clenching her 'Mech's right hand, she drove the steel fist hard into the Highlander 'Mech's damaged shoulder. The *Wyvern* staggered under the blow. Again and again she battered at the enemy machine until it collapsed into a heap.

Panting for breath, as though she had smashed the forty-five-ton BattleMech into scrap with her own hands, Cara glared at her tactical monitor, searching furiously for another opponent upon whom to vent her wrath. The nearest enemy machine was several hundred meters away, and was entangled in a close-range pounding match with a member of her command Star. All around them, the battle raged.

Glancing at the tactical display, the reality of the situation dawned upon her. The Northwind Highlanders had a solid grasp of the effect their abhorrent display of the symbols of the Star League Defense Force and the Royal Black Watch Regiment would have on the Smoke Jaguars. In an effort to reach the Black Watch 'Mechs, the lead elements of her force had bypassed other, more dangerous opponents, and the balance of her command seemed to have the same fanatic determination to come to grips with the barbarians and expunge the Highlanders' arrogance in their own gore. Meanwhile, the balance of the Highlanders had a clear road, straight into Pahn City.

Cara began screaming orders into her communicator, desperately trying to regain some control of the situation, but her words were overpowered, swallowed whole by the skirling wail that jammed the unit's tactical frequencies. Hurriedly, she programmed her lasercom system to repeat her message at the touch of a key, and began targeting the secure, line-of-sight communicator at each of her subordinates in turn. In each case the message was the same: "Break off and pull back."

The idea of ordering her warriors to disengage with a known enemy was so foreign to Cara that she had difficulty in giving the order. Still, she knew it was the right thing to do. If her troops spent themselves in destroying the Black Watch, the rest of the Northwind Highlanders would bypass her troops to sweep into Pahn City and destroy the factory complex she had been charged with protecting.

"Star Colonel," her communicator squawked. For a moment, Cara believed that the jamming had cleared. Then she realized that the message was being sent via a laser-comm relay.

"There are enemy BattleMechs less than three kilometers from the factory." The voice shouting at her from the communications system was that of Star Captain Ezra, the solahma officer she had left in charge of the factory. "We count at least a full regiment, Star Colonel. Some of the technicians here are asking permission to take the field in defense of the complex and their homeworld."

Cara was unsure of what angered her more, the lucrewarriors' display of the ancient, and revered Star League emblems, or the idea of lower-caste technicians and laborers actually asking for permission to assume a privilege afforded only to warriors, the right to pilot a fully armed and operational BattleMech. For now, she could do nothing about the former, but she would die rather than allow the latter. The affront to the Clan's and to her personal honor would be too great to bear, and damn this outdated shell of a warrior for even asking such a thing.

"Neg!" she snarled in reply. "The factory complex, and Huntress, will stand or fall on the strength of our warriors. I will not entrust the safety of either to lower-castemen."

"Star Colonel, may I remind you that some of those lower-castemen were born into the warrior caste?" It took a few seconds for the message and the reply to be relayed across the battlefield. "They are lower caste only because they failed their Trials of Position."

"*I said no,* Star Captain!" Cara screamed, the rage in her heart making her voice crack. "If you *dare* question my decision again, we will meet in a Circle of Equals, *quiaff?*"

"Aff, Star Colonel. I understand. I only hope your decision will not condemn us both to death or disgrace."

* * *

"Colonel, Ah'm gettin' a good bit o' interference here. I think all th' lights and motors and structural steel an' such is malfin' up my sensors."

At least we've got little need for tactical encryption. Colonel William MacLeod laughed to himself at the heavy burr in the voice coming over the commline. *We can understand ourselves an' each other, but I doubt anyone else this side of Glengarry can.*

Indeed, many troopers who had fought alongside the displaced Scotsmen of the Northwind Highlanders had complained, sometimes bitterly, that they could barely understand the broad, rolling burr with which many Highlanders spoke. MacLeod's own speech could easily lapse into the dialect when he was especially excited, angry, or provoked.

"Do th' best ye can, Sergeant. Remember our intel says there's the better part of a Cluster out here, an' we've only seen a couple o' Stars." MacLeod glanced at his tactical display, noting that the recon lance leader to whom he was speaking had breached the chain-link fence surrounding the Highlanders' objective factory. "Keep yer eyes open, boy. I wouldn't trust the Jags any further than I could toss my 'Mech. The rest o' the *sassanach* have got to be around somewhere."

William MacLeod had been pleased with his unit's performance up to that point. They had grounded right on schedule without having to resort to a hot 'Mech drop, and had swept the initial Clan resistance from the field. He grinned inside his neurohelmet at the thought of the Jaguar commanders trying to coordinate their forces, all the while unable to communicate because of the Highlanders' unique form of jamming. Thanks to Trent, who had provided data regarding the Huntress garrison's tactical radio frequencies, the Smoke Jaguars protecting the factory were unable to communicate with each other.

MacLeod had detailed the Highlander bagpipers to flood the Clanners' air waves with the skirling strains of *Sound the Pibroch* and *The Killicrankie*. While the Highlanders might find the sound inspiring, MacLeod could picture the Jag commanders literally tearing their hair out at the blanket of pipe tunes clogging their radios.

"Dundee to all Highland commands." MacLeod had chosen the name of the leader of the first Jacobite Rebellion on Terra as his codename. "Move in on th' factory, but keep yer peepers peeled."

"Contact! Contact!" The excited shout rang across the Highlanders' tactical frequency like a plate of armor steel dropped from a repair scaffold. "Dundee, this is Targe One. I have contact with many hostiles, I say again *many* hostiles. They're comin' outta the bluidy woodwork. Targe Group is engaging. Targe One requests ye get us some immediate back-up."

"What have you got, Targe One?" MacLeod glanced again at his tactical display to see that Targe Group, in reality a company of his own regiment's First Battalion, was south and west of the factory proper. Targe One would be Captain Micheil McClannaugh, the company commander. The tactical feed coming from McClannaugh's *Trebuchet* showed a large number of contacts swarming out of the big assembly building to engage the mercenaries at close range.

Now, that's torqued up, MacLeod told himself. *The contacts are too small to be BattleMechs, and too big to be Elementals.*

"Dundee, I am in contact with enemy units, twenty or more, of an unknown type," McClannaugh replied. "I dinna ken what they are. At first I thought they were Elementals, but they're bigger than Toads, an' they hit harder. Kin ye get us some help?"

"Roger, Targe One, help is on th' way. Claymore, you're closest. Swing 'round on Targe's left flank, then you'll have the *sassanach* between you."

Sassenach was a name more properly applied to the English who had long ago held Scotland in their iron grip, despite the best efforts of such men as William Wallace and John Graham Claverhouse of Dundee. The word, alternately meaning foreigner and enemy, fit the Smoke Jaguars in both translations. To the Highlanders the word was nearly a profanity.

"Dundee, this is Claymore One, we're on th' way, sair."

Before MacLeod could reply, the cry of "Contact!" rang in his ears once more. This time the enemy was much closer. In fact, they were right in front of him.

A dozen misshapen figures, too tall and bulky to be Elementals, yet too small and fast to be BattleMechs, the figures looked to be something out of a nightmare. The squat machine closest to his *Huron Warrior* proved that it was no phantasm by leveling a stubby gun barrel, as thick as its own head, and loosing a terrific blast of raw energy at MacLeod's 'Mech. The blast of laser energy splintered much of the armor covering the *Warrior*'s right breast.

In response MacLeod pointed his right arm at the darting figure and triggered the Grizzard Gauss rifle mounted in that vambrace. The hypersonic slug streaked across the intervening gap to smash his assailant into dust. But, the fast-moving miniature 'Mech wasn't there when the Gauss slug arrived. So rapid was its movement that MacLeod had trouble tracking his target effectively. The head-size chunk of nickel-iron slammed into the ferrocrete pavement of the factory compound, throwing shards of gray, iron-reinforced concrete around like shrapnel. MacLeod tried to walk fire from his pulse laser into the enemy machine, but the Clanner moved too quickly for his 'Mech's pivoting torso to follow. The strobing laser bolts slashed into one of the factory buildings, leaving a series of smoking holes in their wake.

The miniature BattleMech fired again. This time its speed worked against it, as the poorly aimed laser bolt flashed past MacLeod's *Warrior* with several meters to spare. Pivoting to follow the smaller machine, MacLeod unleashed a stuttering volley from his 'Mech's pulse laser. The flickering darts of energy, normally invisible, but detectable only because of the smoke and dust choking the air of the factory complex, slashed into the little aggressor's legs. The Clan 'Mech stumbled, but didn't go down. Instead, the pilot fired yet a third blast from his anti-'Mech laser.

The powerful beam of coherent light savaged the *Warrior*'s left leg, causing MacLeod to miss a step in his pursuit of his tiny, but dangerous opponent. It was that very stagger which brought about the destruction of the miniature 'Mech. While struggling to keep his reeling 'Mech on its feet, MacLeod fired a wild volley from all of his *Warrior*'s weapons. Two blasts of laser fire lanced past the Clanner to scorch the side of a storage shed, but the hastily aimed Gauss slug found its mark. The heavy metal ball smashed into the Jaguar's chest, reducing the enemy machine to scrap.

Bloody hell! MacLeod was open-mouthed in horrified amazement. *It took a bloody Gauss slug to kill that little armored boggart.*

All around him, the members of MacLeod's command company were engaged in close-range battles with the small, 'Mech-like machines. But there were other Jaguar forces on the way, and these newcomers were piloting the defenders' larger, more powerful cousins.

"Dundee to all commands, fall back on Schiltron Group. We've got Jag 'Mechs inbound and we need to regroup. I say again, fall back on Schiltron Group."

Several hours later, the fighting in and around Pahn City subsided. MacLeod successfully reformed his unit and launched a fresh assault on the factory complex. Fifteen Smoke Jaguar Mech-Warriors were sent to the Kerenskys, along with a dozen of the miniature BattleMechs, which the Highlanders had taken to calling Boggarts, after a particularly annoying type of Celtic goblin.

The pilots of the half-scale 'Mechs were thin and wiry, looking more like a Clan aerospace pilot than either a hulking Elemental or a MechWarrior. Dark blue geometric shapes like angular tattoos laced their arms, legs, and faces. It was apparent to the salvage crew that the enhanced-imaging neural interface, whose subcutaneous circuits produced the tattooing effect, must be necessary to operate the miniature 'Mechs.

When Colonel MacLeod learned of the Boggarts' recovery, he passed an order to all of the Highlander recovery crews. Every effort should be made to salvage as many of the small battle machines as was practicable. The teams of BattleMech-supported infantrymen clearing the factory complex itself of the last vestiges of Jaguar resistance were similarly told that the complex itself should be kept intact if possible. Any blueprints, technical readouts, or control programs concerning the miniature Battle-Mechs were to be located and seized. Finally, three of the Highlander DropShips were called in to take aboard the salvaged war machines.

MacLeod acknowledged the order, but there was little evidence of joy over his coup in his voice. He handed the radio handset back to the commo tech and flopped back heavily against the armored sides of the Highlander command truck. Across the narrow strip of ferrocrete that marked the edge of the Pahn City factory complex, MacLeod saw the dark forms of a burial detail carrying heavy bundles toward the forest, where they would be interred. At least thirty of those plastic-bagged bodies belonged to his men. He had no accurate count of how many Jaguars had died in the struggle for the factory.

From his position outside the complex's main administration

building, MacLeod could hear a constant metallic bang and clatter coming from one of the large 'Mech assembly buildings a few dozen meters away. Unlike men, the 'Mechs could be repaired.

MacLeod's report to General Winston stated flatly that, given their losses in men and machines, the Highlanders might be able to hold out against another push by Jaguar BattleMechs, but that if the enemy brought up a sizable force, the mercenaries would be forced to abandon the complex.

═══ 21 ═══

Fox Team Operational Area
Near Falcon Eyrie, Eastern Mountains
Huntress
Kerensky Cluster, Clan Space
12 March 3060

For perhaps the tenth time since arriving in the rock-walled hide overlooking the Jade Falcon installation known as Falcon Eyrie, Sergeant Henry Kramer pulled away from the twin eyepieces of the powerful "big eyes" surveillance binoculars. The sophisticated electronic unit combined all the features of high-magnification, high-resolution binoculars, low-light and thermal imager, and holographic recorder. The unit was also capable of being fitted with a small, portable target designator, similar to the Target Acquisition Gear mounted on BattleMechs and other combat vehicles. Of course, this system was not as accurate as a 'Mech-based designator, and its range was sharply limited, but the man-pack TAG, as it was called, added another weapon to the Fox Teams' already formidable arsenal.

Unfortunately, after about ten minutes of staring into the tiny video display, an operator began to suffer eye strain. After fifteen minutes, the strain turned into blurred vision and a sharp, rasping ache behind the eyes. The effect was especially savage when the low-light or thermal viewers were being used, as Sergeant Kramer was now learning. He and his team mates had been in position for more than five hours, watching the Eyrie for any signs that the Jade Falcons were about to get involved in the defense of Huntress. So far, Kramer's close observation of the base had yielded little more than itchy eyes and a stabbing headache. Accepted procedure with the "big eyes" was to spend a few minutes looking through the device and a like amount of time resting one's eyes. Usually, five-man surveillance teams would rotate in ten-minute shifts, allowing each member a respite from the glaring imager only a few centimeters from his or her eyes.

Again, unfortunately for the Fox Teams, they were so thinly spread over the Eyrie's perimeter that the expected length of their mission forbade them that luxury. As a result, each member of the five-member surveillance teams would have to stand a thirty-minute stint at the "big eyes," alternately staring through the viewer and resting the eyes by scanning the area without the aid of the electronic imager.

General Winston, following the advice of the mysterious Trent, had decided that the Fox Teams would maintain an intensive surveillance of the Eyrie only for the first twenty-four hours of the invasion operation. The conventional wisdom of the day seemed to be that if the Jade Falcons didn't involve themselves in the defense of Huntress in that time period, they were unlikely to do so, unless provoked.

The Falcons were, however, known to be one of the more aggressive Clans. As such, the surveillance and containment teams could expect the Eyrie garrison to make a demonstration or two. Winston thought it unlikely that the Falcons would attack the Fox Teams directly. Instead, she believed they would move their forces right up to the perimeter of the base, possibly even going so far as to lock their weapons onto the Rabid Fox positions. It was the age-old game of cat and mouse. One that opposing forces had played against each other from the beginning of organized warfare.

So far, the only activity that Kramer's men had seen within the Eyrie was the occasional movement of personnel from one place to another. They'd seen a few armored Elementals and a few squads of what appeared to be conventional, unarmored infantry. But the Rabid Foxes had yet to see a single Jade Falcon OmniMech.

* * *

"There, do you see him?"

"Where?"

"Down there, among the rocks, about five meters to the left of that small clump of bushes." The whispered exchange could not have been heard three meters away.

Unknown to Sergeant Kramer, two sets of eyes were watching *him,* although not from within the confines of Falcon Eyrie. A pair of Smoke Jaguar scientists who had been tromping through the Eastern Mountains in search of untapped mineral deposits had spotted five silent black shapes moving across a rocky clearing. More curious than fearful, the geologists had followed the dark forms as they picked their way through the rough terrain toward Falcon Eyrie. Scientist Gary, the younger of the two, believed that what they were seeing was a test run of some new form of Elemental armor, possibly being developed for the Watch.

Vito, the more senior of the pair, contradicted him. He had once been of the warrior caste, but that was before getting seriously injured in his Trial of Position. Having failed his Trial, and been crippled besides, Vito was deemed unfit to be a warrior by the way of the Clan. Though he was consigned to a lower caste, he maintained an interest in things military and was familiar with most new systems being produced by the Clan. He had neither seen nor heard of a program to develop light combat armor either to replace or augment the Elementals. No, he reasoned, these black-armored shapes had to be something else.

At first, he reasoned that the armored warriors might belong to the Jade Falcons; perhaps *they* were working on new, light power suits. But, when the shadowy forms took up positions *outside* Falcon Eyrie, their identity became clear to him. The intruders were outsiders, setting themselves to keep watch on the Jade Falcons. But, who could they be? Members of another Clan? No. No Clan Warrior would resort to stealth and covert surveillance. If any Clan commander wanted to know what the Falcons were doing, he would declare a Trial of Possession and issue a *batchall.*

Could these be members of the bandit caste? Again, no. Bandits could barely provide themselves with 'Mechs, let alone stealth-capable battle armor.

A feeling of cold horror settled over Vito as he arrived at the last possible conclusion. He had heard rumors of filthy spies from the Inner Sphere, creeping along the Exodus Road, feeling out the way to the Clan homeworlds. Those vermin could not have made their way to Huntress undetected. Even if they had, they would have been caught and exterminated by the warrior caste. But the presence of the barely visible shapes huddled in the shadow of Falcon Eyrie gave the lie to Vito's reasoning. If the intruders were not Clansmen, they could only be from the Inner Sphere.

Pulling a small holocamera from his rucksack, Vito recorded the barely visible figures. He would want more positive proof than the word of a failed cadet when making his report of their presence. Vito hated thinking of himself that way, but he knew it was how the rest of Jaguar society saw him. He had no illusions that his discovery and reporting of the intruders would change his status. His actions were no more and no less than those expected of him by his Clan.

Five hours later, Vito was explaining that very thought to Elemental Star Captain Tullain. Like Vito, Tullain was not exactly the cream of Jaguar society. The officer, once a front-line Elemental Star Colonel, was nearly forty years old, well past his prime. As an older warrior, he had been declared solahma after the Battle of Tukayyid and rotated back to Huntress, where he would live out the remainder of his life in useless obscurity, as a mere Star Captain in charge of other solahma Elementals of the Lootera garrison.

When the Inner Sphere fleet appeared at Huntress, the solahma warriors viewed the attack with two thoughts in mind. The first, and most automatic, reaction was one of outrage. The second was an odd sense of gratitude. With the barbarian attack on the Jaguar homeworld, those warriors, who, according to their Clan, had outlived their usefulness would be given one final chance to die as a warrior should, in battle. But, to Tullain's shame, Galaxy Commander Russou Howell had ordered his Star held in reserve, to be brought up should the MechWarriors defending Lootera need reinforcements, or should the barbarians make a flank move and attack Lootera from the south or east. Thus it was Tullain's force that the geological survey team first contacted upon arriving in the Jaguar capital.

Tullain had taken over a small office building in the city's southeastern quarter as his command post. It was there that the scientists presented their information.

Unlike Scientist Vito, Tullain was still a member of the warrior caste, and thus commanded deferential respect from those of the lower classes. His contempt for Vito showed in his body language and tone of voice as he stared at the tiny three-dimensional figures produced by Vito's holocamera.

"So it seems that the Inner Sphere *surats* are taking an interest in the Jade Falcons as well," Tullain muttered. He had to squint a bit to make out the fine details of the holographic image Scientist Vito had brought him.

"That is what I surmised, Star Captain Tullain." Vito nodded his agreement. "The Inner Sphere troops seemed to be some kind of special operation team. They had a large amount of surveillance gear, but few heavy anti-'Mech weapons."

Tullain's head came up in a flash of annoyance. Vito was not a warrior. He should stop trying to act like one. But Tullain quickly got his irritation under control.

"You have served Clan Smoke Jaguar well, Scientist Vito. I will see that a full report is forwarded to your superiors. But, understand that I do not approve of mere scientists playing at warrior, or of your unauthorized interest in military matters."

"Aff, Star Captain." Vito nodded. "I understand."

"You are dismissed."

As the scientist closed the door behind him, Tullain gestured to a lower caste technician, who sat in one corner of the room, a communication headset clamped over her ears.

"Technician Jesse, connect me with Galaxy Commander Russou Howell. Then summon Alpha and Bravo Points. They are to be ready to move in five minutes. Tell them we are going into the mountains. While the Inner Sphere *surats* are busy watching the Jade Falcons, we will take them unaware. We will show them, and the Smoke Jaguar, that we are *still* warriors."

A flat, dull clunk caught Sergeant Kramer's attention, jerking him out of a half-doze. Kramer had been off shift for nearly an hour, and was finally getting over the vise-like headache caused by the "big-eye" viewer.

"Sarge, it's me," Private Luis Daltezze whispered urgently. The sound that had awakened Kramer was the private lightly tapping on his armor's breastplate.

"What?" Kramer lowered the muzzle of his sound-suppressed Imperator submachine gun, which he had snapped into line even as he came fully awake.

"The seismic sensors just went off. We got movement, a lot of it, about five hundred meters south east."

" 'Mechs?"

"Uh-uh," Daltezze replied. From the subtle movement of the powered armor, Kramer knew the communication specialist was shaking his head. "The trace is too small, and there are too many of them. My read is Elementals, maybe two Points of 'em. They look to be headed this way."

Kramer swore. If the seismic trace *were* Elementals, there was a good chance they knew where his surveillance team was, and were on their way to attack them. In that case, his team would have to bug out, abandon their observation post, and lead the hulking Clan warriors away from the rest of the Foxes. Because security might have been compromised, Kramer could not even risk sending a warning to Captain Montjar or Leftenant Fuentes. He swore again.

"Get back to your sensors, Daltezze. Let me know if the contacts get any closer, or any bigger. And, send Whitman over here."

Moments later a camouflaged shape slid into Sergeant Kramer's hide. Private Stacy Whitman was his team's scout, and the one best suited to the job Kramer had in mind.

"Look," he said, "we're probably compromised here. Daltezze has multiple seismic traces, probably two Points worth of Elementals, and he thinks they're headed this way. We're going to have to move. We can't use the radio, and we don't have a direct line-of-sight to use the lasercoms. I want you to head over to Leftenant Fuentes and tell him we had to bug out. Tell him we're going to lead the Elementals away from this position. If we can kill them off, we'll hook back around and resume surveillance. If not, we're going for a link-up with the nearest friendlies. Either way, we'll check in as soon as possible. Got it?"

Whitman nodded her grasp of the situation.

"Good, now move out."

As Whitman slithered out of the natural rock-walled hole in search of Team Four's command post, Kramer snatched up his weapon and made his way across to the sheltered overhang where Daltezze had placed his sensor monitoring units.

"Well?"

"It's definitely Toads, Sarge," Daltezze reported. "And, they're headed straight for us. I count ten Elementals, and no BattleMechs."

"That's something, at least." Kramer peered closely at the jagged series of lines scrawled across the monitor's screen. He understood the basics of remote sensor systems; it was part of the basic training for all Rabid Foxes. But the finer points of reading and interpreting the data was a specialization all to itself. Daltezze, as the team's communications tech, was the most familiar with the electronic sensors. If he said the traces were generated by Clan armored infantrymen, and not 'Mechs, then that was the source of the traces.

"How close?" Kramer asked.

"Close," Daltezze answered. "Three hundred meters, no more. And they're still coming this way."

"That's it, then. We can't wait any longer," Kramer said decisively. "Dal, rig destruct charges to your monitors. We don't want the Clanners getting their hands on our sensor systems. Don't arm the charges until we're all ready to move. I'm going down to the OP to collect Mitts and Santone."

Much to their credit Privates Mitts and Santone didn't give in to the natural human questions of "Why?" and "How?" when Sergeant Kramer told them the surveillance team was being forced to bug out. The troopers simply packed up what gear they could easily carry, and set thermite charges on the rest.

By the time they returned to the monitoring station, Daltezze had shut down his systems and rigged them for destruction. At Kramer's nod, the electronics specialist yanked the pull-rings on a pair of M-95 fuse igniters. The short sections of gray-green fuse attached to the cast-metal cylinders would burn down in thirty seconds, triggering a brace of thermite grenades attached to the monitoring console with "thousand kilometer per hour tape." Each cylinder weighed just under a kilogram, and when detonated sent a jet of white-hot flame down through its base and into whatever object it had been set to destroy. Under ideal circumstances, only one incendiary charge would be needed to destroy the delicate electronics of the console, but Rabid Foxes were trained never to rely on "ideal circumstances."

For good measure, he had also set up one of the team's few directional mines as a booby trap. If for some reason, the thermite grenades failed to go off, and the Clan warriors found and tampered with the monitoring station, the small, slightly curved plastic box would explode, filling the rock-walled overhang with hundreds of steel flechettes. It was uncertain whether the hardened steel darts could actually penetrate the Elementals' thickly armored skins. But the explosion of the mine in such a confined area would stun or possibly even injure the man inside the armor. At the same time, the high-velocity "finishing-nails-with-fins" would abrade the Elementals' viewports, making vision difficult. They would penetrate and jam the joints between the powered armor's moving parts. If nothing else, the mine would completely wreck the monitoring unit.

As soon as Daltezze dropped the smoking igniters, the Fed-Com commandos scrabbled out of the hide. They kept low, moving as quickly as they dared, trusting in the electronic camouflage and IR suppression units built into their power suits. Only one avenue of escape was open to them, and that was due west, between the approaching Smoke Jaguars and the rocky crags of the Eastern Mountains. They moved single file, with about five meters between each team member, so a single missile or burst of gunfire wouldn't hit more than one man.

Private Mitts led the way, then came Sergeant Kramer. Santone followed the squad leader, carrying the team's only anti-'Mech weapon, a heavy short-range missile launcher. The weapons specialist had four reloads for the bulky weapon, one of which was a two-shot clip of napalm-filled incendiary warheads. Called infernos by foot soldier and MechWarrior alike, the missiles did no direct damage to a 'Mech's armor or internal systems, but coated the machine with a wave of burning, petroleum-based fuel. The idea was not to destroy the machine, but to disable it by increasing its heat to the point that its central computer shut it down.

With good reason, infernos were among the most feared weapon on the battlefield. Occasionally, MechWarriors had been literally fried in their cockpits by hits from the incendiary rockets. Only the weight, bulk, and instability of the rounds prevented them from becoming common ammunition loads. A stray round that penetrated the missile's case would ignite the warhead, turning the missile gunner into a living torch. Still, some infantrymen, like Private Santone, felt the effectiveness of inferno warheads outweighed the risks.

Last in line came Private Daltezze. Every few meters, he would pause and half-turn, scanning the team's back-trail. When no trace of pursuit was found, he continued on.

Thirty seconds into the march, a quartet of sharp-flat cracks ripped the night air. Though they had been expecting the reports, the members of Second Squad, Fox Team Four, dropped flat onto their armored bellies as though they'd been brought under sudden enemy fire. Sergeant Kramer cautiously lifted himself onto one steel-clad elbow and looked back toward the team's observation post. In his electronically enhanced viewscreen, he saw the bright glow of burning thermite as the incendiary charges destroyed the equipment left behind by the withdrawing commandos. As soon as he was satisfied that the Jaguar Elementals were looking at the now burning hide rather than his escaping commandos, he signaled his men to move on.

The going was painfully slow. Every dozen meters or so, the team was forced to scramble over large boulders deposited in their path by some long-ago rock slide. Twice, Kramer's men paused to carefully survey their back-trail. Both times, they saw the faint thermal traces generated by the massive enemy power suits glowing dimly against the dark, cool background of the rocky Eastern Mountains. At each halt, the Elementals were drawing closer. At the rate the armored warriors were closing the gap, Kramer figured his team had two hours, maybe two and a half, at the outside, before the Elementals got so close that they couldn't avoid spotting the well-camouflaged commandos.

Kramer intended for the Elementals to pick up his team's trail, in hopes of leading the Jaguars away from the other Rabid Foxes. He even sketched out a plan for luring the armored giants into pursuit. The plan was unnecessary. Even before the dim glow of the ruined and smoldering surveillance gear died out, the Elementals had picked up his team's track. They probably hadn't seen any of the commandos directly, the power suits' camouflage being far too good for that. In all likelihood, one of the Jaguar warriors had spotted a footprint, a scraped rock, or some other physical trace of the team's passage. Kramer had ordered his men not to be too careful to leave no trace of their passage. What he hadn't counted on was the enemy picking up the trail so quickly or following his team so closely. Silently, he gestured to Private Mitts, signaling him to move out.

As they crept across the rocky plateau, Kramer surveyed the ground, analyzing every boulder, every shrub, every clearing. Almost unbidden, his mind formulated, assessed, and discarded plans for laying an ambush against the team's dogged pursuers.

Finally, the commandos could not maintain a sufficient lead over the Clan infantrymen. Fatigue was beginning to set in. If they pushed ahead any further, the Foxes would be in no state to launch an effective ambush against their pursuers.

In a shallow, rocky defile, Sergeant Kramer gave a signal, and the four armored commandos came to a halt. The gap, forming an east-to-west pass through the southernmost ridges of the Eastern Mountains, was too wide for Sergeant Kramer's liking, and its rocky sides were too gently sloped. But he had no other choice. The pursuing Elementals were closing the distance too quickly for his team to find another ambush site.

Quickly they set out the last of their directional mines, sighting them in such a way as to blanket the widest area possible. Moving on, the team advanced another three hundred meters before swerving off the trail, but still they didn't stop. Instead they hooked back into a position that let them see the defile in which they had left their mines. The team spread out. Each man searched for what he thought was the best available firing position, making sure there was at least five meters' distance between each member, then settled down to wait.

For what seemed like hours, the commandos sat in silence, waiting for the Elementals to enter the defile. Patience began to wear thin as it seemed the enemy would never appear. Silently, Sergeant Kramer wished he had taken more time to work with the Draconis Elite Strike Teams. The Draconis Combine's version of the Rabid Foxes seemed to be possessed of infinite patience that could explode into violently, deadly action in less than a second. He was beginning to think the Elementals had either lost the trail, or had somehow bypassed the ambush without either triggering the mines or being spotted by the waiting commandos.

Then, a slight flicker of movement caught his attention.

There. At the edge of the kill zone. A steel claw wrapped itself around an outjutting spur of granite. Slowly, cautiously, the Elemental belonging to that claw leaned around the rock as though some sixth sense told him he was standing on the edge of mortal danger. For long seconds, he scanned the area before him, the multi-barreled machine gun attached to his armor's left wrist tracking back and forth across the gap.

He's not going for it, Kramer thought as the armored warrior stubbornly refused to leave the shelter of the rock. Ignoring the silenced submachine gun slung over his power suit's shoulder, Kramer brought up the Thunderstroke Gauss rifle he'd been issued for dealing with Elementals. Resting the weapon's barrel on the large boulder behind which he was sheltering, he brought the high-tech rifle into line with his enemy.

Though not as effective as the BattleMech version of the "railgun," the Thunderstroke used a series of powerful electromagnets to accelerate a hardened steel spike to more than twice the speed of sound. The projectile was capable of penetrating even Elemental armor if the shot was placed in just the right spot. The weapon interfaced smoothly with the targeting circuits built into his battle armor, bringing a bright scarlet cross hairs into life in front of his eyes. Carefully, he sighted the weapon on the shallow chevron of the Elemental's visor, and began to depress the trigger.

Before the weapon fired, the Elemental moved. Kramer, caught off-guard by his target's sudden change in position, let off the Thunderstroke's trigger. Still moving with infinite caution, the Elemental stepped into the defile. The machine gun swung from side to side, the even motion telling Kramer that the armored giant was still alertly searching for any possible threat. A few seconds later another Elemental stepped carefully into the Fox Team's killing zone, then another. Soon, a full Point's worth of the massive, genetically engineered infantrymen were creeping along the defile. If the Foxes waited any longer the leading warrior would be out of the kill zone.

Taking careful aim, Kramer leveled his weapon at the third Elemental in the short, staggered line. If the Clanners followed typical infantry doctrine, the first two troopers were common grunts. The third man was probably the Point commander. Placing the glowing cross hairs just a centimeter or two ahead of the visor's trailing edge, Kramer took a half breath and squeezed the trigger.

A loud crack split the air as the heavy steel dart broke the sound barrier. The Elemental staggered under the impact, but did not fall. In his low-light visor, Kramer saw a large, pale green splotch where the right half of the Elemental's viewscreen had once been. The Gauss slug had shattered, but failed to penetrate the tough material. The impact had probably sent fragments of plastic, spalled loose from the inside of the visor, slashing into the Elemental's unprotected face and eyes.

Before the startled warriors could begin to react, the defile blew up in their faces. Kramer's single shot had been the signal to initiate the ambush. Daltezze had done his work well. The directional mines all fired at once, filling the shallow trench with smoke and thousands of high-velocity flechettes.

Sighting through the smoke and dust, Kramer settled his cross hairs on the reeling infrared image of the suspected Point commander. A caress of the Gauss rifle's trigger sent another projectile into the Elemental, then another, and another. The armored behemoth staggered under the impacts, but struggled back to his feet after each hammer-like blow. Kramer fired two more shots at the giant, finally dropping him with the last round in the Thunderstroke's five-shot magazine.

This was Kramer's first Elemental kill. He had always known that Elementals were hard to kill, but that one had been even tougher than he'd been led to believe.

Kramer yanked the empty clip from the top of his weapon's receiver and rammed a fresh magazine home. As he brought the Gauss rifle up, in search of more targets, he heard the *crackwhoosh* of a portable SRM launcher being fired. In the defile, an Elemental warrior, his armor already scarred and pitted by the directional mines, virtually disintegrated under the impact of the big, armor-piercing warhead.

The thuttering scream of a minigun filled the air. Tracers, seeming to form a solid line, so rapid was the machine gun's rate of fire, reaching out from the eastern edge of the defile. The tiny, man-made meteor storm reached the shallow hole in which Private Mitts was snapping a fresh clip into his Gauss rifle. The hard, armor-piercing slugs ripped through the light armor as though it were made of cardboard. Mitts collapsed heavily and didn't move again.

Santone swung the SRM launcher and blasted the western end of the ambush site. For a moment, the machine gun was stilled, then it started up again, its murderous fury unabated.

Kramer peered closely at the end of the defile, hoping to catch some glimpse of the Elemental whose long, barrel-melting bursts of gunfire were keeping his team's heads down, while the rest of the surviving Clan warriors closed on the Fox Team's positions. Movement to his right diverted his attention. An Elemental, his right arm dangling by a few strands of myomer and muscle tissue, had crept close enough to the sergeant's position to attack him in a rush.

Distantly, as though he were watching a recording of the scene, rather than acting as a participant in it, Kramer noticed that the Elemental's armor had been deeply scored by the mine flechettes. Even larger holes showed where missile shrapnel had slashed through the tough armor and into the more yielding flesh behind. The triangular missile launchers were empty, and the stubby anti-'Mech laser's housing bore enough holes and dents to tell Kramer that it was not operational, even if the hulking warrior could lift the big weapon with his crippled arm.

But, all the damage seemed to be concentrated on the Elemental's right side. The power armor's left arm, with its light anti-personnel weapon and powerful battle claw, were intact. As he charged, the Clanner lifted the head-sized steel claw over his armored head, clearly intending to bring it smashing down on the commando's more lightly armored body.

Fortunately, Kramer's commando training held true; the Thunderstroke's gaping muzzle had followed his gaze. Twice he jerked the weapon's trigger. The Elemental convulsed and died as the steel darts ripped into his already broken armor. But two Gauss slugs could not break the momentum of his charge. Even as he began to collapse, twisting as he fell, the battle claw whistled down in a lethal arc. Only by the sheerest good luck, the deadly steel fist struck Kramer only a glancing blow to his head and left shoulder. Had it taken the full impact of the attack, Kramer's helmet would have split open like a ripe melon, and his head along with it. As it was, the imperfect blow left him with a ringing headache and a jammed shoulder joint.

The dead warrior took one more step, driven by reflex action only, before he finally dropped. The massive weight of the slain man and his suddenly pilotless armor fell across Kramer's legs, pinning him to the ground. As he struggled to free himself, he heard another volley of missiles leaving their tubes. Then a second pair of rockets were fired, then a third. Four sharp bangs hammered Kramer's eardrums, despite his suit's noise-attenuation systems. High-Explosive, Dual-Purpose warheads exploded, scattering shards of rock and high-speed metal fragments across the hillside. An odd *whoomp* sounded in reply, and Kramer's infrared imager whited out.

Cursing, he heaved the armored corpse off his legs, switching his helmet viewer to visible light as he did. Rolling up to his knees, he saw savage fire burning at the western end of the defile. In the glare of the petrochemical flames, he could see the shapes of no less than four Elementals flailing their steel-and-composite clad arms across their armored bodies in a vain attempt to extinguish the burning, jellied fuel that was roasting them alive. A man-sized shape staggered toward him, black against the yellow-orange glow of the flames.

"C'mon, Sarge, we gotta go. Now!" Daltezze bellowed over the communicator.

"What about . . ."

"Santone's dead, so is Mitts," Daltezze barked, yanking Kramer to his feet. "And so will we be if we don't haul outta here. I'm sure those Toads have got buddies. And, they aren't going to like what we just did to their friends."

"All right," Kramer sighed, nodding his head. Then, as he groped in the flame-cast shadows for his Gauss rifle, he sighed again. "Let's get out of here."

"Right, which way?"

"West," Kramer answered, sadness tainting his voice as he gazed down the length of the defile where his men lay, just as they had been killed. There was no time to bury them, nor could he and Daltezze be burdened with their bodies. "West. We've got to lead the bad guys away from the rest of the team."

"Uh-huh." Daltezze grunted as he angled away into the darkness, following the integral compass display projected onto his power suit's helmet visor.

Kramer took one last look at the mountain pass where half of his squad had died. Speaking quietly, more to himself than his lost comrades, he promised Private Mitts and Santone that he'd come back and take them both home. Then, without another word, he turned his back on the still flickering flames and followed Daltezze into the darkness.

22

Lyran Guards' Operational Area
Near Bagera, Huntress
Kerensky Cluster, Clan Space
12 March 3060

Smoke drifted thickly across the battlefield, partly obscuring the ugly gray buildings and narrow streets of the northern quarter of the town called Bagera. Marshal Sharon Bryan stared angrily out through the dark glazed viewscreen of her updated *Banshee*. At the viewscreen's maximum magnification, she could just pick out the dark rectangles made by the building windows. Here and there, the sophisticated sensors built into her ninety-five ton machine picked up the glowing heat traces of still active Battle-Mechs. Many of those traces belonged to the enemy, the Smoke Jaguars.

Bryan's Eleventh Lyran Guards had been tasked with assaulting and capturing the Jaguar training base near Bagera. Secretly, Bryan believed that Ariana Winston had purposely assigned the only pro-Katrina unit to crack the toughest nut on the Jaguar homeworld. She knew that the Eridani Light Horse was technically under contract to the Lyran Alliance, but Winston's seeming devotion to Morgan Hasek-Davion had given Bryan the uncomfortable feeling that the General might have turned her coat.

Besides, Morgan had appointed Winston as his second in command, even though Bryan outranked her. Bryan had to admit, though, that the ranking was a technicality. The Eridani Light

Horse, as supposed adherents to the "ways of the old Star League," *had* no rank of Marshal. Winston commanded a reinforced brigade, consisting of *three* full combat regiments and a vast support and transportation section. Bryan, on the other hand, had direct command of only *one* regiment.

Sharon Bryan had never really liked Winston in the first place, and there was something distinctly fishy about the way she'd ascended to command of the task force. As a loyal Steiner officer, Bryan was bound by her honor and her oath to look out for the interests of the Lyran Alliance and Archon Katrina. At the same time, as a member of the newly formed Star League Defense Force, she was also duty bound to obey the lawful commands of the officers appointed over her, no matter how that officer got her appointment.

Maybe I'm just being paranoid, Byran told herself. *Maybe all the political wrangling that accompanied the formation of the new Star League and Task Force Serpent is beginning to rub off. After all, there's never been any question about Winston's loyalty in the past.* She shook her head, dismissing the unfounded suspicion for what it was.

The strobing flash of a missile volley brought her back to the battlefield. The Lyran Guards had met with strong opposition on their in-run to their designated landing zone. One of the regiment's 'Mech-hauling DropShips had been badly damaged by a flight of Jaguar fighters during its final approach. With its maneuvering thrusters crippled, the big, ovoid *Overlord* Class DropShip landed heavily, causing its starboard-side landing gear to collapse. Fortunately for the Guards, the ship landed in relative safety, with the loss of only two light 'Mechs damaged by the hard landing.

Bryan's luck held all throughout the initial landing and assault phases of the operation, which was to say, it stayed bad, but not insurmountably so.

The Smoke Jaguars had plenty of information from the aerofighter pilots about the Guards' course and probable destination. The Clan ground forces, in turn, had plenty of time to prepare a defense in depth. The last of Bryan's heavy and assault 'Mechs hadn't yet been broken out of their transport bays when an enemy Supernova Trinary appeared on the edges of the Guards'

LZ. Without a word of warning, or challenge, the Jaguars charged straight into the landing zone.

At first the battle against the mixed force went well for the Guards. There was enough separation between the forces to allow each side the luxury of time to discern the identity of both friend and enemy before engaging a particular target. But as the Jaguars closed with the Inner Sphere assault force, the amount of time available to identify each combatant diminished to nothing. Under ordinary circumstances the swift pace of the battle wouldn't have mattered, even against the Clans. But here, on Huntress, the heart of Clan Smoke Jaguar, the incredibly time-compressed events worked against both sides, for each was equipped with Inner Sphere 'Mechs.

That came as no surprise, however. They'd known about the Jaguars' use of captured 'Mechs as far back as Defiance, a fact verified by the reports of the other commanders who'd already seen combat here on Huntress.

What none of the Task Force leaders had anticipated was the sheer number of Inner Sphere 'Mechs being used by the Jaguars. The force that had attacked the Guards' landing zone was an uneven mix of Clan second-line 'Mechs, Elementals, and seemingly brand-new Inner Sphere designs. Bryan's Guards had pushed the Jaguars back, clearing the LZ, but at great cost to both sides. The Guards had lost fifty-one of their one hundred-twenty 'Mechs, either destroyed or too badly damaged to continue the fight.

"Gauntlet One, this is Stalker One," a shouted message crackled from her communicator. "We have incoming 'Mechs, lots of them, twenty-five or more, with many Elementals. I say again, twenty-five or more enemy 'Mechs, mostly front-line heavy and assault OmniMechs, supported by many Elementals. They are approaching my position . . ." The message broke up in a burst of static, then cleared. ". . . needs help. Gauntlet One, respond please."

"Stalker One, this is Gauntlet One," Bryan replied. "Say again, all after 'approaching my position.' " She knew that the Major commanding the Eleventh Guards' reconnaissance company was not a man given to either panic or exaggeration. If he was calling for help, there must be something desperately wrong. Bryan asked him to repeat the broken portion of his message so she could get a handle on what it was.

"Gauntlet One, Stalker One. I say again; 'They are approaching my position. We are under long-range missile and PPC fire, and are in danger of being overrun. If we are to hold, Stalker needs help.' Over."

"Roger, Stalker One." Bryan keyed up her tactical display as she spoke. Stalker Company was two kilometers west of her position, and just inside the edge of town. "Hang on. Help is on the way."

Rapidly switching channels, Bryan ordered the balance of the Guards' First Battalion to wheel out of line and move to support Stalker. Another quick frequency change, and the order went out to her own command company. Though it was not uncommon for a general officer to engage in combat, it certainly wasn't an everyday occurrence. Too many battles had been lost because a commander tried to lead his or her troops from the front line of battle, instead of from the relative safety of a command post. Still, if Stalker One's report were accurate, they would need every available 'Mech, and that meant the heavy and assault machines of her command company.

Moving at top speed her *Banshee* rocked and heaved like the deck of a sloop in a hurricane, but the long-legged stride ate up the ground in ten-meter strides. In the distance she could see the flash of gunfire and the glare of energy discharges. It seemed that Stalker was heavily engaged. The thick radio cross-talk seemed to bear out that assessment.

"Gauntlet One, this is Stalker Three. Stalker One is down. Please hurry."

"Calm down, boy." Bryan tried to sound reassuring, but it was hard when your insides were being shaken apart by a running assault 'Mech. "Help is on the way."

There was no reply.

A dark shape loomed up out of the smoke in front of her *Banshee*.

Without conscious thought, she saw that the target's image did not carry the electronic Identify Friend and Foe code programmed into every 'Mech in the task force. Instinctively, she brought her 'Mech to a skidding halt and settled the screen-projected targeting discrete onto the target's center of mass. Twin bolts of azure energy lanced into the humanoid shape before her, followed by a hypersonic Gauss rifle slug. The enemy machine, now identified by her computer's warbook subroutine as a *Loki Prime,* took both PPC blasts in the right arm. The shattered limb dropped to the heavy 'Mech's side, hanging limply by a few strands of myomer and rods of metal bone. The Gauss slug slammed into the Jaguar machine's torso with enough force to make the *Loki* stumble.

A wave of heat flooded into Bryan's cockpit, instantly bringing beads of sweat from her pores. Below her feet she could almost feel the high-efficiency heat sinks throbbing to life as they struggled to bring the *Banshee*'s heat levels under control.

The *Loki* began to pivot, bringing its intact left arm to bear on Bryan's BattleMech. Though slowed by its own size and mass, the movement reminded Bryan of a holoshow gunfighter drawing his six-gun. Bryan did not intend to give the Clan pilot enough breathing space to obtain a proper target lock. Dropping her cross hairs onto the 'Mech's scarred left torso, she triggered the Gauss rifle again, this time adding a flight of short-range missiles and a pair of laser bolts for good measure.

Bryan's attack was not quite fast enough to prevent the Jaguar pilot from pummeling her *Banshee* with an eye-searing stroke of artificial lightning and a shower of short-range missiles. Still, the enemy's attack was too little, too late.

The Clanner's anti-missile system automatically clawed the missiles from the sky, but could do nothing about the basketball-sized chunk of nickel-iron that slammed into its chest, nor could it affect the megajoule's worth of amplified light energy that slagged the armor protecting its left leg. The second laser bolt seared its way through the rent in the Omni's right torso. A blast of flame gouted from the *Loki*'s back, scattering shrapnel and two large armored panels across the battlefield.

The laser blast must have touched off his ammo. Bryan smiled in grim satisfaction as the Jaguar pilot ejected from his crippled machine. *I'll bet he's real happy his* Loki *had CASE gear.* Only the presence of Cellular Ammunition Storage Equipment had saved the Clan pilot from being blown to pieces when Bryan's laser touched off the ammo stored in the *Loki*'s right torso.

She had little time to gloat over her kill, however. A volley of missiles slammed into her *Banshee*'s side and legs, announcing the presence of yet another enemy. As she turned to meet the new threat, a burst of autocannon fire ripped open the already brutalized armor protecting the *Banshee*'s left breast. As she recovered control of her staggering 'Mech, the sight that met her eyes made her blood run chill.

There before her was the oddly elegant, bird-like shape of a *Cauldron-Born,* the incredibly tough 'Mech first used by Clan Smoke Jaguar against the defenders of Luthien.

The Clan pilot brought the machine's arms up, seeming to point them directly at her cockpit. Undaunted, Bryan lifted her own weapons. The warriors fired at exactly the same time.

For the briefest moment, all Marshal Sharon Bryan knew was searing heat and eye-scorching light. Then she was lying flat on her back wrapped in the shrouds of her recovery parachute, dimly aware of a dull ache in her left arm. She tried to lift her head to look at the injured limb, but couldn't. The parachute shrouds had not only entangled themselves around her body, but her ejection seat as well. She was as tied as effectively as though someone had done it intentionally. With shock-induced detachment, she told herself that her arm was broken, probably a compound fracture, and was going to hurt like the devil in the morning. Out of the corner of her eye, she could see the smoldering wreckage of her *Banshee,* standing locked in place like a ruined statue. The *Cauldron-Born*'s attack must have breached the assault 'Mech's ammunition lockers, initiating the auto-eject system.

Straining against the nylon spider's web that held her, she groped for the survival knife strapped to her right calf. Only with difficulty, and against such pain that she feared she would black out before she touched the knife's parkerized gray handle, could she free the blade from its cast plastic sheath.

As she began hacking at such of the parachute cords as she could reach, Bryan heard a high, screeching howl, seemingly right in her ears. With visions dancing in her mind of a Battle-Mech about to crush her to death under its armored feet, Bryan began to slash wildly at the tough nylon shrouds. The blade glanced off the metal armrest of the ejection seat, twisting the knife from her grasp.

Then a head appeared, a head wearing the heavy armored helmet of a Lyran tanker. The panic that had so briefly and recently engulfed her drained away like water, leaving Bryan weak from adrenaline shock. The howl she'd heard had not been the actuators of an approaching 'Mech, but the lift fans of a hovertank.

"Marshal," the crewman bellowed. "Take it easy. I'll get you out." Without another word, the man hacked away the tangled shrouds and carefully lifted his injured commander to her feet. As she was freed of the lines, she saw with a measure of relief that though her arm was definitely broken, for a miracle, the fracture was not compound.

"Marshal, can you walk?"

"Walk?" Bryan rasped against the pain. "Give me a minute boy, and I can run."

"I'm sorry, ma'am, we don't have a minute." The young soldier slipped her uninjured left arm over his shoulders and half-carried, half-dragged her toward a grounded Fulcrum heavy hovertank. The vehicle's commander stood in the open turret hatch waving angrily and shouting words Bryan couldn't make out against the din of battle.

The youthful tanker heaved Bryan up onto the tank's hull deck, then swung up deftly after her. Before she had dropped fully through the gunner's hatch, the Fulcrum's driver engaged the fans, and swung the vehicle through a stomach-wrenching turn, going hell-bent-for-leather straight away from the main body of the fighting.

"Marshal," the tank commander hollered over the roar of the vehicle's engines, a radio headset in his outstretched hand. "Colonel Price for you."

"Price? Bryan." Bryan didn't settle the headset in place, but rather held it up to her ear. "What's going on?"

"Marshal, I've ordered the regiment to pull back." If Price was relieved to learn that his commander was still alive, his tone didn't reveal it. "The Jags threw a full Trinary of front-line OmniMechs into the line. Stalker has been wiped out, and the rest of the outfit is pretty badly shot up. We're withdrawing, but the Jags are not. I think they may be regrouping for another attack."

"All right, Price." Bryan's arm was starting to hurt as the initial shock of her injury wore off, but she couldn't give in to the pain. Not yet. She still had a job to do. "Can you give me a tactical feed and patch me through to Dancer?"

"Wilco."

Moments later the feed came through, displayed in much less detail than she was used to on the Fulcrum's tactical display monitor. Bryan knew the image was so grainy because the hovertank's computer was far less powerful than that of her now destroyed *Banshee*.

"Dancer, this is Gauntlet." Bryan set her teeth against the liquid fire that had once been her arm. "Gauntlet has taken severe casualties and is in danger of being overrun. Request naval fire support.   Grid: Mike-alpha-one-eight-seven-three-four-zero, Gauntlet Two will correct. Over."

"Gauntlet, this is Dancer." Ariana Winston's tone suggested to Bryan that she had not concealed the pain of her injury as well as she had believed. "Stand by for hand-off to naval fire liaison."

"Roger. Gauntlet is standing by, but don't make it too long. Aaahh!" Bryan gasped as the broken ends of her humerus ground together.

"Marshal, are you all right?"

"Nothing more than a busted wing, Dancer," Bryan panted. "Just get me that fire support. I'm handing you off to Colonel Price. Gauntlet One, clear."

High above the battlefield, the captured *Whirlwind* Class destroyer *Fire Fang* rolled along her axis, bringing her portside batteries to bear on the coordinates relayed up to her through the naval-fire liaison officer attached to Ariana Winston's command staff. When the ship's weapons officer reported that her surviving naval Gauss and PPC batteries were locked onto the target, the captain gave the command to fire.

In the vacuum of space, there was little to see. A bright spark lit the Gauss cannon's muzzle for only a fraction of a second. Then a brighter, but briefer flare belched from the heavy naval PPC battery. All in all, a rather disappointing show had anyone been outside the *Fire Fang* to watch it.

On the battlefield northeast of Bagera, the effects were a little more dramatic. The Gauss slug, accelerated to incredible velocities, slammed into the red-brown mud with the force of a hundred conventional artillery shells. Less than a second later the PPC discharge savaged the Jaguars' position, flashing the muddy ground into dirty steam.

Colonel Timothy Price, Marshal Bryan's second in command, watched in horrified fascination as the energy released by the blast shattered the Clan 'Mechs unfortunate enough to be near the naval fire's impact point. Though the fire mission had fallen over one hundred meters to the west of Price's designated target, the effect on the Jaguars was nothing less than appalling. Nine of the lighter enemy 'Mechs just ceased to exist, blown to pieces by the unbelievable energies delivered by the *Fire Fang*'s weapons. Any Elemental unlucky enough to be caught in the primary blast area was vaporized. Most of the surviving Clan forces were so badly damaged as to be useless as fighting machines, or even as spare parts.

"Dancer, this is Gauntlet Two." Price paused and swallowed hard against the lump in his throat. These were soldiers, and no soldier, friend, or enemy deserved to die like that, with no way to retaliate or even protect himself. "Dancer, Clan resistance in Bagera has been broken. Gauntlet is moving in, but I don't think we'll have to do anything but mop up."

Huntress' yellow sun was beginning to set, turning the dark gray clouds scudding across the horizon a brilliant orange. The brief sudden rainstorm that struck the Field of Heroes had passed, leaving shallow puddles around the feet of the handful of 'Mechs standing dormant in the shadows of Mount Szabo. Each of the BattleMechs bore the prancing black horse emblem of the Eridani Light Horse and the silver crest of Ariana Winston's command company. Leaning against the doorjamb of her mobile headquarters van, Winston marveled at how the brief but heavy downpour had washed the soot and grime of battle off the command company's armor. The rain settled the dust and smoke of the battle, and brought with it a clean freshness that was so deceptive.

There was nothing clean or fresh about the Field of Heroes. Only a few hundred meters to the north of where her headquarters van now rested on its hydraulic leveling jacks, only a few hours before, men and women had been locked in a desperate life-and-death struggle for control of the stormy homeworld of Clan Smoke Jaguar. Though the rain had washed away the dirt of battle, the green-painted 'Mechs and hovertanks of the command company still bore the laser-scored and explosion-pocked signs of a hard and bloody fight. Broken bits of armor and oily patches of spilled coolant marred the once clean and smooth pavement of the parade ground. Not far away, recovery crews, medical teams, and, most ominous of all, burial details were combing through the wreckage of battle, searching for equipment to salvage, wounded to treat, and bodies to inter.

Looking down at the datareader held loosely in her right hand, Winston realized that similar scenes were being played out all across Huntress. Task Force Serpent had accomplished in less than a single day what most of its warriors would have believed impossible just a year ago. They had attacked and seized the homeworld of the most brutal and aggressive of all the Crusader Clans. But, the price was terrible.

Of the eleven combat units that had grounded on Huntress, all had taken heavy damage. The greatest number of casualties seemed to have been inflicted on the Eleventh Lyran Guards. The Guards had seen nearly twenty-five percent of their Mech-Warriors either killed or so badly wounded as to be unfit for combat duty. Losses among the Guards' infantry and armored battalions were even higher. Half of the surviving Guards had been less severely wounded. Marshal Bryan herself had suffered a broken left arm. Forty of the Guards' BattleMechs had been knocked out, including Bryan's *Banshee*.

The Jaguar defenders had, unknown to the task force or to agent Trent, moved a large, powerful unit, equipped with the latest Clan OmniMechs, into Bagera. Though piloted by just-blooded warriors and their training cadre instructors, the OmniMechs, supported by Clan-built second-line machines and Elementals, ran roughshod over the Lyran unit, forcing Bryan to call for naval support fire. The hellstorm unleashed by the *Fire Fang* broke the Jaguars' back, allowing Bryan's troops to move into Bagera and mop up what little resistance remained. Winston knew that the support and repair crews would be able to restore about half of the Guard's losses to some kind of fighting trim, if they had enough time.

On the other hand, the combined St. Ives Lancers/Fourth Drakøns assault on the training base on Abysmal went off almost better than had been anticipated. One Drakøn and four Lancer 'Mechs had been destroyed in a close-range scuffle with such Jaguar defenders as had been at the camp. Apparently the training camp was a facility only used to temporarily house troops being trained in desert warfare. When the Lancers and Drakøns hit the camp, there were no warrior cadets present, only the training staff. According to Major Poling, the Lancers' commander, the instructors tried to give a good account of themselves, but were simply overwhelmed by the task force's superior numbers.

The rest of Task Force Serpent's assault units fell somewhere between these two extremes. Each had met stiff resistance, but were eventually able to defeat the Smoke Jaguars and seize their objectives.

After-action reports had filtered in throughout the day. The Kathil Uhlans under Andrew Redburn had met a determined security force at the city of Myer, but were able to batter it aside and seize the factory complex. The Com Guard Third Battalion had easily secured the Jaguar facility inside Mount Szabo, mostly thanks to the damage inflicted on that facility by the DEST teams. The Northwind Highlanders had met heavy opposition in their attempt to seize the 'Mech production plant at Pahn City, as had the Knights of the Inner Sphere and Kingston's Legionnaires at New Andery.

In both cases, the assault forces reported contact with a new, totally unexpected type of 'Mech. Smaller, faster, and more agile than even the most maneuverable twenty-ton scout 'Mech, the new "proto-Mechs" had created such havoc among the Knights and Legionnaires that Paul Masters had been forced to call in the Com Guard First and Second Battalions as reinforcements. MacLeod's Highlanders had encountered the proto-Mechs too, but there were far fewer of the little machines at Pahn City than at New Andery. MacLeod's report stated that the mercenaries had managed to take the production facility intact. Much of the equipment used to construct the proto-Mechs had been destroyed and the facility's central control computer purged of all design specifications and blueprints for the miniature BattleMechs. It was possible that the Jags had off-line backups for the software, but there wasn't time to search for it.

The proto-Mechs gave Winston a shiver of concern. Most of the warriors piloting the small, fast, hard-to-hit miniature Battle-Mechs encountered by Task Force Serpent were either trainees or solahma. Even so, they had inflicted severe casualties on the Knights of the Inner Sphere and Kingston's Legionnaires. She closed her eyes and remembered the shock she had felt upon her first encounter with Elementals at the start of the Clan invasion some ten years past. A lot of very good MechWarriors died before the Inner Sphere learned how to cope with the heavily armored, genetically engineered Clan infantrymen.

As tough as Elementals were, the protos were even tougher. Winston shivered again. The proto-Mechs were such an unknown, and unexpected quantity, that she didn't like to contemplate what might have occurred if the Jags had shipped proto-Mechs to the Inner Sphere in any great numbers, with skilled, front-line pilots at the controls.

Though each of the individual unit commanders had reported his or her area of operation secure, she knew that there was secure and there was secure. The main body of resistance had collapsed. At the same time, she was certain that there were those Jaguar warriors who had escaped from the battlefield. She understood that the complex and rigid Clan code of warfare didn't normally permit any kind of guerrilla campaign against an attacker, but she couldn't be certain that the surviving Jaguars wouldn't launch such hit-and-run attacks against the task force units.

One odd note appeared on her list of after-action reports. Sandra Barclay's scouts reported seeing an explosion and fire on the horizon, coming from the direction of Lootera. The 71st's commander knew that there were no task force units in the area, and had asked if it were possible that either bondsmen taken from the Inner Sphere during the Clan War might have rebelled and committed some act of sabotage, or if Jaguar civilians might have been responsible for the fire.

Winston assured Barclay that she didn't know the cause or location of the fire, but granted her permission to send a scout team in for a look. The lie gave her an uncomfortable queasy feeling. It was the first time she hadn't been entirely truthful with one of her subordinates. Winston knew full well that the explosion and fire were the handiwork of the shadowy nekekami. The presence of such highly trained saboteurs and assassins with her task force, especially given that she had never met them face-to-face, made her uncomfortable. But Morgan had seemed to trust them, as did Theodore Kurita. To Winston, they were like a big ugly dog. You could trust the dog to protect you and your family from an intruder, but could you trust the dog not to attack you himself?

Dismissing the disquieting question, she made an entry on her noteputer to advise the various unit commanders to post sentries.

She would also recommend that they send out patrols with the intent of running the fugitive Clansmen to ground.

Winston turned her back on the glowing sunset, and sighed her satisfaction. The Eridani Light Horse and the rest of Task Force Serpent had passed into history. They had not only carried the war to the direst foe the Inner Sphere had ever known, they had, like a street fighter, hit him where it hurt the most. They had attacked, and in less than twelve hours, conquered the enemy's homeworld.

For the moment, the planet was secure, the invasion of Huntress was over.

23

With an easy grace that belied her twenty-nine years as a combat soldier, Ariana Winston turned away from the open door of the mobile HQ standing in the shadow of Mount Szabo. Making her way into the van's dark and cool interior, she then dropped into a padded seat just behind the driver's position. Were she like far too many commanders in these degenerate days, it was from that seat that she would have commanded the Light Horse's part in the invasion of Huntress. Some commanders even chose to oversee an operation from the relative safety and comfort of an orbiting DropShip rather than subjecting themselves to the heat and stench and danger of leading their troops from the sweat-drenched cockpit of a BattleMech.

For a moment she tapped idly at the keyboard set into the command station, causing the holotable built into the HQ's central data processing and display system to flicker between the task force's various landing zones. Though not as detailed as the holotank dominating the *Invisible Truth*'s bridge, the table-top holographic projector showed graphic images of the various forces assigned to Task Force Serpent and their surroundings.

Had there been anyone else in the van, they might have thought

Winston was delaying some major decision or announcement. Fortunately for her, the mobile HQ was empty. She had ordered the various technicians out, ostensibly for them to get a breath of fresh air and a bite of chow. What she really wanted was a moment alone. With a sigh, she blanked the holotable, shoved a datachip into the system's reader, and keyed in a new set of commands. The computer obediently displayed the document she had requested.

Shaking her head, she re-read the contents of the file for perhaps the hundredth time since taking command of Task Force Serpent. The words, frozen in the electronic memory of the chip, stubbornly refused to change.

Blast, Winston swore silently, and tapped another control.

"All commands, this is Dancer. Attention to orders." She paused for several breaths to make sure all unit commanders were on line and listening.

"All regimental commanders," she continued, "are to meet me at the planetside command post for a new mission briefing at zero-nine-hundred tomorrow, one-three march, thirty-sixty. Respond and confirm."

One by one, the acknowledgments trickled in. Inside of two minutes all her regimental commanders had signaled their understanding of the order and indicated that they would be present for the briefing.

With another silent oath. Winston shut down the communicator. She wished that she could pass along, by radio, the next set of orders she would be obligated to give, but something in her makeup forbade such a cold and detached action. Though all of the commanders by now had to know, or at least suspect, what she would announce to them tomorrow, she believed that an officer had the right to look into his commander's face while receiving such an order.

Far to the southwest, at the Com Guard command post near Pahn City, Colonel Regis Grandi nodded slowly at the commtech who had brought him the message. He had been expecting it.

"Send for Major Lewis and Captain Ho. Tell them to get ready to leave for Lootera, by oh-five-hundred tomorrow," Grandi instructed an aide, who saluted his understanding and left.

Grandi slumped heavily into a convenient camp chair. The

plastic stool was cool against his back, its chilliness a byproduct of the compressed gas-foam used to fill the seat's hollow plastic structure enough to make it rigid and usable. Though he had been anticipating the order from Winston, it was not a joyous, eager sort of anticipation. Grandi knew what had to come next. In fact, his infantrymen were already at work preparing to carry out the General's commands as soon as the formal word was given.

An identical somber mood hung over the steel-walled command van belonging to the Knights of the Inner Sphere. Parked beneath a vine-shrouded tree, the Knights mobile HQ was hot, humid, and stuffy inside. The vehicle was built on the chassis of a tracked armored personnel carrier. Instead of the rear section being an empty steel box, fitted with bench-type seats for a squad of infantrymen, the after compartment was jammed with sophisticated communications equipment.

Its environmental control system did little to affect the quality of the atmosphere in the vehicle's steamy confines, however. The air smelled of rotting vegetation and burnt rocket propellant. With night coming on, gossamer-winged bugs the size of a large man's fingernail were beginning to collect around any light source. Like the mosquitoes often found on other worlds, the pests seemed to live on blood, but unlike mosquitoes, it hurt when the Huntress bloodsuckers bit you.

All this only contributed more gloom to Masters' already bleak humor. He, like Grandi, had been expecting General Winston's orders. His normally fair, handsome face turned dark and stormy upon hearing the word that Winston wanted her commanders to attend a strategy session in the morning. The timing and the order to meet at Lootera could only mean one thing, and Masters didn't like it.

"Well," he said, looking across the vehicle's cramped interior at Samuel Kingston. "At least she had the courtesy to want to tell us in person, rather than putting it out over the radio."

"C'mon, Masters," Kingston said, with a chuckle. The Capellan officer had been nearly intolerable ever since the Jaguars were driven from the field in disarray. Before the invasion, Kingston had been only annoyingly self-important and argumentative, but with the end of Clan resistance, he had become downright obnoxious. He slapped Masters on the shoulder in what was obviously intended to be a friendly gesture. Masters only found it irritating. "What could be so bad? I'm sure the good General wouldn't order you or your men to do anything that might offend your 'delicate knightly sensibilities.' "

"You think so?"

Masters could tell from Kingston's face that he wasn't sure whether the Knight was sharing in the joke. With a slight shudder that might have been a qualm of fear, Kingston allowed Masters to slip past him, out of the command van, and into the gathering jungle gloom.

As he walked, Paul Masters wrestled with himself over the orders he knew were to come. His vows as a Knight of the Inner Sphere bound him to protect all who were weak and helpless, to show mercy and compassion to a defeated foe. But those same vows obliged him to obey the lawful commands of those lawfully appointed over him. He'd known from the time Task Force Serpent was being formed that its ultimate goal was the annihilation of Clan Smoke Jaguar's warriors and the destruction of the Clan's ability to make war. He was fully prepared to carry out those orders, but his preparedness did not change the fear he felt inside.

Masters was not afraid for his own safety, nor for that of his troops. He, and they, were warriors, and it was their place to risk their lives in service to their lord. No, the fear that chilled his soul was something else, something of a less primal nature. Paul Masters feared that the task force would have a hard time getting the genie of destruction back into the bottle once it was unleashed against the military capabilities of Huntress. He feared that the destruction would spread to the civilian areas of the targeted cities, even to the civilians themselves. He feared that once the warriors who destroyed not only a Clan, but that Clan's homeworld, returned to the Inner Sphere, the idea of utterly destroying an enemy's hearth and home would become acceptable. Masters was afraid that the seeds of ruin sown on Huntress would come to full bloom in the Inner Sphere. The Knights had been formed to combat mankind's slow slide to annihilation. How could he participate in the acceleration of the self-destructive process?

Masters nodded silently as he passed the sentry who had been posted on the edge of the Knights' bivouac area. The young woman reminded him that the area was not one hundred percent secure, and that he should be alert for any signs of trouble. He smiled gently at the sentinel, lightly tapping the black nylon holster worn cross-draw fashion on his left hip. The picket smiled back, as though she understood her commander's gesture as a promise to take care.

He walked only a few more meters before he stopped and looked up. Here and there, strange stars showed through the thick canopy of leaves. Huntress' single moon had not yet risen, leaving him alone in the dark with his thoughts.

For a long while, Masters leaned on his left forearm against the rough, scaly trunk of a jungle tree, no longer aware of the biting insects that buzzed hungrily around his head. He gazed sightlessly at the warm, cheery glow of campfires built by his men, not so much for warmth, as out of the fact that they were soldiers, and soldiers had always built campfires whenever time and conditions would permit.

"So what do I do?" he asked aloud. "How do I look my Knights in the face and tell them to obliterate their enemy? And how do I live with myself once this is all over?"

Perhaps it was the audible stating of the turmoil in his heart that brought the answer. Perhaps it was something far greater. Paul Masters was never certain, but he had his solution.

"We signed on for this operation, knowing what was coming." Masters sighed and pushed himself erect. "All we can do is obey orders, and make sure that the whole thing doesn't turn in on us."

Patting the tree trunk as though it were an old friend who had just given him some wise advice, Masters walked softly back toward the Knights' picket line. He was careful to answer the sentry's challenge correctly. The commander of the Knights of the Inner Sphere had finally gotten his heart settled about the next phase of the operation, and didn't want to end up getting shot by one of his own men.

The sun was barely a hand's span over the horizon when the last of the shuttles carrying the unit commanders touched down on the Field of Heroes. Already the humid, oppressive heat was beginning to rise, burning away the coolness of night. The Star League battle flag hanging from the corner of the command truck hung limply, its nylon folds stirring only slightly in the nearly nonexistent breeze. Thick clouds had enshrouded the sunrise, turning the sky a dull, angry orange and presaging a day of rain.

Well, that'd be just perfect, Ariana Winston snorted to herself. *It's setting up to be a lousy day, and it isn't going to get any better as it goes.*

Though Bagera, the last Jaguar pocket of resistance, had been reported secure at eighteen-thirty hours the previous evening, Winston had gotten little sleep. In the fifteen hours between the secure signal and the arrival of the first shuttle, she had reviewed preliminary after-action reports and had written her own. She was constantly interrupted by reports of sporadic fighting between elements of Task Force Serpent's ground units and the survivors of the Smoke Jaguar garrison. Twice gunfire sounded along the Light Horse's own perimeter. Once, it turned out that the nervous sentries had been firing at shadows.

The second incident, though a bit more humorous in nature, was no less disturbing than the first. A Light Horse MechWarrior, a veteran of the original Clan invasion, spotted what he believed to be a Jaguar *Mad Cat,* running cool and approaching his sentry post. Twice he shouted a challenge to the enemy 'Mech. Twice he received no answer. Finally, the guard leveled his *Watchman*'s heavy laser at the target, and blasted the *Mad Cat* into glowing shards of rock. In his jumpy, keyed-up state, the picket had mistaken one of the stone statues lining the edge of the Field for a live enemy.

Winston, though mildly amused over the incident, resolved that the statues would have to be torn down before anyone else opened fire on one of the monuments and touched off a fratricidal "mad-minute."

I guess they'd have to go anyway, she told herself. *We can't leave a bunch of monuments to the heroes of the Smoke Jaguar Clan standing. The Clanners just might get some idea of recapturing the glory of their past.*

Though a reasonable political decision, the idea of destroying monuments to the Jaguar's heroes grated on Winston's soul. Aside from going counter to the Ares Conventions, the act of destroying the Jaguars' heritage was in direct opposition to the Light Horse tradition of respecting the legacy of the past.

Absently, she rubbed the knuckles on her left hand where it gripped the dark gray-green casing of her personal data unit. The joints often pained her in the morning, having once been broken in a fouled-up ejection during her younger days. Nine pairs of eyes turned toward her as she ducked under the edge of the green-camouflaged, polypropylene tarp her troopers had set up as a field command post. None of the commanders, save Colonel MacLeod, seemed to have gotten any more sleep than she had. For some reason, the Highlander commander seemed well-rested, despite her knowledge to the contrary. She knew that he'd been up half the night, checking on his wounded and writing the inevitable letters to the families of the dead. That was one task she was still putting off.

On the other end of the spectrum was Marshal Sharon Bryan, who looked pale and drawn. A hand-sized bruise, just coming into its full, colorful splendor, marred the left side of her face. A white plastic air-cast, supported equally by a drab-green sling, immobilized her left arm.

"It's one of those stupid, *stupid* accidents." Bryan smiled thinly and shook her head when Winston asked about the injury. "The medics don't want to let me back into the cockpit until this heals, but we'll see about that."

Then Bryan's back came up again, as though she regretted letting down her guard even for an instant and was now trying to recover.

"What's this all about, General? What are these new orders that you can't put out over the air?"

Winston was rattled a little by the directness of Bryan's question. A glance around the command post told her that the other commanders were just as impatient to hear the orders, even though she was certain that each already knew what she was about to say. She had, in a way, intended to put off the actual moment for giving the order by asking after the condition of each unit under her command. The faces of her commanders told her that she had run right out of breathing room.

"Very well. Pursuant to General Order, number TFS oh-one-oh-five-one," Winston read from the data display unit she had laid on the table, "upon completion of the initial assault on the planet Huntress, the units comprising Task Force Serpent are to take every measure possible to eliminate the war-making ability of Clan Smoke Jaguar. To this end, the units of Task Force Serpent are to destroy all barracks, 'Mech hangars, fighter bays, command, communication, and control centers, and military repair facilities. Likewise, all factories, warehouses, armories, shipyards, and any other facility or installation that may be used for the construction of war materiel, or the storage, or transport of the same, must be destroyed or rendered unusable by Clan Smoke Jaguar.

"Such stores of weapons, ammunition, spare parts, food, and other military supplies, as well as those military assets that can be captured intact and transferred off planet by the units of Task Force Serpent should be secured by the units of Task Force Serpent and protected from deliberate sabotage by the forces of Clan Smoke Jaguar.

"The commander of Task Force Serpent is charged with the initial disposition of all captured materiel. All combat losses not provided for by a unit's Table of Organization and Equipment will be made up out of captured materiel wherever possible. All other captured materiel will be shipped for transport back to the Inner Sphere, where it will be disposed of by Star League Defense Force command.

"Such captured materiel that cannot be used by the units of Task Force Serpent and that cannot be shipped for transport back to the Inner Sphere is to be likewise destroyed."

There, I've said it, Winston thought, putting down the data unit. *Now comes the storm.*

For several long seconds the storm did not break. It was as though the commanders had been struck dumb by the orders, though each knew that the commands had to be given.

Then, Colonel Paul Masters spoke up. "General Winston, I formally ask you to reconsider the order.

"Such widespread destruction will cause unnecessary hardship for the Jaguar civilians. Many of them live within the confines of factory complexes or military bases, just as some workers do back in the Inner Sphere. If we raze those complexes, the civilians housed at those facilities will be left homeless."

"Colonel Masters," Winston interrupted. "No civilian homes are to be touched. This task force will make every effort to ensure that the civilians of Clan Smoke Jaguar are affected as little as possible by our operations. You know this has always been my intention."

"Yes, General, I know that." Masters lapsed into a stiff, formal manner of speaking, just as Winston had.

"However, may I remind the General that as a matter of historical fact, troops ordered to carry out such operations tend toward one of two attitudes. Some become so enthralled by the act of destruction that they run amok and begin to destroy private, civilian property. Others are so overcome with what can only be called blood lust that they engage in looting and theft, some even going so far as rape and murder of civilians.

"If they do not become a rioting mob, troops ordered to raze occupied territories will often do so only under protest. As a result, they will become sullen, withdrawn, and intractable. They will begin to protest *every* order, not just the ones they disagree with on a moral basis.

"Either way, General, if we enforce this order upon this Task Force, we will risk losing our troops as an effective fighting force. Therefore, I must respectfully ask that you reconsider this order."

Then MacLeod jumped in even before Winston could respond to Masters. "I'd have to agree with that, General," he said. "It's not that I don't understand the need for keeping the Jags from rebuilding their war machine. I just don't know as how we'll be able t' carry it off without we risk becoming the very barbarians the Clanners claim us t' be."

"Come off it, MacLeod," Bryan snapped. "Everybody's heard by now. Your Highlanders captured that Jag factory almost intact. You want to ship it home piece by piece and start building your own Clan 'Mechs, especially those proto-Mech things. You know as well as I do that if we leave the Jaguars even one piece of warmaking technology, they'll use it to rebuild their society. Then, we'll end up having to fight them all over again in a couple of years."

"That's ridiculous," Andrew Redburn snapped. "I agree that we have to wipe out the Jags' military industry. Not because they're going to rise up like a phoenix and become a threat to the Inner Sphere again, but because we have to completely destroy them as a Clan if we're going to make a legitimate claim to the Star League. You were at the Whitting Conference, Bryan, you know the reasons as well as I do. This isn't about conquering worlds or capturing technology. This is about making the other

Clans sit up and take notice. We *have* to wipe out the Smoke Jaguars for the rest of the Clans to realize that we're a threat, to make them realize how horrible total war can be, and to make them realize that is exactly what they'll have on their hands if they *ever* renew their offensive against the Inner Sphere."

"Now hold it . . ." Winston's attempt to regain control of the meeting disintegrated as a general argument broke out among the commanders. Masters, Kingston, and, surprisingly, MacLeod protested what Masters called "the wanton destruction of Huntress," while Ryan, Poling, Sleipness, Bryan, and Redburn argued for the razing of the Jaguar military assets. Through her frustration and quickly mounting anger, Winston noted bitterly that this was perhaps the first time Bryan and Redburn had agreed on anything since the mission began.

Blang!

As the echoes of the pistol shot died away, the only sound that could be heard inside the command post was the steady drip of water as the thin, bell-like clatter of a spent cartridge case danced across the map table.

"You may have gotten away with this crap with Morgan, but by the Eternal, you aren't going to get away with it with me." Winston lowered the big, black, evil-looking Mauser autopistol. A pale tendril of smoke drifted from the weapon's blunt muzzle, which seemed to glare at the officers with an intensity rivaled only by her angry scowl. "Now sit down and be quiet."

When the chagrined and startled officers, who were too stunned to protest, resumed their seats, Winston safed the pistol and threw it onto the table with a snort of disgust.

"You all knew the orders when you signed on for this mission," she snarled. "And by the Lord God, you're going to carry them out. Colonel Masters, your holier-than-thou code says you're supposed to defend the defenseless, right? Well, what about all those defenseless lives you're going to be saving by wiping out the Smoke Jaguars right here and now? Kind of easy to forget about them when you're so far away, isn't it?

"And, oh, by the way, doesn't your code say something like, 'Defense of any charge unto death'? As I recall, Thomas Marik charged you with supporting this task force and its commanders. Is this how you defend that charge? You were on Tharkad, you know that the Captain-General signed off on these mission orders. If you don't like the orders, fine. You can take it up with him—but you'll have to wait until we get back to the Inner Sphere, *if* we get back to the Inner Sphere.

"Gentlemen, I don't like these orders any more than you do, but I must remind you that we are an *army,* and the purpose of an army is to kill people and break things. If we kill enough of the enemy's people, and break enough of his things, we just might be able to convince him that we'll kill and break whatever he has left if he ever bothers us again.

"Now, the order stands. Whatever can be salvaged will be salvaged. The rest is to be destroyed. There are about a dozen salvageable DropShips on the tarmac at Lootera. I'm sure there are a few more at other, smaller facilities. Load whatever salvage you can pry loose aboard those ships. As for the rest, the destruction of this planet's industry *must be* and *will be* aimed at concrete and steel. No humans—warrior, scientist, technician, or civilian—are to be harmed, so long as they do not pose a threat to this task force. Is that understood?"

The officers indicated that they would comply with Winston's orders, with a degree of enthusiasm in direct proportion to his or her original position regarding the destruction of Huntress.

"Good," Winston grunted. "Dismissed." Leaning heavily on the map table, she waved a salute at the departing officers.

For a long moment, she stayed where she was, gazing sightlessly at the holographic map of Huntress. The next few days would determine her place in history. If the razing of the Jaguars' war-making capability went smoothly, and with a minimum, or hopefully, even no civilian casualties, then she might be remembered as one of the greatest military leaders in history. If the Jags resisted, or if, as Paul Masters feared, her own troops ran wild, she'd be remembered in one breath with Adolph Hitler and Stefan Amaris.

"Fffuh," Winston snorted with disgust, and cursed under her breath. Collecting her sidearm from its resting place in the center of the map table, she stalked out into the growing heat of the day to pass the orders along to the Light Horse regimental commanders. She noticed that the gaping black muzzle of the weapon had come to rest pointed straight at the Field of Heroes and the Eridani Light Horse's Area of Operations.

Almost physically, she cast off the odd sense of foreboding. She might be a soldier, and soldiers might be, by nature, a superstitious lot, but she refused to view the accidental aiming of the pistol's ugly business end at her brigade's AO as anything more than an odd chance.

24

W*hy, with all our advanced technology, can't we come up with a better way of treating broken bones?* Marshal Sharon Bryan cursed the heavy plastic cast immobilizing her left arm. It was bad enough that the Eleventh Guards' senior medical officer had removed her from the regiment's combat roster because of the injury. But even if he hadn't, the bulky cast, which stuck almost straight out from her shoulder, would have prevented her from crawling through the narrow cockpit hatch of the salvaged *Zeus* the Guards' repair teams had cobbled together for her.

Leaning heavily against the side of the regimental command van, she told herself it didn't matter all that much. The Smoke Jaguar defense of Huntress had collapsed after less than a single day's bloody fighting. Though the Jags had put up a valiant struggle, the outcome was a foregone conclusion. As much as she hated to admit it, Precentor Martial Anastasius Focht's shadowy agent known only as Trent was right. The Jaguars had only about two Galaxies of combat troops available to defend their homeworld. To top it off, those troops were solahma, warriors either too old for front-line service or who had somehow stained their honor. Apparently, due to some Clan military code, the solahmas were forbidden to pilot anything but second-line 'Mechs.

Bryan snorted ruefully as she remembered her own reaction when she was told the Jaguars would be defending Huntress with second-line gear. She had actually laughed out loud. She realized now how foolish she had been. She had mistaken second-line for second-rate, something the Clan 'Mechs certainly were not, as her broken arm could attest.

Still, the very idea of leaving so small a garrison to protect a world that was the heart and soul of the Smoke Jaguars brought a bitter grin to her sunburned face. There were a few Clusters of unblooded warriors undergoing training at the planet's various training camps and bases, and they had been equipped with OmniMechs, some of them the latest models off the assembly lines. And, there had been the "proto-Mechs" MacLeod and Masters had encountered in their respective Areas of Operation.

Taken as a whole, the defense of Huntress, though courageous, had been doomed to fail from the beginning. Now, the warriors of Task Force Serpent had to turn their attention to the next phase of the operation—the destruction of the Smoke Jaguars' ability to make war.

Across the parade ground in the center of the Bagera training base, Bryan watched tiny black figures as they moved in and out of the large, ugly ferrocrete administration building. She knew that those figures were the Guards' surviving combat engineers. Until just a few minutes ago, those same men had been ransacking the offices of the Smoke Jaguar training command, searching for any bit of data the new Star League Defense Force might find useful.

Unfortunately, most of what they uncovered was of limited value. Training manuals, operating procedures, course curricula, and the like were interesting, but not particularly useful. Clan training programs were based on the premise that the instructors were teaching warriors who were the product of the Clan breeding program.

The Inner Sphere certainly had nothing like that. The Lyran Alliance required that all soldiers, of any branch, undergo a sixteen-week basic training course, even if a warrior had already graduated from one of its prestigious military academies. The purpose of the basic training was to make sure a soldier was physically and mentally ready for combat duty before he was passed on to a so-called "A-School," where he learned the skills of his Military Occupation Specialty. Once a soldier passed his A-School, and was given his MOS, he was assigned to a unit, where most remained for the rest of their term of service. Not much in the way of cross-training occurred, and what little was provided was usually limited to the members of elite forces, such as the Lohengrin anti-terrorist squads.

The Jaguars, on the other hand, with their system of genetic engineering and sibkos, seemed to have found a way of streamlining the process. Warriors were created using DNA that predisposed the resulting individual for one specific field of endeavor, be that MechWarrior, Elemental, or aerofighter pilot. The products of such genetic manipulations were placed in groups of varying sizes, called sibkos, where their natural tendencies were encouraged, and shaped, much as a swordsmith fashioned a billet of steel into a sword-shaped blank. From a very early age, the sibko members entered training together. Very few survived the grueling ordeal, and the failures were, sooner or later, reassigned to one of the "lower castes." Those who completed their training were like a well-fashioned sword, strong, sharp, and deadly.

The whole process of making a Clan warrior struck Bryan as far more efficient than the old, established Inner Sphere method. Unfortunately, it required the Clans' selective breeding and genetic engineering processes in order to work. Still, according to orders, she had the training base's offices cleaned out, and any data that might be even remotely useful loaded aboard the Guards' command DropShip.

Secretly, though, Bryan had ordered several copies of each file be made and stored in the safe in her personal quarters. Whatever useful information those files might contain was not going to be placed solely in the hands of Sun-Tzu Liao, the current First Lord of the Star League. Some of the hotter files were not copied, but were simply removed from the data intended for delivery to the SLDF and were placed whole in her personal safe.

She felt no qualm of guilt over the copying or pilfering of what was to become Star League property, an act that some might call treason and espionage. Bryan was a true Steiner loyalist, and as such, she considered it her duty to secure for the Lyran Alliance any military or scientific information she came across. If that information gave the Alliance a military or scientific edge over the rest of the Successor States, so much the better. Sharon Bryan believed that Archon Katrina Steiner would reward her handsomely for procuring such sensitive and valuable information.

"Marshal?"

"Huh?" The single word, spoken in a low, respectful tone, yanked her out of her self-congratulatory daydream. The man behind her wore a black-centered blue chevron, as well as the blackened metal castle insignia of the Combat Engineers. With a crisp wave of her hand, she returned the man's salute. "What is it, Hauptmann?"

"Marshal, we've finished stripping the 'Mech hangars and repair bays of all useful materiel, and we're about finished setting the demolition charges. We should be ready to blow them in about twenty minutes." The junior officer paused long enough for Bryan to nod her understanding of the report. "It's going a bit slower in the administrative buildings and barracks. There's such a wealth of information to be garnered in the admin offices that it's taking a long time to sort through it all. Colonel Price suggests that we pull some of the walking wounded out of the hospital and assign them light duty going through the stuff we haven't been able to look at yet."

Bryan mulled over her second-in-command's suggestion. Taking those troops who were only slightly wounded out of the hospital and putting them to work rummaging through the mounds of intelligence yet to be evaluated was a three-edged sword.

The additional manpower would speed up the process, thereby allowing the demolition teams to proceed with their tasks. But the use of untrained personnel in gathering and analyzing data would increase the chances that something critical would slip through the sieve, and at the same time increase the work load of those few trained intelligence analysts she did have when the data could finally be reviewed.

Lastly, the use of the common line-soldiers would increase the chances of a security leak, and security had to be especially tight, given Bryan's program of securing particularly vital information for the Alliance, and the Alliance alone.

That would be all I need, some ground-pounder bragging to his buddies that he saw the specs on some kind of hot new Clan weapon, and then that data doesn't make it to the Star League Defense Force.

Bryan looked at the engineer officer and realized that he was waiting for an answer.

"All right, Hauptmann, go ahead and destroy the 'Mech facilities as soon as you're ready. But for now, let's hold off on dragging any of the wounded out of the hospital. I'd rather not risk making their condition any worse by having them sort through piles of old Jag records." Bryan gave a short, explosive laugh that carried just the right note of exasperated bitterness. "I'd rather take a little longer in destroying the planet than risk losing any of my wounded for the sake of speed."

"Very good, ma'am." The Hauptmann saluted again and turned away.

As she watched the young man striding confidently across the parade ground, Bryan felt a slight chill in her soul. Though she had not compromised her loyalty to the Lyran Alliance, she could not escape the feeling that she had betrayed the Star League. Perhaps she should reverse her earlier decision and remove the carefully garnered information from her safe and place it with the rest of the data.

No, it's too late for that, she told herself. *If I do that now, I'll have to explain why I was redacting the intelligence in the first place. No, it's best that we just carry on as usual.*

Just over thirty minutes later, the Hauptmann returned with word that the demolition charges were all set and the training base's hangars and 'Mech-repair bays were all set for destruction.

Bryan gave a short nod. "Do it."

The man nodded in return. Pulling a small communicator handset from his drab green field jacket, he spoke a phrase as old as modern warfare.

"Fire in the hole."

Within the space of a slow breath, Bryan saw a dull white flash illuminate the inside of a low-slung 'Mech hangar on the south end of the parade ground. The building seemed to shiver, like some kind of small dog caught in a sudden freezing draft. Smoke billowed from the open bay doors. The low, grinding thump of detonating explosives came a second later.

When the smoke cleared, the heavy ferrocrete roof of the hardened 'Mech bunker sagged in the middle like the sway-back of an old, hard-ridden horse. With the aid of her binoculars, held awkwardly in one hand, Bryan could see specks of dark gray dotting the tarmac before the hangar doors. She knew that those specks were large chunks of steel-reinforced concrete that had until only recently been part of the hangar bay's thick walls. So powerful were the explosive charges set by her combat engineers that the outer-wall surface of the hangar bays had spalled away under the high-velocity shock wave created by the demolition blocks. She knew that the scene inside the bays would be absolutely hellish, a maze of broken support girders, shattered 'Mech cradles, and twisted repair gantries. Fortunately there were no human beings inside the bay. The massive explosion that had savaged the incredibly tough hangar bunker would have mashed to a bloody pulp any living creature caught in its swiftly expanding shock waves.

The thick, white smoke of the first series of bombs had barely begun to roll away on the gentle east wind when a second series of blasts further gutted the hangar, bringing down the roof a thousand meters away with a thud Bryan could feel in the soles of her feet.

Like ripples on a still pond, she felt rather than heard four more of the double thumps as the rest of the demolition charges were detonated in sequence by the engineers. When it was over, the Bagera training facility lay in ruins. Off to the east, a thick column of black oily smoke rose into the overcast sky, marking the smoldering ruins of what had been the Jaguar cadet barracks. Only the two-story administration building remained undamaged, but that too would be destroyed at the proper time.

With a long sigh, made of equal parts satisfaction and pain, Bryan levered herself erect, tried again in vain to ease her cramped, sore left shoulder, and turned away from the infernal tableau. Walking around to the open back door of the command van, she stopped at the bottom of the ramp. There was no way she was going to try to maneuver her jutting left arm into the vehicle's cramped interior.

"Get a message through to Dancer," she called to the technician manning the communication console. "Tell her the training base at Bagera has been destroyed."

"Very well, Marshal," General Ariana Winston replied to Bryan's dispatch, trying to keep the sadness over the destruction of the Clan military installations out of her voice. "Continue repair and salvage operations, and let me know as soon as your outfit is back up to fighting strength. In the meantime, take every reasonable precaution against guerrilla actions by the Jaguars. They say the Clanners aren't *supposed to* engage in such tactics, but I think we're in kind of unfamiliar territory here. No one's ever invaded their homeworld before. Even in the days when they were only fighting among themselves, it sounds like all they ever did was wrangle for some particular thing, and then withdraw, win or lose. But us? We've not only attacked Huntress, we've moved in for what has to seem to the Jags like the long haul. We know they aren't too happy about us hitting their homeworld in the first place. I gather our coming in under the banner of the Star League is an order of magnitude worse yet, at least to the Clan way of thinking. I've heard a number of prisoners talking about it. They just might throw their precious code of honor out the window and start harassing attacks.

"You can go ahead and interrogate any high-ranking Clan officers you managed to capture, but I want to be kept informed of the results. You might want to post a few MPs in the center of Bagera as well. Don't let them make pests of themselves. Just post enough of them to keep order, and let the civilians go about their business.

"Also, we'll need a breakdown on all the prisoners, er, um, bondsmen, you've taken." Winston stumbled over the Clan term even though the word had long been part of Task Force Serpent's vocabulary. "And I'd like an accounting of all the material you salvaged from Bagera. We may have to do a gather and distribute operation to refit all of the units that took damage during the invasion."

"Understood." Even allowing for the clipped, formal speech common to many high-ranking Lyran officers, Bryan's reply was curt. Winston wondered if she had inadvertently touched a nerve, or if the irascible Bryan's arm was especially painful right now.

Whatever the problem, Winston had no chance to inquire about it. Bryan cut the connection and was gone. For a few seconds, Winston considered having her commtech reestablish contact so she could find out what, if anything, was eating Bryan. The notion was short-lived, cut off by the raucous buzz of an incoming communiqué. William MacLeod was calling to report that the Pahn City factory complex had been stripped, almost to the bare walls.

"We've yanked out just about everything we could pry loose,

and a few things we had to cut." MacLeod's words were difficult to hear over the metallic crackle and hiss of the communicator. "We've downloaded everything the Jags had in their computers. As soon as we get a chance to look at it, I'll be sending you a copy, with our analysis. We managed to grab about a half dozen of those proto-Mech things intact. We've got a couple dozen more in various states of destruction. We might be able to salvage a couple more of those. The thing is, I don't think we'll be able to use 'em. All the pilots I saw had them enhanced-imaging tattoos. The couple we captured alive who were willing to talk said that the EI stuff was necessary to make the little armored boggarts work."

Winston chuckled a bit at MacLeod's colorful description of the nasty, dangerous, miniature war machines. Boggarts she knew was an old Gaelic word for "goblin" or "bogey-man." Leave it to MacLeod to give an enemy's most recently developed weapon system a humorous nickname. Secretly, Winston preferred Paul Masters' more elegant reporting name, Ocelots.

"Very well, Colonel," she replied, astounded at how much difference there could be in the tone of the identical phrase she spoke to Bryan. There was something about MacLeod that instantly made you want to like him, while Bryan's cold, taciturn nature inspired the opposite effect. "How are you coming at dismantling the plant?"

"We're not dismantling it, General." MacLeod's voice suddenly shifted tone, assuming the quality of a doctor's pronouncement of an incurable, fatal disease. "We'll be ready to set a torch to the factory in a couple of hours. I expect we'll have a bit of trouble with the locals when we blow it up, but not too much."

Winston's heart sank at MacLeod's abrupt frankness. She took neither delight nor pride in the idea of destroying the Jaguars' capability to make war. The task force was destroying factories that were turning out equipment that was decades ahead of anything the Inner Sphere and the renewed Star League could boast. Such destruction, to Winston's tradition-bound, history-conscious mind, was what had led to the original Star League army's abandonment of the Inner Sphere and the rise of Clan culture. Now here she was committing the same crime, after living over thirty years with the deeply ingrained belief that all technology that was beneficial to humanity in any way was to be preserved and nurtured until the benefit became a common blessing.

"I hope you haven't let the locals get anywhere too sensitive," she said, partly out of concern for the mission, but more to get her mind off the depressing thought that she was personally responsible for the destruction of a culture that was nearly three hundred years old.

"Nah, Gen'ral. I know better than that. We're letting them drive power lifters, loaders, and the like. No ammunition handlers, no armed trucks, nothing like that. We're not even letting 'em into the LZ. We're having' 'em haul their cargoes right up to the edge of the landing zone and drop it. My ships crews are taking over from there.

"My take on the whole thing is that the civilians seem to view the invasion almost as though they've been absorbed, if that's the right Clan term. We won the battle, so we get the spoils, and the spoils seem to include the lower castes. That would mean that they're part of our Clan now, part of Clan Serpent, and they're doing everything they can t' serve their new Clan as befits a true Clansman."

"All right, Colonel, just keep an eye on your 'new kinsmen.' I don't particularly want to believe that the captured Clanners will simply switch their allegiance to the Task Force, and then wake up with a knife in my throat."

"Aye, General, I'll do that."

With that MacLeod shut down the communications link.

After the Highlanders came Andrew Redburn, with a report that the Kathil Uhlans' AO was secure and the razing of the Clan's military industry was progressing apace. After Redburn came Regis Grandi, then Paul Masters. With each new report that the Task Force was systematically destroying the Smoke Jaguars' military infrastructure, Winston became more sad and withdrawn. For one who, in her own words, killed people and broke things for a living, she abhorred the almost wanton destruction now being loosed over the planet Huntress. She felt as though she was being unfaithful to the Eridani Light Horse's single-minded dedication to the preservation of all possible aspects of the Star League, and that meant protecting the industrial assets of a captured planet. She had even gone so far as to send Light Horse troopers into Lootera to destroy the secondary command center.

Briefly, elbows on the map-table, she rested her face in her hands. The muffled sound coming from behind her masking palms was neither laughter, nor weeping. The tech nearest her chair believed she was praying.

At that moment, Captain Dane Nichols tapped her on the shoulder. While the gesture would normally be considered far too familiar between a General and a junior officer, Nichols, a member of Winston's personal staff, could get away with quite a bit more than the average trooper.

"General, I've got the preliminary reports from the repair and salvage crews."

"Sit down, Dane." Winston pushed out a chair for the young officer, and leaned back in her own. "Now, go ahead."

"Well, ma'am, the Twenty-first Striker took the heaviest casualties. Colonel Amis reports eighteen dead and thirty-nine critically wounded. Most of his combat losses were among his infantry platoons. Five of his 'Mechs were destroyed. Eight more are damaged beyond his ability to repair. He has his salvage crews stripping them out for spare parts. Fifty-four of his surviving 'Mechs sustained varying degrees of damage and are under repair. Colonel Amis says he's taken a few minor casualties from Jaguar Elementals who ambushed one of his combat engineer teams. The engineers got pushed away from the military spaceport at Lootera, and Colonel Amis had to send in 'Mechs and armored infantry to root the Jags out. He says the spaceport and city are secure, but not very."

Winston chuckled in spite of her weariness at Amis' characteristic reporting style.

"Colonel Antonescu says he has five dead and thirty-six wounded," Nichols continued. "Nine 'Mechs destroyed or damaged beyond repair. Forty-one damaged but repairable. Colonel Antonescu reports no activity in his area south of Lootera.

"Colonel Barclay seized the Jaguars' genetic repository and the Field of Heroes. She took some heavy losses among her mechanized infantry platoons. The Jags must have put up a pretty stiff fight at the repository. According to the Colonel's after-action report, the Jaguar 'Mech forces fought a delaying action while the Elemental forces assigned to the repository sealed the facility. Her infantry units were forced to blast their way in and fight the Toads room-to-room. She's got thirty-one dead and forty-eight wounded. That's almost twenty-percent casualties."

"Mmm," Winston hummed sadly. "PBIs."

"Yes, ma'am," Nichols agreed. Poor Bloody Infantry.

"Colonel Barclay's losses among her BattleMech forces were considerably lighter," he said. "Two pilots killed and eleven wounded. Seven 'Mechs destroyed or unrepairable, fifteen damaged.

"All in all, the Light Horse got off easy."

"Uh-huh. Easy, but not scot-free," Winston said softly. "Tell the regimental commanders to keep me posted on the repair process. If the Jags manage a counterattack, I want to be ready for them."

"Wilco." Nichols made an entry on his noteputer. "I've also got a listing of the prisoners taken, or bondsmen, or whatever you want to call them."

Winston took the noteputer and scanned the list. There weren't all that many entries. Most of the Jaguars, it seemed, preferred to die fighting rather than accept the dishonor of being captured by the Inner Sphere forces arrayed against them. The highest-ranking officer accounted for was a Star Colonel captured by the Com Guards at the New Andery training base.

"No word on the garrison commander, what's his name? Russou Howell?"

"No, ma'am." Nichols shrugged. "He's supposed to be the head honcho for the whole planet. If he's like most other Jag officers, he'd be right out in front, leading his troops to death or glory. Some of the prisoners say he was at New Andery when the Knights hit the training base. He may have been killed in the fighting, or he may have escaped and is trying to reform enough of his forces to launch a counterstrike."

Winston nodded, considering the possibilities. "You don't suppose the Jags have sunk so far from 'the way of the Clans' that this guy Howell would pull back into the mountains and launch a guerrilla war, do you?"

"Dunno, General." Nichols shrugged again. "That's not my department."

Nor hers either, Winston thought. She'd have to refer the matter to what few intelligence specialists the task force did have.

Winston turned slightly in her chair, and gazed through the open door of the command truck. The accessway gave a limited view of the shattered monuments lining the Field of Heroes, and the smoke-palled city of Lootera beyond.

It can't have been this easy. The thought sent a shiver of disquiet crawling along her spine. Then an even more disturbing specter crept into her mind.

If it was this easy for us to seize the planet, how hard could it be for the Jags to take it back?

Shaking off the odd premonition, she gave Nichols an order that was to be passed along to each Inner Sphere unit commander on the planet.

"I want every effort to be made to find these missing Clan officers. If they're dead, fine, if not I want them run down and captured. There are far too many variables here, far too many things we don't know. It's going to take a couple of weeks to finish destroying the Jag's war-making capability. We can't risk having the Jags start up with partisan attacks against the task force. We don't know if they got out a call for help, and I don't want to be chasing a little band of guerrillas around the hills when and if a relief force does get here."

About the Author

THOMAS S. GRESSMAN lives with his wife, Brenda, and a lance of cats, in the foothills of western Pennsylvania. When not chained to his computer, he divides his time between leather-crafting, living history reenactment, and a worship music ministry *Sword and Fire* is his second novel and the sequel to *The Hunters*, previously published by Roc Books.

Don't miss the next exciting book in
the Twilight of the Clans series!

Shadows of War

by Thomas S. Gressman

General Ariana Winston's attack force
from the Inner Sphere has secured the
Smoke Jaguar Clan homeworld. But
as the 'Mech warriors prepare to destroy the Jaguars' war-making ability
once and for all, none of them are
aware that a new threat is bearing
down on them. . . .

Coming from Roc Books
in September 1998!

Daishi

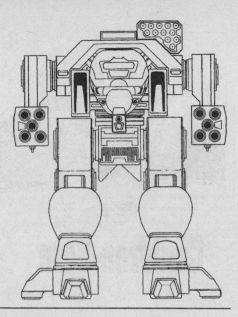

Clan Elemental

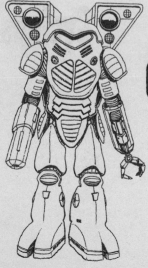

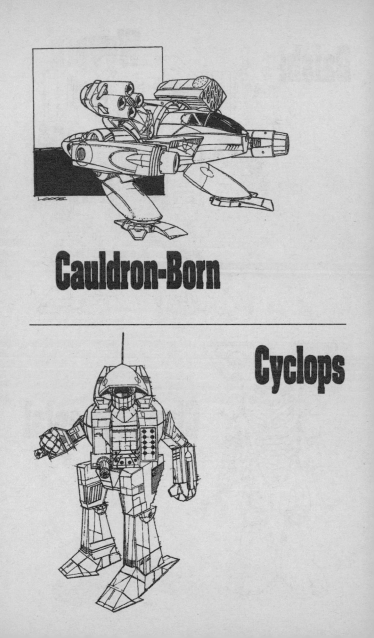

Cauldron-Born

Cyclops

Wyvern

Viper

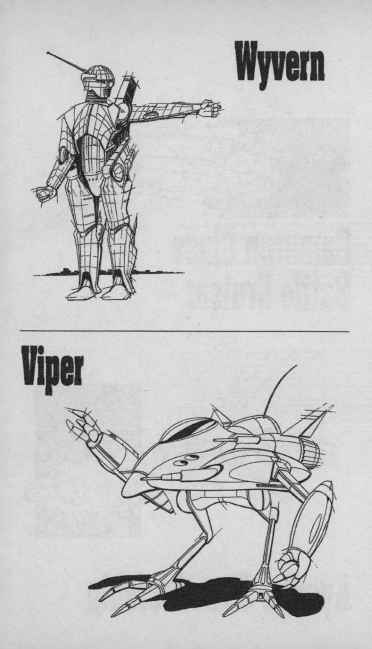

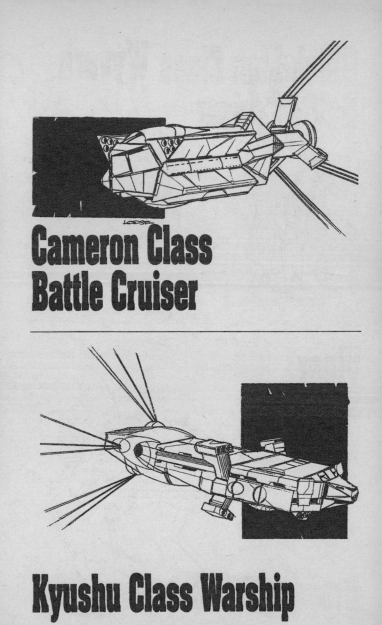

Cameron Class
Battle Cruiser

Kyushu Class Warship

Black Lion Class
Battle Cruiser

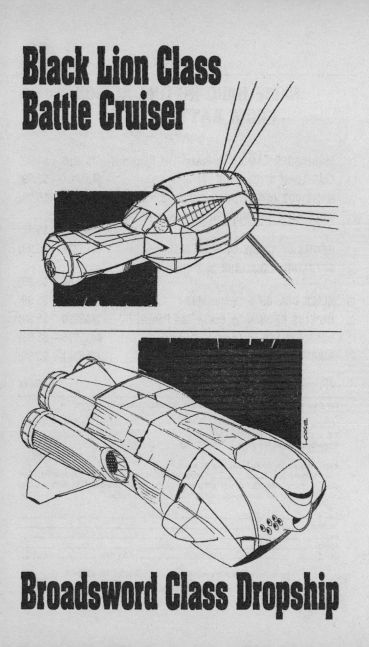

Broadsword Class Dropship

MORE HARD-HITTING ACTION
FROM BATTLETECH®